DALIT WOMEN'S MOVEMENT IN MODERN INDIA

DALIT WOMEN'S MOVEMENT IN MODERN INDIA

Dr. Indu Baghel

JNANADA PRAKASHAN (P&D)
NEW DELHI

Published by :
JNANADA PRAKASHAN (P&D)
4837/2, 24, Ansari Road, Daryaganj
New Delhi-110002
Phone : 011-23272047
Mobile : 9212137080

Assisted by :
TEXT BOOK PROMOTION SOCIETY OF INDIA
4837/2, 24, Ansari Road, Daryaganj
New Delhi-110002
Phone : 011-23272047
Mobile : 9212137080

Edition: 2009

Dalit Women's Movement in Modern India

ISBN : 978-81-7139-267-4

Typesetting by :
Vardhman Computers
New Delhi-110017

Published by Mrs. S. Chowdhary for M/s. Jnanada Prakashan (P&D) Daryaganj, Ansari Road, New Delhi-110 002 and printed at Balaji Offset, Navin Shahdara, Delhi-110032.

PREFACE

It is common knowledge that even today there exists deep discrimination against Dalit Women in India. Keeping in mind this fundamental reality, the author has critically examined the social, economic and political position of Dalit women and its overall impact on India's political system.

Democratisation has, undoubtedly, played a pivotal role in enhancing the level of political participation by the Dalit women. More particularly, the reservation of one-third seats in the Panchayati Raj institutions has provided enormous space for Dalit women in the decision-making process.

However, the level of economic and educational advancement of Dalit women is a matter of serious concern and in the author's view need special treatment. The Government of India must adopt a comprehensive policy framework for the economic, educational and social upliftment of Dalit women.

The emergence of various non-governmental organisation dealing with different issues concerning the Dalit women like violence, illicit human-trafficking, divorce etc. is a matter of great satisfaction. This is mainly because of the fact that these organisations have been largely successful in highlighting the key issues and problems being encountered by Dalit women in India.

The author is confident and fully convinced that this book would be a significant contribution to the proper understanding of Dalit movement.

CONTENTS

1

DALIT WOMEN IN INDIA

The Dalits

In India and other countries in South Asia, Dalits have been systematically discriminated against on the basis of their work and descent for centuries. Over 200 million people are Dalits, also known as untouchables or outcasts. They experience violence, discrimination, and social exclusion on a daily basis. Economic growth in India has been strong over the past decade. Ironically, the caste disparities are increasing.

Dalit Women

The situation of Dalit women in India needs special attention. They are one of the largest socially segregated groups anywhere in the world, and make up 2 per cent of the world's total population. Dalit women are discriminated against three times over: they are poor, they are women, and they are Dalits. Dalit women constitute half of the 200 million Dalit population, and 16.3 of the total Indian female population. The traditional taboos are the same for Dalit men and Dalit women.

However, Dalit women have to deal with them more often. Dalit women are discriminated against not only by people of higher castes, but also within their own communities. Men are dominant in Dalit communities. Dalit women also have less power within the Dalit movement itself. Women are active in large numbers in the movement but most leadership positions in the organisations, local bodies and associations have until now been held by men.

Human Rights of Dalit women

India is a democratic country and is a party to most of the major human rights treaties. These treaties provide the same rights for men and for women. Because India is also a Party to the Convention on the Elimination of All Forms of Discrimination Against Women (CEDAW), the Government has an extra obligation to make sure that women can realise their rights. It is generally accepted in international law that governments have to do more than just pass legislation to protect human rights. The Government of India has an obligation to take all measures, including policy and budgetary measures, to make sure that women can fulfil their rights. It also has an obligation to punish those who engage in caste-based violence and discrimination. The Government of India, as a modern country with a growing economy, has the means to fulfil its obligations.

Civil and Political Rights

India is a party to the International Covenant on Civil and Political Rights. Based on this treaty, the Government of India has an obligation to make sure that Dalit women can enjoy a whole range of human rights, such as the right to life, freedom from torture or cruel, inhuman or degrading treatment or punishment, freedom from slavery, the right to be equal before the court, the right to recognition as a person before the law, the right to privacy, the right to marry only with free and full consent, and the right to take part in public affairs. The life and dignity of Dalit women depends on the realisation of these human rights. However, they are breached systematically.

An essential precondition for the realisation of civil and political rights of Dalit women is registration. Article 24 (2) of the Covenant provides that every child shall be registered immediately after birth. In India, 46 per cent of all children are not registered. There is also no system of registration of marriages. This is not only a barrier for the realisation of civil and political rights; it also prevents the protection of Dalit girls from sexual exploitation and trafficking, child labour and forced and early marriages.

Economic, Social and Cultural Rights

India is also a party to the International Covenant on Economic, Social and Cultural Rights (ICESCR). This treaty not only identifies a range of economic, social and cultural rights, but it also requires that all people have these rights, without discrimination. The treaty also discusses the ways in which states must work to realise the rights. The rights outlined in the ICESCR include the right to work and to just and favourable conditions of work, and to form trade unions, the right to social security, protection of the family, the right to an adequate standard of living, including food, housing and clothing, and the right to health. Dalit women hardly enjoy any of these human rights.

Millennium Development Goals and Dalit Women

In 2000, one hundred and eighty nine countries accepted the Millennium Declaration and agreed to take the necessary action in order to attain eight specific goals: the Millennium Development Goals (MDGs). The realisation of human rights of Dalit women will have a major positive effect on the realisation of the MDGs. Dalit women are extremely poor, and make up 2 per cent of the world's population. In India, 60 million children do not attend primary school; the majority of these children are Dalit girls. India's child mortality rate is one of the highest in the world and with its vast population and a rate of 540 maternal deaths per 100,000 live births, India accounts for more than 20 per cent of all global maternal deaths. A greater availability and accessibility of healthcare for women, including Dalit women, is needed.

Violence against Dalit women—impunity

Certain kinds of violence are traditionally reserved for Dalit women: extreme filthy verbal abuse and sexual epithets, naked parading, dismemberment, being forced to drink urine and eat faeces, branding, pulling out of teeth, tongue and nails, and violence including murder after proclaiming witchcraft, are only experienced by Dalit women. Dalit women are threatened by rape as part of coll ctive violence by the higher castes. However, sexual assault and rape of Dalit women and girls also occur within their own communities. For Dalit men, the suppression and rape of women could be a way to compensate for their own lack of power in society. The Devadasi system of temple prostitution is the most extreme form of exploitation of Dalit women. Dalit girl children are forced to prostitution. The majority of cases of violence against Dalit women are not registered. The lack of law enforcement leaves many Dalit women unable to approach the legal system to seek redress. Women are often unaware of the laws and their ignorance is exploited by their opponents, by the police, and by the judiciary system. Even when cases are registered, the lack of appropriate investigation, or the judge's own caste and gender biases, can lead to acquittal.

Action by Dalit women

Dalit women have been active throughout history, though often this has not been recorded. They were actively involved in the anti-caste and anti-untouchability movements in the 1920s. Today they are the strongholds of the Dalit movements in thousands of Indian villages. They continue to play a critical role in the movements for land rights. They are making their mark as independent thinkers and writers in the literary world and visionary leaders in the Panchayati Raj institutions. However, they are unable to put an end to the structural discrimination and exclusion. Violence and impunity are used to keep them in their place.

Getting Organised as Dalit Women

Since the late 1980s, therefore, Dalit women have increasingly felt and articulated the need for a separate platform—created, developed and controlled by themselves —through which they could forge their own identity, fight for their rights and find solutions to their particular problems as Dalits and as women. Conscious that the call for a separate platform could be interpreted as a divisive move by both Dalit men and non-Dalit women, the proponents of such a special forum emphasise that their initiative must not be mistaken for a separatist movement. Rather they assert that there is need for strong alliances between the Dalit movement, the women's movement and the Dalit women's movement if their common vision of socioeconomic and political equality and justice for all is to be realised.

The National Federation of Dalit Women (NFDW) was launched by Dalit women themselves and committed itself to undertake several tasks to bring about positive changes in the lives of Dalit women, such as legal action against caste based atrocities, political empowerment of Dalit women, economic empowerment against growing pauperisation, building self-confidence and leadership.

DALIT IN WESTERN INDIA

This study contains very broad and tentative commentary on Dalit question in western India, and on complexities surrounding this question. Second intention behind this note is to attempt and explore hidden and not-so-hidden alternatives to restore life of dignity and freedom to Dalits in India, not only Dalit men, but also Dalit women and children, whose life experiences are pathetic beyond words More often than not, Dalit women and children have remained neglected in our understanding and analysis Dalit male world and its world view dominate our focus. This attitude is changing, but it is changing at a snail pace. This situation needs to be altered consciously.

Defining Dalits

Who are Dalits? Traditionally, they include the member of scheduled castes, or ex-untouchables in India. This term 'Dalit' was first coined by Dr. Babasaheb Ambedkar, champion of the downtrodden, and crusader for their rights. In 1970s, the

Dalit Panther movement led by Namdeo Dhasal and Raja Dhale brought this term in common parlance Now, human and dalit rights groups have further popularised its usage. Interestingly, there is continuous attempt to expand Dalit canvas to include other socially and culturally oppressed groups like nomadic, advises, women, minorities, etc. in last three decades. We should appreciate these efforts wholeheartedly. The term Dalit includes individuals, groups and communities suffering from social and cultural oppression. This oppression can be visible or invisible, open or concealed, manifest or latent. It may cause material or non-material injury or handicap; and contain multiple levels of hardships; such as encountering verbal abuse, physical violence, humiliation, insults, moral stigmatisation, mental torture, victimisation, and even liquidation or death. Being Dalit means facing these insufferable, inhuman and downright degrading conditions on the basis of one's birth in a particular polluting caste or cluster of castes.

This state of being can also be labeled as Dalais. It means existence steeped in social and cultural marginalisation. Interestingly, it is legitimised through supra-human agencies in the garb of divine intention and thereof *karma*. Scriptures and religious practices of the Hindus, specially empowering the *Savarnas* to exercise complete power over others, and relegating the lower castes, *Shudras* and Ati-Shudras to positions of servitude and humiliations, buttress this dehumanisation. Birth is the basis of one's entry into castes, and hence it is well nigh impossible to exit one's caste during his lifetime. Social and cultural ranking is therefore immutable, at least in theory; though in practice there were vital breaches in some quarters due to efforts of some lower castes to upgrade themselves through what Srinivas called 'Sanskritisation'. But in the long run, it appears to be fickle and failed project, as some scholars have argued.

One must admit that the situation of the Dalits has not remained the same in recent historical past. There has been a good deal of churning within civil society and social and cultural upheavals. There are even bloody confrontations between the Dalits, the oppressed, and the non-Dalit Savarna castes, the oppressors.

How does one perceive and interpret this interface and encounter? Should we say that the situation at ground level has remained stationary and moribund, with persistent setbacks and defeats for the Dalit communities, and the untenured victory for the oppressed groups in all regimes? One needs to fathom deeply into empirical ground realities and perceptions of the Dalits involved into these confrontations.

Moreover, it calls for careful sifting of the evidences and identify the critical markers both at the level of agenda and mobilisation strategies of groups involved in these struggles, and also at the level of epistemological underpinnings. The impact of these struggles on social and cultural landscape in various parts does reveal the presence of both positive and negative trends and tendencies. The picture one obtains has several shades within. Social scientists have just begun to capture these complexities, while especially Dalit literature [self-narratives and poetry in articular] have much earlier arrived at this assessment.

In Maharashtra, works of Baburao Bagul, Raosaheb Kasbe, Annabhau Sathe, Yeshwant Manohar, Narayan Surve, and Daya Pawar already contain seeds of discovering the strengths and capacities of Dalits and Dalitism to transform the present social reality into more humane, egalitarian, gender sensitive and stress-free society. Such moral and emancipatory message is also available through writings of Dalit women, notably Jyoti Lanjewar, Kumud Pawde, Urmila Pawar and Minakshi Moon. Issue of Dalit identity formation, its consolidation and assertion need to be located within this larger matrix of changed environment, both within Dalits and outside.

How does one grapple with Dalit social and economic realities and changes occurring within them? Here one must distinguish between urban and rural landscape. Some Dalit groups, like Mahars of Maharashtra, Ezavas of Kerala, Nadars of Tamil Nadu and Mahyavanshis of Gujarat had relatively better exposure and contacts with urban, industrial world and its opportunity structures compared to other Dalit groups. Scholars have noted the migration and lateral and sometimes upward social mobility of Dalits through their entry and association with military establishments, textile and other industrial sectors, and entry into British houses as butlers and cooks. They were the first to settle down in the towns and cities of Bombay, Nagpur, Chennai, Agra, Ahmedabad, Kanpur, etc. A few of them went abroad as personal servants of British army officers, some specialised in bakery and confectionery products. A few among these early migrants with better socioeconomic opportunities took the lead in spearheading change within their own immediate kinship groups and caste circle. They also knew the value of liberal education then, and made conscious efforts to educate their own children and also other Dalit children by opening night schools, hostels, etc. Gavli and others have documented these early efforts of social and other reforms among the Dalits in Vidarbha region.

When Dr. Ambedkar arrived on the scene, there were already considerable efforts both in Gujarat and Maharashtra within some Dalit groups to ameliorate their conditions from the status of servitude and slavery. Dr. Ambedkar himself has noted these legacies in his writings, But these changes mainly occurred among Mahars, Chamars, Mahyavanshis, Mochis, and few other castes whose members were fortunate enough for early contacts with modern institutions. In some places, Gandhian workers and missionaries brought about perceptible changes within the life space of Dalits. They became literate and conscious of their needs and rights. Early recruits in all political parties were the members of these upcoming conscious Dalit castes. But, question of social and cultural degradation of even these so-called liberated castes was not resolved fully, despite their educational achievements and assumption of public office. Social scientists told us that the unsociability was incompatible with rapid urbanisation and modernisation. Education is a gateway for higher status and life of dignity and self-worth. These remained at best the half-truths, to say the least. Daya Pawar who wrote the first openly and subtly in several localities in Bombay. Dalit dead bodies were taken to cemetery Worli, and not at Chandanwadi in Girgaum in 1960s. Former was the burial ground for the Dalits, and the latter for others, non-Dalits, he disclosed.

Even in slum settlements of Golibar, at Santa Cruz, there was rigid residential zoning along caste lines. *Dalits bastis* were separate even within slum settlements. *Bhangis* or *Mehtars* doing scavenging and sweeping job were either settled in rickety municipal quarters, or in isolated slum pockets at Chembur, Dharavi or Goregoan, again away form the lower castes mainly OBCs, equally or more poor than Bhangis, but who ranked themselves socially higher. This situation remains more or less unchanged even today. In urban areas of Gujarat, the situation is equally grim. Untouchability is practiced in more subtler ways than what was the case in fifties, when textile mills in Baroda had three separate drinking water tanks within its premises, one for *Savarnas*, second for Harijans, and the third for Muslims. Even mill canteens had separate cups and saucers for the Dalit workers. Now that situation no longer persists. It is however, difficult for even educated Dalits to secure at ease house in a *Savarna* locality, though he may have means to purchase or hire one. Subtle comments are passed against the Dalit employees. They are referred to as Godmen, an acronym for Harijan, or *Sarkari Jamais*, i.e. son-in-laws of the government, etc.

In slums of Ahmedabad, Surat and Baroda, the *Vankars* stay in separate clusters, away form *Bhangis*, another Dalit caste. On many occasions they do not see eye to eye. Some have strong biases against each other. *Vankars* consider themselves higher in status compared to Bhangis. Bhangis owe allegiance to BJP, while Vankars are mostly with Congress and Samata Party. Though *Bhangis* and *Vankars* worked together in same textile mill, they hardly had relations of inter-dining.

It was a common knowledge that in caste violence in Gujarat during mid-eighties, the *Patidars* and other *Savarna* castes to settle score against the *Vankars* used the *Bhangis*. So one Dalit caste was used against another.

Situation of Dalits in rural areas was more depressing and critical. Most of them worked as landless labourers doing hard work whole day, and receiving pittance for their grueling labour. They were treated with lesser mercy than the cattle of their landowners. They lived in the eastern end of the hamlet, and suffered several indignities at the hands of their employers and village fellows belonging to *Savarna* castes. The situation did not much change even today in terms of their basic necessities like drinking water, assess to firewood and fodder, and participation in social and cultural activities in the village. Account of one Dalit college teacher, P.E. Sonkamble who later became principal of the college in Aurangabad is heart-rending. His self-narrative, Athavaniche Pakshi is a pointer towards how mercilessly Dalit agricultural labourer is treated by the Savarna farmers. Sonkamble himself belonged to poor Dalit family and slogged as farm labourer in his childhood. He was accommodated in a cowshed, and was given stale food as part of his wages. Exposure to such unsanitary and obnoxious conditions resulted into many physical ailments, including his succumbing to perennial complaints of scabies, infections in digestive tract, and other illnesses associated with his childhood occupation as agricultural labour.

Relationship between Dalits and Non-Dalits

What about relations between Dalit and Non-Dalit poor? Indications are that both in Gujarat and Maharashtra, they are economically equal, but socially and culturally separate. They believe in and nurture these distinctions assiduously. One instance is sufficient to bring this point home. Baba Adhav, noted social activist form Pune has recalled his experience with workers doing road construction labour under EGS. The working gang included Marathas, Dhangars, Malis and also Mahars. The first three castes belonged to Savarna category, while the last consisted of a Dalit group. All were workers, all were paid same wages, and all encountered similar work situations. But, when the work stopped during the recess, the Savarna workers assembled in one corner, ate their food; while the Dalit Maharssat separately. Not only that, the Savarna workers refused to take drinking water form Panodya, a water carrier, because they came to know that he was Mahar by caste. Adhav's book *Ek Gaon, Ek Manavatha* is a perceptive document revealing mind-boggling contradictions within rural working class.

So much was the caste rigidity even among workers working on the drought relief sites and being organised by the socialist leaders. When the relief workers organised protest march on *tahsil* office, or organised big processions with slogans like down with imperialism and capitalism, or down with high-handedness of bureaucracy or sugar factory management, all of them moved together, jostling with one another. They castigated the rural capitalists and their henchmen with full-throated voice. But, with equal alacrity, they refused to share food and water with their own colleagues on work sites. When they went back to their village, they were separate beings; they were upper castes, touchable, divinely ordained with higher social and cultural status. They were unwilling to disturb the pollution code.

Caste is a thin but tenuous dividing line among them; the *Savarnas* and the Dalits. The *Savarna* castes cannot abandon their age-old beliefs. They cannot disrespect the social and cultural codes of behaviour handed down form generations. They, the *Savarnas* distinguished economic issues form social ones, fighting for economic justice is one thing; affairs of social and cultural living were a separate domain. This situation has remained unaltered even today. This is a worrisome situation indeed. Economic relations do not tear through, and realign social and cultural relations to render them mutually compatible. This is indeed a sordid rural reality in Maharashtra, Gujarat, and Karnataka. Maybe, other states demonstrate similar tendencies. In this seminar, we may pursue this question with more rigours, as it has vital implications for Dalit struggles for social equality and justice.

A brief reference to social and cultural arrogance of the Savarnas is necessary here. Particularly this was evident in situations of caste agitation and ensuing violence Caste violence in Marathwada took place in July 1978. It enveloped every single *taluka* towns and many villages under their jurisdiction. The was renaming the Marathwada University after Dr. Babasaheb Ambedkar. Battle lines were drawn between the *Savarnas* and the Dalits, and the Dalits suffered heavily through damages to their house, cattle, crops, shops, etc. In some villages, they were chased and hounded out of the village. Dalit men took shelter in outlying agricultural fields, while their womenfolk witnessed the village *savarna* mob ransacking their home, and destroying their standing crops.

Not many savarna villages who took part in this vandalism knew about the renaming issue; they were least affected by that decision at that juncture. Their fury was against something, for which they were harboring the feelings of animosity and hatred against the Dalits. They had grievance against upward social, economic and cultural mobility of the Dalits living in the village, especially the younger generation. They disliked that the Dalits were taking higher education, and securing government employment or jobs in the industry in cities of Aurangabad, Jalna, Nanded and Pune. They strongly disapproved the behaviour of the upwardly mobile Dalits who visited their native place attired in better dress, with combed hair, and moving in the village with sense of self-confidence and dignity. They compared these young educated and employed Dalits with their aged parents who had served the village society with servility and meekness. This socioeconomic change angered them the most.

How can they move in a village in upright posture, and with air of independence? How can they behave differently than their parents who did not disobey or disrespect the village traditions, and command of elderly *Savarna* leaders of the village? How can they go straight to their Maharwada, and leave the village without paying respects to village Patil, and other upper caste gentry? They are a spoiled lot; they have become disrespectful, recalcitrant. They consider that village society is no longer relevant to them; they can live their own life with sense of independence and freedom. It is with these feelings, the Savarnas attacked their houses, torn and trampled on their school and college books, set fire to photo frames of Dr. Ambedkar and Buddha, and vandalised their Buddha viharas. And in this mob violence, the non-Dalit poor were equally active and belligerent. Studies on Marathwada episode by Vibhuti Patel, Dipankar Gupta, Gail Omvedt, and others bring forth this outrageousness eloquently.

This is also noticed in instances of forced exodus of Dalit communities from Gujarat villages. It is called Hijarat, and during last two decades there are scores of forced collective migration among the Dalits due to both economic as well as social and cultural reasons enumerated above. Instances of Hijarat form villages of Bilia, Bhojpura, Toda, Chitrodipura and Vavadhara from districts of Bhavnagar, Mahesana and Banaskantha constitute a testimony to this process of social, economic and cultural oppression of the *Savarnas* against the Dalits. This has been happening since 1981, and the situation is equally critical even today. It is important to mention here about two narratives depicting the conditions of Dalits in Gujarat. First is a narrative on the hardships and struggles of the Dalits in Sabarada involving Vankars or Mahyavanshis. It was titled *Sabaradathi Swamannagar*. Harshad Desai and Chandu Maheria wrote it. Dalits of Sabarda were forced to evict their village homes due to caste repressions. A Dalit professor Parmar, teaching at Morbi College of Engineering, led Dalit struggle in Sabarada. He is no more, and his untimely death is an irreparable loss to Dalit movement in Gujarat. Second is a comprehensive commentary on long drawn battle of Bhangis, a scavenging community at Ranpur village in North Gujarat.

These two documents immensely valuable documents for future researches in this area. The activists meticulously prepared both these documents with financial and moral support for Centre for Social Studies, Surat. It should be noted that two of the three writers mentioned above were not trained social scientists as defined in our mainstream vocabulary. But then work reveals a great deal. It is capable of shattering our conventional wisdom and notions on doing research on subaltern classes, and also on our ways of reporting the outcome. One can place these documents parallel to another epochal narrative I came across. The ordinary workers and activists from Mumbai also opine that. I am here referring to very sensitive account on the conditions of scavengers in Maharashtra. The book is titled, *Narak Safaichi Gost,* written by Mohamed Dhadas and Thakur. This book received raving reviews both in academic and literary journals in Maharashtra and outside.

How can we alter this situation of Dalits suffering social, economic and cultural oppression? What can be envisaged to counter the atrocities on Dalits by the *Savarna* castes and their hatchet men? Are there durable and effective institutional mechanisms to restore relations of normalcy between the non-Dalits and Dalits, and restore the status of self-worth and dignity among the Dalits, to enable them to enjoy their civil and democratic rights? In my view, these are significant questions for all of us to ponder over, and come up with relevant and rights-respecting solution to Dalit question in India. But can we answer these questions with some degree of certitude and confidence? To answer this question is to question the hitherto received answers on Dalit problematic in India. And I humbly feel that such questioning is the need of the hour.

Burden of this note is to uncover complexities surrounding the question of Dalit world, its own worldview, and its interface with wider mainstream society, essentially the *Savarnas*. Historical Dalit Social reality is mainly influenced by and constructed around their economic and socio-cultural profile.

This profile was essentially rooted in social and economic slavery, the parameters of which were exclusively determined by the dominant castes within Brahminical mode and code of thinking. Lowly economic status was cleverly matched with subhuman social and cultural status with denial of and exclusion from all regenerative, creative processes of unfolding human potentialities Ambedkar theory of broken men and their attributes do voice this concern, and many of the hardships suffered by the Dalits in mid-1930s and earlier still continue till date, despite considerable efforts ranging form social reforms to regulatory institutional mechanisms based on constitutional guarantees and legal protection.

Positive outcome cannot be underplayed. Some Dalit individuals and groups have come up with distinct material gains and leverage. Some traditional servile occupations have been abandoned; thanks to ceaseless efforts of Dr. Ambedkar and his colleagues. There is also political gain through open democratic process which enabled some Dalits to occupy the seat of power at various levels of decision-making structures; be they local village panchayats, district level bodies, legislative assembly or parliament. At least theoretically they are free to speak, argue and decide. They can participate and make critical contribution in the governance of civil society, both in urban and rural setting.

Indicators of Socio-economic Advancement

Increased literacy and education, their representation in government employment and political party, their mobilisation on labour front are all indicators of some social and economic improvement. The fact that violence against Dalits receive prominent attention from the print and electronic media; the fact that available to them as a matter of right: are all signs of presence of some desirable environment; presence of liberal, progressive tendencies and respect for democratic institutions and ethos.

But, having said this, we must admit that there are ruptures and distortions. Setbacks far outweigh the significance and relevancy of success stories of Dalits. Injuries seem to run far deeper in Dalit, payshe, and children are disabused. And somewhere behind all these injuries, there is present a question of their caste and its ascriptive attribute of sub-human identity defined by others, the mainstream and mainly *Savarnas*. Hence we come across instances of *Savarna* castes even tolerating cases of economic mobility among the Dalits; but not their social and cultural assertion. Mainstream intolerance of Dalit assertion and assertiveness is largely rooted in this mindset; reminiscent of Brahminical hegemonic thinking. It is this mindset which Phuley and Ambedkar and others wished to demystify and demolish through organic solidarity and collective struggles of all subaltern classes including Dalits.

Emergence and some consolidation of Dalit identities in recent years owe their birth to instability and failures on both fronts; economic and social-cultural. Economic setback is demonstrated through increasing pauperisation of Dalit households in rural areas through land alienation and distortions in input and output markets; and increasing shrinkages in urban and industrial labour market. The Dalits are under acute survival pressures, the intensity of which has increased in the era of globalisation and privatisation. Dalits are not alone who feel this heat of down turn in urban and rural economy. But, strangely Dalit and non-Dalit poor are not coming together to resolve this crisis together, in genuinely participative and democratic spirit. I have narrated earlier how the relief workers do not abandon their caste mentality, and how *Savarnas* in the village project their anger against Dalits by burning their books and destroying their icons. As long as this mentality and consciousness among the *Savarnas* prevail, there is hardly any space for social relief and reconstruction, no matter how massive and multi-focal the economic programmers. And that shall give further twist to Dalit identity assertion and associated political expressions.

What is the way out? First is more vigorous, multipronged and widespread social reform movement within *Savarnas*, principally directed towards transforming their reactionary worldview. Also public debate on religion and cultural practices of mainstream society is the need of the hour. Second relates to coming together of all subaltern classes to seriously address the question of globalisation and its perceived threats to toiling classes including the Dalits. Dalit identities must seriously examine the nature and implications of this globalisation process, as it would determine the current and future prospect of Dalit identities. A word about the role and relevance of social sciences in addressing Dalit question is in order.

Dalit and non-Dalit activists are coming forward with their own perceptions and interpretations on Dalit question. They are not formally trained in social science theories and methodologies. All the same, their works reveal so much of insights and introspection, often found missing in social science literature. This also suggests strongly that depiction of social realities is not the monopoly of only formally trained social scientists. There are others, perhaps better equipped and with deeper organic linkages. The ordinary men and women can construct social reality. They can do that with better grasp and orientations. Often these writers reveal impulses and innate abilities to interpret them. It is imperative that social scientists begin to learn from them, and develop sustained linkages with such creative workers. Indeed, both society [including Dalit community] and social sciences are gainers in this enterprise, a value of which has begun to dawn in some circles in recent years.

DALIT AGENDA

The term Dalit as used here is comprehensive and secular enough to describe the phenomenal number of castes and sub-castes in India who stand suppressed and oppressed for centuries. Their usual characteristics as well as stigmas are: untouchability, segregation, poverty, helplessness, exclusion, and seclusion. These are offshoots of the age-old caste system that thrives on the purity-pollution syndrome, sometimes borrowing heavily from racial theories and rationalising from divine prescriptions of spurious theological validity. In terms of demographic, legal, and constitutional terminology the Dalits comprise the Scheduled Castes (SCs), Scheduled Tribes (STs), and in certain cases even the Other Backward Classes (OBCs).

These are variously called as: the deprived groups of the Third World situation; the poorest of the poor; the umbra within the penumbra; the non-Aryans; the anaryans; the aborigines; the 'mlechhas'; 'the indigenes'; the sons of the soil; the original Indians, the Fourth World. They have the longest history but the shortest life cycle; the oldest civilisation but lowest literacy standards. They live amidst some of the wealthiest men in the world but are paid the poorest wages. They live in a country where the high-caste elite advocate the abolition of apartheid from the world but practise untouchability and slavery at home. The Dalits can climb up the tallest mountains but are challenged by the toughest social battles. They live amidst contrasting situations, paradoxical value systems, oppositional politics and distorted perceptions.

The External Forces

Three phenomena stand out in the Dalit-non-Dalit relationship: internal colonialism, symbiotic oppression, and ethereal diversity. These act as the centrifugal forces which have a bearing on the unity of the Dalits.

Domestic Colonialism

Internal colonialism, based on the pernicious race-caste-class nexus, determines the Dalit-non-Dalit socioethnic relationship. Under this doctrine, domination and discrimination of the Dalits are justified on the questionable premises of eugenics, Manu's socioreligious theories, and the division of labour, or rather, 'labourers'. Domestic colonisation, as described by Robert Blauner, has the following features: colonisation begins with an involuntary entry of the colonisers (conquest) or colonised (slavery); the colonising power deliberately constrains or changes indigenous cultural forms;

the lives of the subject group are controlled by the colonisers; there is separation in labour status between the colonisers and the colonised; and racial or cultural superiority is used by the colonisers to justify exploitation, control and oppression of the colonised.

In Indian conditions, the consequences of colonisation, starting with the external and moving to the internal, have been disastrous to the very existence of the Dalits. The Aryan invasion created a victor-vanquished and friend-enemy relationship, and it remains so immutably. This is why Dalits are located outside the victors' ethnic and even territorial boundary. The SCs are kept on the outskirts of the village and the STs in distant forests. The process of 'Hinduisation' and' Sanskritisation' unleashed by the non-Dalits has, in addition, destroyed the indigenous culture and social resources and imposed dominant traditions to the near total obliteration of their 'little' traditions. Dalits are skilfully manipulated into divisions and groups along caste and ethnic lines and are thoroughly subjugated by a process of divide-and-destroy. Lately, the open-market economy has been introduced, in which development is dependent on the market forces, based on a trickledown paradigm. In this paradigm, there is no distinction between the capitalist caste of traders and the Western capitalist societies. About 10 per cent of India's population controls 90 per cent of the country's resources, its services, its economy and politics and also the trade and market.

Many eminent authorities on economics of discrimination have asserted that market is not neutral to caste; it discriminates, the labour market specifically. Hence, both the elite and the rich, the large industries and big trades determine the fate of the Dalits, their life and labour. Dalits simply happen to be the colonised, because caste, class and capital have moved together leaving only the crumbs of development to the Dalits. Finally, the Hindutva model carries with it the traits of a casteist, and Fascist society, instances of which range from demolition of the Babri Masjid, the burning alive of the Staines family, genocidal murders of Dalits, and their enslavement in the hierarchical caste-based society. These are the usual consequences of domestic colonialism in the Indian context.

Symbiotic Oppression

The oft-repeated rhetoric of integration of the country and homogenisation of all groups of people, under a single banner of Indianism or Indianisation, or cultural nationalism, emphasises forced conformity to majority cultural norms. *Cultural integration* occurs when the Dalits change their cultural patterns and substitute with the core-culture norms of the non-Dalits. *Structural assimilation* occurs when there is large-scale entrance of the Dalits into the societies, associations, institutions and primary groups of non-Dalits. In India, only a microscopic minority of the middle- and the upper-middle-class Dalits have achieved some amount of cultural integration, but not structural assimilation.

Integration may effect uniformity, but its social and economic costs for the Dalits are enormous, since they will be placed lowest in the hierarchy. Integration, cultural or structural, leads to the illusory concept of equal opportunity, but social justice becomes the consequential casualty. *Equal opportunity and social justice are antithetic,* since the Dalits have no capacity to compete with non-Dalits. Integration only legitimises the existing power pyramid of society, and results in competitive and oppressive relationships along the various ethnic horizontals on the pyramid and diverts attention from the oppression and exploitation of the larger class system.

Ethnic Diversity

India is a pluralist society, with multiple cultures and traditions co-existing, each with its identity and independence (as against the theory of melting-pot) with or without political and social equality. The euphemistic slogan of unity-in-diversity is well known. But, the unity in this slogan is ethereal, while the diversity is real. The ethnic diversity is reflected in caste alliances and majority-minority relationships.

The pluralist principle governing the Dalit-non-Dalit relationship perpetuates a perennial conflict, making the life of the Dalits "poor, nasty, brutish and short" under the non-Dalit hegemony. The history of Mahenjodaro and Harappa, of the Jains and the Buddhists, speaks of how the Brahminic Hindu violence eliminated the rich Dalit civilisation from this country and packed it off to China, Japan and Sri Lanka. The recent Brahminic Hindu revivalism, to bring back the "errant" Christian Dalits to Hinduism with systematic violence or 'Talibanisation' of education and other anti-minority measures, continues this historical trend.

Internal Dynamics

The basic features of the intra-Dalit situation can be discussed in terms of *(a)* dispersed territoriality, *(b)* fragmented society, and *(c)* stratified solidarity. These features reflecting the internal dynamics of the Dalit situation also work against Dalit unit.

Dispersed Territoriality

Dalits, who constitute the majority—the Bahujans—of the country's population, do not live in one place. They are scattered. Except the tribal people of the North-East and in some parts of central India, the tribes are also scattered more or less throughout the country. The unrestricted invasion and entry of non-Dalits to these areas reduces them to minorities. The SCs are distributed very thinly throughout the country. Their regrouping is impossible. Similar is the situation of the other weaker sections. There may be some villages where Dalits dominate in numbers, but these are exceptions. The majority of their villages are unrecorded and unnamed hamlets.

This settlement pattern hinders their unity. Large industrial or irrigation projects scatter the tribes and destroy them. Most educated Dalits have migrated to the cities or even abroad, thus depriving the community of their presence or proximity. Thus, territoriality as a factor is not available to them to build a Dalit community, and therefore, the communities remain mere statistical artifacts, rather than a real society. Even where Dalits are made to live together, supportive social, economic or political institutions, which could have brought about proximity and thus unity, are non-existent. Indira Awas Yojana, for example, failed to provide schools or medical institutions to the Dalits' habitations, leaving the houses deserted. In the urban areas, wherever Dalits are concentrated as labourers and slum-dwellers, the extremely scanty infrastructural facilities compel them to scatter. Most Dalits live in rural areas, where the resources and programmes do not reach. Finally, the territorial interpenetration sometimes gives rise to an interpersion of Dalits as a set of multiple enclaves in a region, making it impossible to draw a single continuous boundary that separates or unites them.

Fragmented Society

Even where Dalits live in physical proximity, they fail in mutual confidence, loyalty and interpersonal trust. Dalits are probably deficient in developing a spirit of cooperation, trust, unity of purpose and gratification in the basic social relationship of marriage and family life. Their friendship bonds also indicate the same ethnic exclusivity as marriage. This is but a manifestation of victimology. Ordinarily, an educated or *nouveau riche* Dalit does not entirely connect in friendship with an uneducated Dalit, except may be only as a nearest member of a family set-up. 'Sanskritisation' is another alienating factor. Nevertheless, generally, social relationship among Dalits has proved to be an asset, since Dalit families are always large enough to accommodate and help out children of poorer relatives. This factor can act as a foundation for greater social solidarity among the Dalits, although may not always prove to be a reality.

Lee Rainwater writes that in close relationships there are greater risks of exploitation: relatives are a greater danger than friends, and friends a greater danger than neighbours or acquaintances, because the closer the person, the less likely one is to be on guard. In poor communities, violence moves horizontally. The Dalits are engaged in in-fighting and have no time or strength to fight the real enemy.

For example, the Dalits are yet to challenge legally or politically the existential arrangements of land reforms, the on-going programmes of privatisation, the principles of reservation in joint sector or private sector companies and the larger issues of Dalit human rights, the casteism in India, and a host of other issues crucial to the survival and growth of the Dalits. But not much is being done by them in these fields as in-fighting takes a lot of their resources and energy, e.g. the feud between Malas and Madigas in Andhra Pradesh or the that between the Kondhs and Panos in Orissa.

Stratified Solidarity

The caste divide extends to the Dalits also, with not only sub-caste differences, but also sub-culture and occupations-based differences, variations in communication and other criteria. Social solidarity is founded on four basic segments: self-identity, self-concept, self-love and self-determination. Only by fulfilling the self-needs can the social needs be formulated and fulfilled. Identity needs, for example, could be met through physical designs that capture and incorporate the symbols, experiences, values and traditions of the sub-cultural group to be served. Self-concept needs could be met through environmental design that makes people feel more positive and more respected in their society. Self-love needs could be met through special arrangements and materials that encourage companionship. Similarly, self-determination needs could be realised when the cultural symbols of the members dominate their environment. From self-identity, we could easily move into group-identity and solidarity.

An Agenda for Action

Against the backdrop analysed above, a few instruments of cohesion and unification are suggested for urgent action. It is time that Dalit intellectuals strive for self-discovery by thinking globally and acting locally, understanding the social dilemmas and the local situation. Only introspection will enable Dalit unity. This requires consensus, focusing on commonalities. Self-definition of their attitudes and self-determination of their ideas will evolve a collective identity and their own political processes, and lead to economic progress and social cohesion. These intellectual strands must necessarily reflect the ordinary Dalits at the grassroots and contain the seeds of tangible improvements in their lives. A common political and social platform, exclusively to cater for their needs, will catalyse Dalit unity, in turn bringing about greater political victory through better positive self-image and greater individual achievements.

Historical Continuity

Tradition and history constitute a great source of strength and social resource. The struggles of Periyar, Phule and Ambedkar are yet to create fully a community spirit among the Dalits, who now appear to be somewhat more alienated and fragmented than ever before. In the interest of a common struggle, they need to realise the importance of consensus, to exhibit a united front. We might take it as axiomatic that if two persons (or communities) always agree, one of them must be a fool; but if two persons always disagree, both are fools. Unity has to be achieved, learning from the strategies set forth by great men like Periyar, Phule and Ambedkar. Dalits may be disagreed among themselves—within families, groups, villages, districts, or states— about various issues. But they need to unite the injustice perpetrated on the Dalits as a whole.

Leadership Structure

Poor communities normally become authoritarian and ethnocentric. To redeem such communities, different types of leaders should be encouraged to emerge. Some Dalit leaders are remote, undemocratic, non-responsive to local community needs and slow to respond to change. Some also remain pedantic and theoretical. The new breed of leaders, emerging from within the community, must be very humanistic, more far-sighted and more democratic. Intellectual militants and social activists are required, not the traditional patronising benevolent status-quoist leaders. The Dalit leaders of today must determine the probable, delineate the possible, and define the preferable.

Intellectual Integrity

Few Dalits have a clear notion whether or not they stand for social integration, separate caste identification or amalgamation with non-Dalits. They are not clear whether casteism should be abolished, the market should be fought against, or socialism brought back. They are not sure whether they are superior to non-Dalits, whether they have a true God to worship or a good religion to follow. This ambivalence can be attributed to their cultural existence, of being members of the Dalit community and of the national mainstream. Depending on the context, a person may shift his allegiance or change his loyalty. Formulating a comprehensive and workable strategy may seem difficult, because of such unsettled ideas and floating emotions. Hence, the Dalits must study in depth, take a clear stand and make their positions clear. This stand should be above one's own caste or sub-caste, income level, educational status, position in a job hierarchy, access to information, age or gender, local problems, political office and party affiliation, whether he is a charismatic leader or a grassroots worker, rich or poor. He should be a-religious, a-caste, anti-caste, a-political and a-local.

Instilling Dalit Pride

The Dalits must take pride that they have a distinctive cultural heritage, indigenous and pre-Aryan. As Ambedkar put it, the Dalits are part of Indian society, but they are a part apart. They are similar in some respects, but very different in many crucial aspects from non-Dalits. Dalits, in a word, constitute a varying complex of cultural conditions, but are capable of responding to different natural and social environments. Thus, the Dalit communities are unique entities compared with non-Dalit communities. The very fact that, despite several millennia of onslaughts they have survived, proves this uniqueness and is a matter of pride.

Atitudinal Flexibility

An ethnic identity may shift, where an individual may change his/her ethnic affiliation on the basis of a perception of some strategic advantage, individual or social, to be gained. Sharply defined differences, relatively unchanging, do not constitute a universal characteristic of a community. Even otherwise, change is a sign of life and flexibility is the hallmark of dynamism. Dalits must change with the changing times, come out of their ghettos and shells and strive for unity and a united struggle.

Constructing Dalit Identity

Continuous variations take place in culture and linguistic characteristics, which means there are in effect no boundaries between the different Dalit groups, but there may be differences of languages, religion or family patterns or temporary occupational divergences. It is, therefore, desirable to emphasise ethnicity and ignore the divergences, give importance to similarities and overlook differences, and highlight positive images and minimise negative ones. Dalit social identity should not be negatived.

Handling Contradictions

There may also be some non-congruent variations, differentiating various Dalit groups. Every single variation does not create a bigger divide and need not be over-emphasised. At the same time, these variations need not be overlooked, but grappled with, lived with and be used to their advantage. For example, casteism may finally be abolished one day, although not in the immediate future. But it has to be handled now squarely. Caste is a double-edged sword by which one can kill or be killed depending on how one wields the sword.

Evolving A Dalit Ideology

The Dalits can create for themselves a true collectivity, in which the good of the whole is the highest value they can achieve. Mutual mistrust, born of generations of Dalit experience, has poisoned the attempts to overcome mutual hostility. Yet, Dalits can be mature enough not to undermine Dalit consciousness and Dalit power, which will result in a new value based on Dalit identity. It is, therefore, assumed that there are internal forces in the community, which promise mutual trust and togetherness and help in the evolution of unity. The vicious circle of Dalits being inferior and internalising their own inferiority complex is to be broken. A Dalit value system needs to be conceptualised, a positive self-image should be created and a strong cultural identity needs to be articulated in order to create collective strength and to overcome casteism and caste conflict. The age-old superior-inferior dichotomy should be reversed and a new Dalit social charter, a new philosophy, a theology and an ideology based on Dalit identity evolved.

Individual and Institutional Networking

During the 1970s extending to the 1990s, I have witnessed retrograde activities among Dalit communities and individuals in Orissa and Andhra Pradesh. In Orissa, a dozen people died in conflicts between Konds and Panos. The conflict only strengthened the non-Dalits in the caste society of Orissa. When the new economic policy was introduced and inflation occurred, Dalits were hit hard, but they did not revolt against the non-Dalits but fought among themselves. The conflicts in Andhra Pradesh between the Malas and the Madigas is well known and nationally publicised. We, therefore, need a judicious mixture of self-love and altruism and dedicate ourselves to a mutual support system, move away from the current destructive feelings among the disunited Dalit communities. There should be a network of people and groups among these communities for mutual understanding and social enterprise, the old assumptions need to be reassessed, old inadequacies overcome and old bickerings left behind and new processes of Dalit empowerment initiated. Only then can we construct a mutually acceptable definition of Dalit unity, organize Dalits into a great people and move forward towards a great destiny.

CONCLUSION

It is widely expected that the future will see a political, economic and social unity of the Dalits. The atrocities and incidents of violence will gradually vanish as Dalits organise themselves politically, socially and culturally as united fronts, alliances or partners and move forward towards progress and development.

REFERENCES

Blauner, Rebert, *Racial Oppression in America,* New York, Harper and Row, 1972, pp. 82-110.

Grecer, Colın, "Remembering Class: An Interpretation" in Colin Greer, (ed.), *The Divided Society: The Ethnic Experson in America,* New York, Basic Books, 1974. p. 35

Hogg, Michael A. and Dominic Abrams, *Social Identification,* Routledge, London and New York, 1998.

Karolson, B.G., *Contested Belonging,* Curzon Press, Surrey, UK 2000.

Nayak, R.K. (Ed.) *The Fourth World: Appraisal and Aspirations,* Manohar, Delhi, 1997.

Rainwater, Lee, *Behind the Ghetto Walls: Black Family life in a federal slum,* Chicago Slum, Chicago, Aldine, 1970, pp. 68-69.

2

DALIT WOMEN : ISSUES AND CHALLENGES

Introduction

All human beings have the right to live with dignity. The concept of human rights aims at protection of rights like right to life, liberty and property. These rights are attributed to human beings irrespective of class, caste, gender, colour and religion. The Universal Declaration of Human Rights was unanimously adopted by the UN General Assembly on 10 December, 1948. The preamble of Indian constitution adequately empowers the central and state government to eliminate human rights violation in the country.

In spite of these international and national declarations and resolutions, human rights are violated in different countries all over the world. In Indian society, due to the social barriers such as casteism, untouchability, patriarchy, disparity, superstition, religious exploitation and class variations, specific groups are becoming weaker and marginalised. These groups are facing the problems of identity crisis, deprivation, discrimination and atrocities. These marginalised groups are also identified and recognised as dalits, SCs (scheduled castes) STs (scheduled tribes), OBCs (other backward castes) NT (nomadic tribes) DT (denotified tribes) religious and linguistic minorities.

Violence on human beings in any form results in violation of human rights. Human rights of dalits and women in general are normally violated by high castes and powerful communities to practice and exhibit patriarchy and castetism. But human rights of dalit women are violated extremely and in peculiar form. Dalit women are in worst position than dalits in general, in terms of sex ratio, wages, employment, occupation, assets, education, health, social mobility and political participation. Hence, it is important to discuss the status of dalit women and various problems they face even after 60 years of Independence.

This study makes an attempt to discuss basic facts, issues and concerns related to dalit women to suggest some alternatives to combat violation of their rights for social justice and equality. Explanation of relevant terms such as 'dalit', 'dalitism', and 'dalit women', is given below to broaden understanding about the issue. Further, the vulnerable situation of dalit women is also discussed in detail.

Dalit

Dalit ('oppressed' or 'broken') is not a new word. Apparently it was used in the 1930s as a Hindi and Marathi translation of 'depressed classes'. The British used this term for what are now called the scheduled caste. Dr. Ambedkar chose the term 'broken men', as English translation of 'Dalit', to refer to the original ancestors of the untouchables. Dalit Panthers, the youth activists from dalit community revived the term and in their 1973 manifesto expanded its reference to include the scheduled tribes, neo Buddhists, the working people, the landless and poor peasants, women and also those who are being exploited politically, economically in the name of religion (Omvedt cited in Webster, J, 1999).

Dalitism

Dalitism essentially implies conditions of subjugation; economic, political, social and cultural. Dalitism also embodies different degrees of marginalisation. It includes not only marginalised status in the economic sphere but also in cultural, political, religious and social domains. That means Dalitism symbolises marginalisation. It is a well-known fact that marginalisation denies basic human rights and social justice.

Dalit Women

Dalit women are one of the most marginalised segments in the society. The condition of dalit women is more vulnerable than non-dalit women. Dalit women are suffering from multi-disadvantages :

(*a*) of being dalit i.e socio-economically and culturally marginalised section,

(*b*) being women and sharing the gender based inequalities and subordination.

To explore these and other crucial issues concerning dalit women there is need to discuss some basic facts concerning the vulnerable situation of dalit women.

Vulnerability of Dalit Women

It is easy for the historically dominating caste and gender to violate human rights of dalit women who are at the lowest rung of the hierarchical ladder. The type of violence inflicted on dalits is in the form of severest violation of human rights. Dalit and tribal women are raped as part of an effort by upper caste leaders, land lords and police to suppress movements to demand payment of minimum wages, to settle share cropping disputes or to reclaim lost lands. The recent incident of Khairlanji Massacare is not something new. A dalit family had refused to let upper caste villagers built a road through their fields. Hence on September, 29th, 2006, Bhaiyalal Bhotmange's family comprising his wife Surekha, daughter Prinyanka and two sons were killed by the villagers of Khairlangi in Bhandra district of Maharashtra. They were first attacked with huge iron chains and than abused by the other caste women of the village. Surekha and Priyanka were paraded naked and raped, and later, their bodies were mutilated and thrown into a pond.

This shows that dalit women are easy targets for any perpetrator upper caste considers them to be sexually available. Hence, they are largely unprotected by the state machinery. Further, there is prevalence of violence, making dalit women eat human excreta, parading them naked, gang- rape, murder, dacoity, robbery and burning of their huts or communities. These are the types of crime, which violate their human rights. According to SCs/STs commission report between 1981 and 1986 about 4000 dalit women became victim of rape. In 1993 - 94, this figure rose to 798 and 992 respectively. This means annually about 700 dalit women fall prey to sexual assault by high caste people.

The main complaints of the poorer dalit women are that they have no good houses. In urban areas, most of them stay in unhygienic slums and in rural areas, their houses are away from mainstream society. Under conditions of grinding poverty and severe exploitation at workplace, dalit women also suffer caste specific ban on water access from upper castes and may be beaten up in their own houses as well. A poem by a dalit poetess Teressama, a teacher from Guntur puts the situation in the following words:

> We go to work for we are poor. But the same silken beds mock us, while we are ravished in broad daylight. Ill-starred our horoscopes are even our tottering husbands lying on the cots in the corner Hiss and shout for revenge. If we cannot stand their touch.

At the outset, prevailing caste and secondary status of women in the society is largely responsible for violation of human rights of dalit women. To understand the root cause of the situation it is essential to examine basic factors responsible for their vulnerability.

Socio-cultural and Religious Factors

First and foremost dalit women are victims of social, religious and cultural practices like Devdasis and Jogins. In the name of these practices, village girls are married to God by their helpless parents. These girls are then sexually exploited by the upper caste landlords and rich men and directed in to trafficking and prostitution. In his autobiography, Kale (1994) has described a ritual called 'chira'. The literal meaning of the word 'chira', is to cut or break. In this ritual, when a girl from the lower caste community reaches the age of puberty, an elderly prestigious man from the higher caste breaks the hymen of the girl child by sexual act. This ritual is performed in a way to make the girl accept this fact as a routine practice.

The 28th report of SC/ST commission reported that in February 1986 there were about ten thousand Jogins belonging to SC in Nizamabad district of Andhra Pradesh. The survey submitted by the district collector to Schedule Caste Finance Corporation revealed prevalence of 15,850 cases. Eighty per cent of these Jogins belonged to SC (Pal and Bhargav,1999). This data is just an example of one district of the country. Practices such as Chira, Jogins, Devdasi which are prevalent even today are harmful and threaten the dignity of dalit women and violate their human rights.

Educational Status

Low level of education is a problem in itself and in turn gives rise to many other problems. In 1991, literacy among the dalit women was indeed quite low. In rural areas only 19.46 percentage women were literate. A report published by Ministry of Welfare, Government of India in 1998 showed that there is much difference in the literacy rate of dalits and non-dalits in general, and gender specific. Literacy rate of non-dalits is 64.13 per cent and literacy rate of women is 39.29 per cent, where as dalit women's literacy rate is only 23.76 per cent (Paswan and Jaidev, 2002). There is a large disparity in the literacy rate due to widespread prejudice based on castetism and patriarchy against dalits and women in general and dalit women in particular.

Economic Deprivation and Unemployment

A careful look at the economic situation of dalit women reveals that their work force structure is such that they rarely own any land. A large majority of them wor as agricultural labourers. The rate of unemployment among them is also quite high. About 90 per cent of women working in unorganised sector are mainly from lower castes. In 1991, about 71 per cent of dalit women workers in rural area were agricultural labourers. Only 19 per cent of them owned land.

A prominent researcher and sociologist while sharing her experience from a research on gender and land issue, informed that, when she enquired with dalit women about land owned by them in their names, they wondered about permissibility of owning land in their name. This indicates that neither do they own any land nor are they aware of their rights on land. When enquiries were made with *Stri-mukti* sanghatana and Prerana, Mumbai based organisations working on the issue of rag picking and prostitution respectively, to ascertain the proportion of dalit women in these occupations, it was learnt that NGOs usually do not keep record of caste.

However, Human Rights Watch Report (1998) mentioned that a large number of dalit women are engaged in unclean, inferior occupation such as sweeping, scavenging and working in dumping grounds, rag picking and also in prostitution. These women have to face steep discrimination in the matters of social relation and employment due to their engagement in these occupations.

Health and Nutrition Status

Dalit women's daily diet is the leftover of family meals, inadequate in quantity and quality. Health services are either not available in case of illness or unaffordable even if available. In addition, due to early marriage and too many pregnancies their health is always at risk. If birth control is practiced at all, 91 per cent cases of tubetomy are performed on the women who have to carry the burden of family planning. In an overall situation where dalits are prone to ailments in general, women suffer from more serious and more varied kind of sickness. More than 80 per cent of women in reproductive age group

(15 to 45) are anaemic. Poor health status of dalit women pushes her into more vulnerable situation.

Political Position

Women constitute half of total population, but are unable to get equal share in active politics. Their socioeconomic status directly depends on their participation in politics. Political parties in India speak much about equality of women but have totally ignored the dalit women.

Traditionally, leadership in the village was confined to 'rural elites', who were aged and belonging to higher castes. In the year 1993, 73rd amendment in the constitution granted reservation to dalits, tribals and women in local government. This amendment made it compulsory that one-third of the seats reserved for dalits be filled by dalit women.

In some states, there has been little or no acceptance of reservation for the lower castes and dalit women by the upper castes. This has resulted in atrocities against panchayat members including women. Dalits who stood for election were beaten, and dalit women were raped and ill-treated. The members of the higher castes, who are not prepared to relinquish power to the lower castes, grabbed their land. An easier method to retain power is to put-up proxy candidates but keep the control in the hands of the dominant castes, always men.

The incapacity of women, particularly dalit women, to assert their rights is at the root of the problem. The reservation for dalits, particularly for women, is accepted in form but seldom in substance. Any change in the status quo is resisted. Dalit women's sitting on chairs is seen as threat to social hierarchy. So, the upper castes in the village vetoed chairs in the panchayat office.

Dalit women also faced many problems in performing their duties due to illiteracy, lack of information and dependency on the male members of their families. An important obstacle is the no-confidence motion against dalit women as *pradhan* by the dominant sections. Rural elites are unable to accept the power, which has been given into the hands of the poorer and disadvantaged women. Despite recognition and legal sanction for political rights, rigid caste system and patriarchy directly and indirectly has been suppressing dalit women and violating their political rights.

This proves that human rights of dalit women are violated right from her family to the society at large by one and all. All these factors are largely responsible for the precarious position of dalit women as far as their social, cultural, religious, economic, health and political status in the society is concerned. These factors force them to mutely allow violation of their civic and human rights. Thus, they become victims of universal violence.

Efforts to Protect Human Rights of Dalit Women

With the realisation that violence is one of the potent threats to the peaceful existence of human beings, whole hearted and all round efforts are made at international, national and local level. The preamble to the Universal Declaration of Human Rights (UDHR) serves as a foundation and philosophy of Human rights. There are a host of international conventions including those for prevention and punishment of genocide and elimination of all forms of racial and gender-based discrimination.

The World Conference Against Racism related to racial discrimination, xenophobia and intolerance held in Durban, South Africa in 2001, brought the issue of caste and untouchability based discrimination on the agenda of UN Conference in Durban. Among the several organisations, the National Campaign on Dalit Human Rights—a collective of dalit NGOs, other NGOs, academicians', activists and large number of supporters spearheaded the national campaign in India for inclusion of the issue of caste and untouchability based discrimination in the Durban Conference.

The preamble of Indian constitution adequately empowers the central and state government to eliminate human right violation in the country. Article 17 of the constitution provides for removal of untouchability. Based on this article, Protection of Civil Rights Act' (PCR), was passed in 1955. However, there was no conviction/under this Act hence, Thirty-four years after the introduction of PCR Act, the Scheduled Caste and Schedule Tribes Act 1989 was enacted to bring various forms of atrocities to an end. In this Act, the complainant is given more weightage. There are stringent provisions against the police for negligence.

Emerging Identity of Dalit Women and Formation of Dalit Women's Organisations

The focus on education of low caste women is one of the important factors responsible for the emerging identity of Dalit women. Reformist intervention by Savitribai and Mahatma Phule of opening school for untouchable girls way back in 1848 was a turning point for changing status of dalit women. Dr. Ambedkar's thought and action made important differences in the lives of dalit women. His movement and especially his organisations encouraged many dalit women to become educated to be active in public life and to gain leadership, self respect in the contemporary period encouraged women to participate in organisation for dalit women at regional, state and national level.

After Independence in 1960s and 70s, the dalit movement and women's movement emerged to demand their rights against caste and gender respectively. However, specific problems of dalit women were not acknowledged by these movements. Hence in 1990s there were several special, independent and autonomous assertions of dalit women's identity; a case in point is the formation of National Federation for Dalit Women (NFDW) and All India Dalit Women's Forum (AIDWF) at the state level. The Maharashtra Dalit Mahila Sanghatana (MDMS) was formed in 1995. A year earlier, the women's wing of Bhartiya Republican Party (BRP) and the

Bahujan Mahila Sangha (BMS) was set up the Bahujan Mahila Parishad.

In December 1996, at Chandrapur, a Vikas Vanchit Dalit Mahila Parishad (WDMP) was organised and a proposal to commemorate 25th December (the day on which Ambedkar had set Manusmriti on fire) as Bhartiya Smriti Divas was advanced. The Christi Mahila Sanghatana, an organisation of Dalit Christian Women was established in 1997. These organisations have come together on several issues such as celebration of Bhartiya Stree Mukti Divas and on the issue of reservation for OBC women in parliament bodies. Indian Association of Women Studies (IAWS) network with dalit feminist across different regions had brought special issues on problems and identity of dalit women.

Several efforts have been made since Independence to secure human rights of women in general and dalit women in particular. Despite this, human rights of dalit women are seen to be violated in different forms. Such infringement of human rights echoes the need of evolving suitable mechanism to empower dalit women to assert for equal rights and justice in order to live a dignified life.

Empowering Dalit Women

To be human is to respond to human sufferings and pain with compassion and effective concern. It is not enough to feel with the dalit women in their pain, There is more need for effective action, otherwise it would be just sentimentalism' says Sequeira in his article 'Human Response to Dalit Women. The needs and the problems of dalit women differ with city, village, area and caste. It is essential to keep in mind that dalit women are not mere individuals but belong to a sociological and dialectical system. Therefore, to recognise the system and to prohibit violation, first and foremost proper perspectives about the issues has to be developed among all by considering following suggestions:

Awareness for Assertion

Extensive reading of available literature can be done by young generation to understand the profile and problems of dalit women. Factual incidents and success stories of dalit women namely, 'We made History Too' by Meenakshi Moon & Urmila Pawar can be included in the educational texts.

Access and Exposure Visits

Special exposure visits to dalit localities can be organised for school and college students to assess basic amenities accessible to dalit women namely, water, electricity, health and hygiene. Similarly dalit women's visit to urban structured colonies can be arranged to impress upon the importance of standard of living of non-dalits. Such purposeful visits will broaden their horizons resulting in improved living of marginalised section.

Academic Activities

Academic institutions need to be encouraged to undertake studies to assess the problems of violence and atrocities against dalit women as also the reasons therefore and to work out ways to overcome them. Thought-provoking sessions on harmful social religions practices namely, Chira, Devdasi, Jogin need to be held for basic understanding and effective interventional strategies.

Campaigns and Sessions

Campaigns for equal and rational distribution of natural resources among weaker sections can be organised to secure their rightful means of livelihood. Proper rehabilitation and shelter can be provided to those communities, which are out of the social periphery (NT/DT) to protect them from the risk of sexual abuse.

Inclusion of Dalit Women in Various System

More dalit women in their population proportion (16.5% SC, 7.5% ST) should be given chance to enter in the system like police, judiciary, education, health and politics.

Sessions can be organised for dalit activist and women activists to sensitize them about the magnitude of torture and oppression faced by the dalit women. Legal education dealing with protection of human rights of dalits and Prevention of Atrocities Act (1989) can be organised to prevent the problems of castism.

CONCLUSION

At the beginning of new millennium, it is absolutely necessary that common people need to be sensitised about the prevailing atrocities against Dalit women. There is a growing need to capture violation of human rights of dalit women, so that talent and potential of Dalit Womens can be used for development of nation.

According to Vippal, a nation does not prosper only on fertile soil, dense forests and everflowing rivers. It is the healthy people who make a nation. A society is made up of both men and women from all states. If women from whichever state is weak and exploited, it is not a healthy society. And when a society is healthy, then the nation will march ahead. To fulfil these dreams women in general and particularly from weaker section need to be empowered for development of the nation.

REFERENCES

Ahuja, R. , *Violence Against Women,* Rawat Publication, New Delhi, 1998.

Bandhu, P., *Dalit Women's cry for Liberation: My Rights Are Rising like the Sun, will you deny this sunrise"?* Edited in Rao (2003). *Caste and Gender,* Kali For Women, New Delhi, 2003.

Chakravati, V., *Reconceptualising Gender, Phule, Brahmanisam and Brahminial Patriarchy,* edited in Rao (2003) *Caste and Gender,* Kali for women, New Delhi, 2003.

Chitnis, V., *Human Rights of the vulnerable groups,* Futuristic Digital, Pune, 2005.

Dietrich, G., *Dalit Movement and Women's Movement,* Edited in Rao (2003): *Caste and Gender,* Kali for Women, New Delhi, 2003.

Jogdand, P., *Dalit Women, Issues and Perspectives,* Gyan Publication, New Delhi, 1995.

Kale, R., *Kolhatyachrepor,* Granthali Publication, Mumbai, 1994.

Kumar, N., *Dalit Policies, Politics and Parliament,* Shipra Publication, New Delhi, 2004.

Kumar, N. and Raj, M., *Dalit Leadership in Panchayats,* Institute of Dalit Studies, Rawat Publication, New Delhi, 2006.

Michael, S., *Dalits in Modern India, Vision and Values,* Vistar Publication, New Delhi, 1999.

Omvedt, G., *Dalit Women and Communalism,* edited in Jogdand (1995) *Dalit Women, Issues and Perspectives,* Gyan Publication, New Delhi, 1995.

Pal, R. and Bhargav, G., *Human Rights of Dalits: Societal Violation,* Gyan Publication, New Delhi, 1999.

Paswan, S. and Jaidev, : *Encyclopedia of Dalits in India* (Vol. No. 10 education), 2002.

Pandit, V., Handbook on Prevention of Atrocities (SC/ST) Vidnayak·Sansod Prakashan, Ujgaon, Maharashtra, 1995.

Punalekar, S., *On Dalitism and Gender,* edited in Jogadand (1995) *Dalit Women's Issues and Perspectives,* Gyan Publication, New Delhi, 1995.

Pillai, T., *Ambedkar's Daughters: A Study of Mahar Women in Ahmednagar District of Maharashtra* edited in Michaels (1999) *Dalits in Modern India, Vision and Values,* Vistar Publication, New Delhi, 1999.

Thorat, S. and Umakant, *Caste, Role and Discrimination, Discourses in International Context,* Rawat Publication, New Delhi, 2004.

Webstar, J., *Who is Dalit* edited in Michael (1999) *Dalit's in Modern India, Vision and Values,* Vistar Publication, New Delhi, 1999.

Zelliot, E., *Dr. Ambedkar and the Empowerment of Women,* edited in Rao (2003) *Caste and Gender,* Kali for Women, New Delhi, 2003.

3

DALIT WOMEN AND SOCIAL DEVELOPMENT

In India the challenges to those engaged in building a women's movement are formidable. Activists who seek to capture political space for women's issues must work to have their voices heard alongside and as part of the multiplicity of class, linguistic, religious, ethnic and caste claimants that make up the Indian polity. The purpose of this article is to consider the kind of power and resources that the Indian women's movement has utilised in the struggle to bring attention to women's subordination.

It has been argued that what has given the Indian women's movement influence far in excess of its numerical strength or organisational cohesiveness has been its ability to "name" issues, to call particular attention to aspects of women's lives that journalists, intellectual and political elites, and a large cross-section of the general population could no longer ignore. Beginning in the late 1970s, women activists undertook to organise around issues of gender violence—rape, dowry deaths, wife-beating, sati (the immolation of widows on their husband's funeral pyre), female-neglect resulting in differential mortality rates, and, more recently, female foeticide following amniocentesis. Raising such issues won the movement its share of critics but without the protest against gender violence. It is questionable whether the growing awareness of gender issues which now exists in India would have developed.

Issues of violence against women by no means constitute the whole or even the primary focus of the contemporary women's movement in India. Only recently, at the third annual women activists conference in Patna (February 1988) and at the Fourth National Conference on Women's Studies in Andhra (December 1988), the debates ranged broadly across questions of poverty, employment, work, property, health and ecology, com-munalism, culture and religion, political representation, law, reproducdon, as well as issues of gender violence. But, it was the focus on violence against women, beginning in the late 1970s, that propelled the movement forward and endowed it with much of its present strength.

Indian Women's Movement: An Overview

The contemporary Indian women's movement is constituted by a panoply of organisations—urban and rural, academic and activist—drawn from upper, middle, and lower-income segments of society (with the leadership stratum largely upper-middle class). Although on particular occasions thousands of women can be mobilised for protests, rallies and mass meetings, the numbers of activists with sustained movement involvement as well as supporters who identify with a collective feminist consciousness are limited in comparison with such numbers in the West. In structure and ideology, the movement resembles its European more than its American counterpart in that feminist groups in India are dispersed (there is no central organisation like NOW) and political commitments and language are distinctly more leftist than liberal. Both ideologically and structurally, however, the movement is marked by heterogeneity. As Susie Tharu observes, "the movement as it has emerged today, has no centralised organisation, no commonly acknowledged leadership, no unifocal programme.... Groups do not share a commitment to any one analysis of women's oppression, or its relationship with other forms of oppression/exploitation, or the strategies necessary for action or change. In fact, even an intra-group consensus is often not assumed or demanded."

The movement is multi-associational, ideologically diverse, regionally broad, and concerned with a vast array of issues. Taxonomically, it can be thought of as embracing six organisational sectors each with particular strengths and weaknesses.

Women's Organisations

These encompass both older and newer organisations ranging from the venerable All-India Women's Conference (AIWC) associated with Congress to the newer Mahila Dakshata Samiti formed as a women's wing of the Janata Party in 1978. Founded in 1927 as a social reform organisation committed particularly to the promotion of education for women, AIWC declared itself apolitical. There were, nevertheless, many prominent members of AIWC who were also active in the nationalist movement. Over the course of particular periods mutual support existed between the movement and the conference. Since Independence, the conference has been closely connected to the Congress Party.

Under CPI leadership, the National Federation of Indian Women (NFIW) was formed in 1954. Following the Communist party split, CPM women worked in the All India Working Women's Coordination Committee and later also in the All-India Democratic Women's Association (AIDWA), formed in the 1970s under pressure from the newer women's movement. The national organisation has been less active than particular subunits such as the Janwadi Mahila Samiti in Delhi whose protest against dowry deaths and whose work in slums is well known. The Mahila Dakshata Samiti, led by Promila Dandavate, whose socialist and later Janata affiliation links organisation to party has also been very active in Delhi.

Other loosely affiliated organisations existed such as the Progressive Organisation of Women (POW) linked to Naxalite student groups in Hyderabad which were in turn succeeded by the more autonomous Stri Shakti Sanghatana (SSS). A recently formed Samagra Mahila Agadhi (the "All-Women's Front") affiliated with the Sharad Joshi-led Shetkari Sanghatana (a powerful opposition force in Maharashtra) has been formed to contest panchayat elections.

Leftist party commentators, particularly, argue that women's groups associated with parties have the potential of being more effective because of their connections with mass organisations. Without these party connections, feminist activism would "remain isolated [and] middle class with limited fields of perception and activity." Whether or not this charge is valid, it is clear that these party-connected groups are far better able to mobilise huge numbers of women for demonstrations. During the controversy over the Muslim Women (Protection of Rights in Marriage) Bill in 1986, for instance, the leftist party-connected women's groups mobilised large numbers of women for demonstrations, numbers which the Delhi-based autonomous groups could not have brought out. Similarly, in 1986 the Sharad Joshi-led groups of Shetkari Sangathana in Maharashtra brought forty-thousand rural women together in a women's meet in Chandwad.

Autonomous Women's Groups

Beginning in the late 1970s, feminists came together in what were later termed "autonomous women's organisations." These groups were independent of party affiliation although individual members often had party links. The distinction between party-linked and autonomous groups is not always clear-cut. Such groups as POW, for instance, mentioned above, might arguably be categorised as "autonomous" rather than party-linked but most of the autonomous groups do not have the clear party affiliations that the Janwadi or Mahila Dakshata Samiti have.

These newer autonomous organisations are largely urban-based. In Delhi, in January 1979, a small group of women began the publication of *Manushi* (in English and Hindi) that was soon to achieve a circulation of several thousand. Saheli, formed in 1982, concerned itself particularly with issues of dowry and domestic violence; Mediastorm with documentary films covering current controversial issues; Ankoor with adult education; Jaguri with the collection of feminist documentation, film and literature; Kali For Women devoted itself to the publication of original feminist literature and analysis. Stree Sangharsh staged street plays about dowry murders, rape and "eve-teasing" (harassment). The list of Delhi organisations is long.

In Bombay, the Forum against Oppression of Women, organised in 1981, took up issues of rape (particularly police and custodial rape), dowry deaths and harassment of women commuters. The Women's Centre in Bombay has provided legal help and counselling to women in need. Also active earlier in Maharashtra was the leftist Purogami Street Sanghatana that started *Bayza,* a Marathi women's journal.

Groups elsewhere in India include the SSS in Hyderabad (mentioned above); Vimochana (Bangalore); Pennurima Iyakkam (Tamil Nadu); Chingari Nari Sangathan (Ahmedabad), the Ahmedabad Women's Action Group; the Stree Jagruti Samiti (Bangalore and Bombay) among many others.

The membership of these groups is small. Many have between ten and twenty active members; some are scarcely one- or two-person operations. But when activists from these different groups come together, their numbers can be impressive. The Bihar conference in February 1988, for instance, drew 750 representatives of different autonomous groups with 8000 people attending the final rally. But generally, the strength of these autonomous groups is not based on their ability to mobilise large numbers in protests or demonstrations but rather stems from their capacity to reflect on, to name, and to publicise movement issues as will be detailed in the later discussion of the movement's politicisation of the issue of gender violence.

Grassroots Organisations

An important force that works for women's interests is located in the grass-roots political movements of India in which women play a major role. These have included the well-known Chipko (tree-hugging) movement that protested deforestation in Uttarkhand then UP in 1978, and the Shramik Sanghatana movement in Dhulia District of Maharashtra in which activist Bhil women and others organised against wife-beating, male drinking and harassment. Activist Dalit women were important in pressuring the J.P. Narayan-formed Yuva Sangarsh Vahini in Bodh Gaya, Bihar, to address issues of drunkenness and wife-beating. Similar movements in Marathwada also took place in the late 1970s under the guidance of the Kashtakari Sanghatana.

These grassroots groups have undertaken energetic campaigns for rise in wages, an end to wife beating and the alcoholism of their husbands, and to protest incursions of outsiders on their livelihood. But such efforts are fragmented, only occasionally linked by national meetings or gatherings.

Women's Research Institutes

Over the last ten years a number of institutes have become a home to large research efforts for the study of women's issues. In New Delhi, these include the Centre for Women's Development Studies (CWDS); the Institute of Social Studies Trust; the Indian Social Institute Programme for Women's Development (a research and networking organisation associated with the Jesuit social action institute and in Bombay); and the Research Centre for Women's Studies which is associated with SNDT Women's University in Bombay.

Each of these centres has research and activist components as part of their broad agenda. CWDS, for example, is involved in two "action research" projects in West Bengal and the Punjab where staff members help in the coordination, networking, training programmes and evaluation of women's employment and production projects. In contradiction to the image sometimes entertained of these organisations—that they are narrowly-focussed on middle-class concerns—many, indeed most, of the research and activist projects address issues facing rural and poor women.

These research organisations function in an interesting "place" in the movement. Unlike women's studies faculty in the United States, the research staff of these institutes (there are exceptions) do little teaching. They are, however, much more closely linked to the extra-university sections of the women's movement than is true of their U.S. counterparts. Their role in creating feminist consciousness occurs not through the classroom but through the dual links that many feminist researchers in these institutes have, both to those in policy-making positions in government and to activists in different sectors of the movement itself.

Women's Development Organisations

The last decade and a half has also seen the formation of a number of nongovernmental, largely urban organisations which attempt to enhance the economic situation of women workers in the informal sector. The Self-Employed Women's Association (SEWA) organised in 1972 and led by Ela Bhatt in Gujarat; the Working Women's Forum in Madras, initiated in 1978 and directed by Jaya Arunachalam; and the Annapurna Mahila Mandal in Bombay founded in 1975 by veteran trade unionist Prema Purao have organised approximately sixty-five thousand women who are petty vendors, hawkers, home-based producers, and labourers. A large number of smaller but important organisations such as the Mobile Creches started by Mina Swaminathan in Delhi are also dispersed in cities and towns throughout India.

The Numerous "Old" and "New" Voluntary Organisations

These include religious, caste, ethnic and nonsectarian organisations that offer services to poor women (job training, legal aid, health clinics, etc.). Although, the targeted beneficiaries of these volunteer groups are usually low-income women, certain projects are aimed at a more middle-class clientele, as for example the fund-raising schemes in Bombay to construct dormitories for working and professional women.

The inclusion of this kind of voluntary organisation within the definitional parameter of the women's movement might be debated. These "charitable" organisations tend not to see themselves as explicitly mobilisational and do not begin to be as self-conscious as the autonomous women's groups about breaking down the stratification between volunteer and client. Unlike the more autonomous organisations or development projects sponsored by the women's studies research institutes, there is less self-reflection about the dangers, as Maitreyi Krishna Raj observes, of "becoming intermediaries for others' uplift."

At the same time it is important to recognise that the functional distinction between these more traditional voluntary groups and the more "feminist" organisation groups is not always so clear in practice. Many of the more "traditional" voluntary organisations do empower women through their services. By the same token, many of the newer feminist organisations express frustration at becoming principally social service associations unable to retain the participation of clients after personal problems have been addressed.

Several general points can be drawn from this synopsis of the women's movement. (1) The movement in India is highly diversified among party-affiliated groups, autonomous feminist organisations, grass roots organisations, private voluntary and development groups and institutions of academic research. (2) This diversity is echoed in the ideological character and political concerns of the movement. Organisational agendas span the range from reformist to radical and target a broad range of concerns from the economic livelihood of poor women to sexual violence across social groups. (3) Each of the movement's organisational sectors has distinct strengths. The party-affiliated groups are of course able to draw on political leverage which established political parties can exert and mobilise funds and people for protest demonstrations more readily than the autonomous groups can. The development groups (SEWA and WWF, for instance) as mass organisations also have far greater numbers than the autonomous groups.

The autonomous groups, however, have acute political savvy and connections to professional, media, and governmental circles which enable them to politicise issues with an effectiveness that belies their numerical "insignificance." (4) The distinction between voluntary and autonomous feminist groups according to whether they serve social services rather than mobilisational functions is more a matter of degree than of kind. (5) Similarly although the "old" movement could be thought of as being less explicitly mobilisational and more directed toward women's welfare concerns than toward the articulation of women's interests as such, this functional distinction is far from absolute. The politics of social reformism and the politics of mobilisation and empowerment have coexisted in the period before 1975 and afterwards with the rise of the more autonomous organisations.

Expanding Feminist Agenda : Protest Against Violence

The year 1975 is often thought of as the beginning of the contemporary "feminist" movement in India. The term, feminism, is usually associated with the autonomous sector of the movement—groups like Saheli, Manushi, the Forum Against Oppression—that emerged in the late 1970s and that mobilised around issues of gender violence. It is true that in some senses 1975 was a beginning. In anticipation of the 1975 International Women's Year declared by the United Nations, the government or India commissioned a report that was to play a catalytic role in the emergence of the contemporary feminist movement in India. Published in 1974, the report dramatically called attention to existing gender inequality with its documentation of a declining sex ratio (read as an indicator of differential female mortality) and its presentation of evidence of inequalities in education, income, access to health care and political representation.

The report galvanised both academics and activists. Not only did it cite patterns of inequality that had not been widely recognised but no less important, the process of preparing the report caused several women members of the commission to redirect their scholarly and activist energies entirely. Having previously neither reflected on nor undertaken research on women's issues Lotika Sarkar and Vina Mazumdar were to go on to occupy positions among those at the forefront of the women's movement.

That year (1975) two conferences on gender were held—the first in Pune, sponsored by various parties of the left, and the second in Trivandrum, run by the Indian School of Social Sciences. The national Emergency, imposed in 1975, spawned the birth of numerous civil liberties groups that protested the abrogation of democratic rights. These events in the mid-decade produced an upsurge of interest in and organisation around gender issues.

Between 1975 and 1980, the movement focussed largely on economic and demographic issues. The two important conferences in 1975 in Pune and Trivandrum had given due attention to issues of violence, dwelling largely on economic questions brought to the fore as a natural part of the left's agenda. At these conferences and elsewhere prior to the turn of the decade, there was some discussion of dowry issues, the sexual exploitation of women in advertising and of "atrocities perpetrated against women" largely as part of upper-class exploitation of untouchables and the poor, but the general issue of sexual violence was given little attention. It was not only the left parties that glossed over such concerns. Several of the authors of the 1974 *Towards Equality* report have reflected with retrospective surprise at their own inattention to sexual violence. One member comments,

> "I realise now that there were other things which we should have investigated. We did not include rape in our enquiry. We took some note of suicides when they were brought to our notice, but no one mentioned a single case of dowry murder. Harassment, even torture was reported but never a murder.

> Today I realise that the issue of violence of crimes against women did not feature in our report as we have not investigated it. Even the practice of dowry was not in our initial questionnaire —it was forced on us by the women we met".

More than dowry, when I look back I am shocked that we have not taken up the issue of rape at all. As far as I can recollect, nowhere in our discussions on women, the problem of rape was ever brought up. Rape was brought up from time to time only in the context of prostitution. I cannot say that I was not aware of rape as an instrument in subjugating the lower classes and lower castes, but what has come to light since the publication of the report, I was not aware of.

In 1979-1980, the movement shifted gears. As Gail Omvedt observes, "the year 1980 can be considered to be an important dividing line." It was at this point that the women's movement led by the autonomous women's organisations brought issues of sexual violence to the forefront of the feminist agenda. This broadening of the feminist agenda was catalysed by the political mobilisation around the Mathura case. Mathura was a tribal girl of between fourteen and sixteen years old when she was called to a police station in a small town of Maharashtra where she was raped while in police custody by two constables. The lower (sessions) court held that she was "of loose morals" and found the policemen innocent, a judgment overturned by the high court. However, on appeal the Supreme Court ruled that Mathura had consented to sexual intercourse. This verdict was protested by four Delhi University law professors who in 1979 wrote an open letter to the Chief Justice of India. The four included one of the women, Lotika Sarkar, who had served on the Status of Women commission earlier in the decade. The letter was followed by country-wide mobilisations around the Mathura rape case and around the issue of custodial rape. *Manushi* and other feminist newsletters and journals carried exposes and personal accounts of women who had been victimised. Others told the tragic stories of daughters and sisters who had been ill-treated, assaulted, or burned to death. These were accounts of what the women's movement came to term "bride-burning" or "dowry-deaths," where in-laws dissatisfied with the young wife and/or with the dowry she had brought would pour kerosene and set fire to her clothing causing her death in incidents made to look like accidents from the explosion of the small kerosene stoves many households use for cooking.

Between 1979 and the present, feminist activists mobilised around different aspects of gender violence. The anti-rape protests were followed by the anti-dowry campaigns of 1981-84. Feminist groups have continued their support of women who are victims of family violence and have extended their protest to other issues such as the practice of sati and female foeticide.

Shifting Agenda : An Explanation

The movement's turn-of-the-decade shift towards protesting violence against women evoked criticism largely from leftist quarters where it was argued that feminists pandered to bourgeois concerns. Lost in the criticism was any real attempt to explore the political logic that steered the women's movement in this direction. This logic was two-pronged: on the one hand, forces *external* to the movement made a "discourse" around violence common currency for movements that sought political attention. By 1980, the threat and/or use of violence by ethnic, religious, and class-based organisations gained currency. Violence was not new to political activists of the 1970s as the bloodshed of partition and the violent demonstrations erupting out of the linguistic state protests of the 1950s and 1960s remind us. But it is clear that by the late 1970s, direct action, frequently violent, became established as one proven method by which government attention to group grievances could be secured. Intensification of conflict and strikes preceded the Emergency in 1975, subsided briefly and again increased.

Second, the movement's concern with issues of violence also follows logically from developments that were *internal* to the movement. Not simply in India but in the experience of other feminist movements as well, feminists appear to address issues of violence only when the movement has established a strong degree of autonomy from the state and party actors. Whether in India or elsewhere, when the state or political parties "sponsor" feminist concerns, concerns about violence against women is rarely a priority.

In Sweden, for instance, where the state has perhaps more clearly than anywhere else declared its commitment to gender equality, and where feminists have been the beneficiaries of close ties to a strong labour-dominated corporatist state structure, issues of violence against women have been low on the agenda. Similarly, in the United States, the first two major legislative initiatives around gender equality (taken in 1963 and 1964 respectively) concerned equal pay and employment and both preceded the emergence of the women's movement. It was only later with the efflorescence of an independent feminist movement that the issues of rape, harassment, and battering came to be articulated and addressed. The more closely tied women's issues are to state and party, the less likely it seems to be that issues of violence will occupy central attention.

The turn to issues of violence, then, followed a logical progression in India as sectors of the women's movement that were autonomous of party politics gained strength. With the emergence of the autonomous wing of the movement, publications and discussion groups provided a forum where personal experiences of battering, rape and dowry violence could be voiced (The attention to dowry-related violence has its own specific history that is linked to the spread and increase in dowry and cash transactions at marriage which may have contributed not only to dowry deaths but to wife beating as well. Hence, the attention to dowry and wife beating could be said to have emanated in part from the changing economic bases of marriage. But the attention to rape that preceded the anti-dowry campaigns cannot be said to have emanated from the same sources.) The pages of *Manushi*, most notably, became the repository for extensive personal accounts of women's experience of violence that had earlier been silenced.

Movement's Strategy

The autonomous groups took up issues of sexual violence through a combination of political strategies that were both radical and pragmatic. The radical dimension of the movement was manifest in that Tharu calls its "commitment to intra-group democracy" as well as in its agitational style of politics, a style nevertheless laced by a strong pragmatic approach to getting things done. The politics of the mobilisation against sexual violence is most clearly illustrated through a depiction of Saheli, one group in Delhi that made gender violence its central issue. Founded in August 1981, it now operates out of a small unimposing upstairs office above a neighbourhood shopping esplanade in a middle/lower-middle class section of New Delhi. The organisation has four to five paid staff members, several full-time volunteers and an extended group of part-time unpaid workers. Earlier Saheli activists spent much of their time on dowry and bride-burning issues. Activists also organised around rape and battering, and in 1984-85 worked with widows in the Sikh resettlement camps and among women in the aftermath of the Sikh massacre. More recently Saheli has considered discontinuing work on dowry murders in order to concentrate resources on women "who live to struggle." The support for victims of battering continues (Saheli's one-room shelter is in continuous use) along with mobilisation around health, housing and other concerns.

Saheli's radical pragmatism has been evident in many dimensions of its political organising. Apprehensive about the cooptative dangers of work with government officialdom, some Saheli activists prefer strategies of agitational politics such as the demonstrations that the organisation once mobilised outside the houses of husbands where a wife had been burned to death. At the same time, Saheli volunteers have met with supervisory officers of the Delhi police urging the instituting of new investigatory procedures. Moderate and agitational politics are sometimes combined as in the case of Asha Rani, a young woman who had left her family and refused to go back despite the vehement attempts of her two brothers to secure her return. In 1982, the brothers together with the local police ransacked the Saheli office in an attempt to find information about their sister's whereabouts. A confrontation between police and Saheli workers ensued followed by a Saheli-led demonstration of fifty shouting and placard-carrying women outside the local police station. The demonstrations and complaints lodged led to the transfer of a senior police officer. Saheli's connections to the media and the newsworthy confrontational politics ensured coverage and won Saheli notoriety and clout. From this point, women identifying with Saheli were able to exact some (not always willing) cooperation from their meetings with local police.

Saheli is also versed in the less public style of politics—using connections to get things done. Saheli's personal connections, for instance, to the Delhi Police Commissioner, Ved Marwah, led to many mutual consultations over police actions concerning the handling of dowry complaints. Letters requesting meetings with Indira Gandhi, ministers and government secretaries were an integral part of Saheli politics. The daily importance of contacts is illustrated by one of the earlier entries to the Saheli diary or log: "March 13, 1983: Spent the whole day making phone calls to every bureaucrat from Director to Joint Secretary in trying to admit Shanti to the Stay Home. We now have a complete list of phone numbers."

Debates in Saheli recur over the acceptability of foreign and governmental funding. The organisation's insistence on the importance of autonomy has periodically led it to refuse such funding or to accept it only for one-time expenditures and only when Saheli has full control over its direction. Extensive discussions are also held about the importance of non-hierarchical methods of organising. During one open meeting held on Saheli's annual August birthday, discussion was invited about the enlargement of the shelter facilities.

New activists argued for setting up different small facilities in several neighborhoods in the belief that this would avoid the necessity of a bureaucratic operation with supervisory wardens overseeing a larger facility. Others with longer experience spoke pragmatically about the greater ease of communication and support services possible with a single if necessarily more "professionalised" facility.

Analogous debates occur over the role of law. Some activists endorse legal reform strategies of the kind that led to Section 498a—that provision in the Indian Penal Code which mandates immediate arrest and severe punishment of family members accused of cruelty towards women. Others see the route of legal reform as, at best, a necessary tactic given existing political constraints. Although there has not been unanimity over tactics and political orientations, the commitment to the mobilisation against gender violence has been maintained.

Consequences of Anti-Violence Organising

The radical pragmatism of the autonomous women's movement has worked quite well given at least two realities such organisations face. First, unlike organisations linked to parties or broader movements, the autonomous women's movement cannot organise vast *numbers* of supporters in protest. Unlinked to party organisations, moreover, the autonomous feminist movements do not have ready access to party leadership and parliamentary votes.

Second, a further constraint the movement faces in its effort to protest violence against women is a state which is *at best* willing but weak. American feminists, particularly those who have come of age as feminists under the reactionary policies of the Reagan administration, cannot help but be impressed by the many highly placed officials and intellectuals in India who have proved to be deeply committed to women's interests. The late J.P. Naik, Margaret Alva of the Ministry of Social Welfare, Ashok Mitra, and former Census Commissioner K.G. Krishnamurthy of the Planning Commission are some of the many names that come to mind. Nevertheless there is a wide gap separating declared policy and its effective execution. India is not short on legislation. There have been reforms in the rape law (the Criminal Law Amendment Act of 1980), 1984 amendments to the Dowry Prohibition Act of 1981, a revision of the Indian Penal Code (Section 498a dealing with the cruelty of a husband and his relatives), and a law prescribing the death penalty for anyone abetting sati and directing the removal of sati temples, etc. Even with some reforms now having been instituted, weak enforcement gives little hope for those who wish to see profound changes in societal practices around gender issues.

Given these constraints, the radical "realpolitik" of autonomous feminist groups has proved quite successful, particularly in three areas. First, it has provided an important source of support for some number, probably not very large, of low-income and middle-class women whose marriages or home life have been rent by violence and abuse. Even if middle-class or lower-middle class women have been the predominant beneficiaries of such support, the importance of such crisis services is undeniable. Yet, it is curious how readily such activities on the part of feminist groups are criticised even by liberals and by the left as anti-family and as presumed evidence of the bourgeois character of the women's movement.

Second, the movement has assisted in successfully pressuring the courts and legislators to begin to take violence against women seriously. In 1983, an additional session judge in Delhi made history by handing down a death sentence conviction in the Sudha Goel dowry murder case, a judgment overturned on appeal. In 1985, the Supreme Court handed down a sentence of life imprisonment for two of the three defendants in the Goel case. In Delhi alone, police figures record between 400 and 630 "accidental" burnings each year for the first part of the 1980s. Although the number of court convictions remains paltry, it is of no small symbolic importance that the courts have begun to reach such verdicts.

By working for the reform of rape law, for the revision of police protocol around allegations of dowry deaths and for changes in the law dealing with violence in the family, feminist groups have helped to remove some of the legitimacy the legal system gave to practices of violence against women.

Third, the greatest impact of feminist activism has been to capture public attention. Violence which had been simply obscured and silenced before has now been named. Feminism's turn to issues of violence has caused a surge in newspaper attention. A study of *The Hindustan Times* (a random sample of twenty days in each year between 1977 and the present) vividly illustrates this dramatic surge in media attention. Three changes occurred: (1) The shift in feminism's agenda coincided with a sharp increase in newspaper coverage. In 1977 and 1978, of the twenty days read, there were only *three* articles on women in the former and *one* in the latter year. In 1979, the year the movement took up issues of violence, the number of articles rose to twelve and stayed constant through the 1980s. (2) The broadening of the movement's agenda to include issues of violence invited newspaper coverage not simply around issues of rape, dowry murders, battering, etc., but also around a range of other movement concerns. Reports on violence comprised between two-thirds and three-fourths of the article coverage. But coverage of other gender issues increased as well. (3) Coverage of violence against women became highly influenced by the movement's construction of violence as a problem. What had earlier been reported as "police blotter" assault or suicide came to be "labelled" as involving a suspicion of dowry murder or forced suicide stemming from family quarrels. What might have been earlier described as sexual assault came to be denoted as rape, and special note was made of police involvement, using the term "custodial rape." The movement's role in "naming" violence seemed to have a clear impact on press reporting.

There can be no doubt that movement-prompted newspaper attention has contributed to the widespread popular recognition of dowry harassment and violence. Newspapers convey consciousness far beyond the direct reach of feminist organisations themselves.

At the same time, as these demonstrations and protests have been of critical importance in eliciting media attention and in shaping a new consciousness around gender violence, they have provoked criticism of the movement as well. Generally this criticism portrays feminist activism as originating out of a Western, bourgeois, modernist perspective. This kind of critique has been articulated most recently in connection with the feminist demonstrations against the sati incident that took place at Deorala, Rajasthanin in September 1987. A sophisticated version of this criticism is set forth by Ashis Nandy. He begins with the observation (in consonance with the argument of many feminists) that sati in these times is likely to occur in the presence of direct or indirect coercion or at the least in the absence of attempts to deter a woman from this act. He also remarks on the likelihood that social dislocation and societal stress provoke families to use such rituals to assert their status in a social hierarchy which is in flux, an analysis echoed in the pages of the feminist journal, *Manushi.* He further stipulates that an analysis of and political response to present-day sati must incorporate the knowledge of the heroic meaning of sati in mythological times—which Vina Mazumdar evinces in her analysis of the dual heroism and oppression of women who undertook to become a sati in earlier times.

Nandy finds the anti-sati demonstrations, however, evidence of the shallow understanding of rural India by feminist and middle-class protestors. He criticises the call for a government ban on the glorification of sati as presumptuous, questioning whether such a ruling would bar the reading of the Mahabharata's treatment of Madri's sati or the ritual worship of the goddess Durga (a question Nandy must have meant largely as a rhetorical flourish rather than as a prediction of any probable government action). But Nandy's more fundamental point deserves serious consideration: when traditional norms and customs that are a source of people's historical identity conflict with prevailing norms about how life is or should be lived now, which values should be privileged? When erstwhile models of the heroic that enshrine a widow's self-immolation as an act of religous devotion confront current secular models of equality, what political praxis would embrace respect for both the old and new? Nandy does not suggest what a preferable response to the Deorala sati might have been. Should there have been no demonstrations? Should feminists have eschewed any appeal to the government for action? If some political and public expression of the view of sati as violence to women was warranted, what form could this expression have taken that might also have acknowledged the mythological tradition that has in the past given the acts of sati its heroic meaning? From a feminist perspective, Nandy's analysis is ultimately inadequate because it does not seek to address questions that are central to political praxis.

CONCLUSION

What gives a social movement strength is not just the existence of organisational networks, strong leadership, access to funds—those attributes usually thought of as movement "resources." Just as critical is the capacity of a movement to produce new meanings in interaction with the political system of which it is a part. The ability of women's organisations in India to act as signifying agents, naming experiences that had been earlier unrecognised, is at the root of the movement's emergence as a growing force in Indian society and politics. By giving prominence to women's experience as victims of violence—of rape, battering, dowry-harassment, murder, and sati—the women's movement has begun to review the way women across a broad spectrum of Indian society see themselves as well as the way women's experiences are understood by those in positions of dominance in society and within the state.

In the first half of this chapter, I have sought to explore the political logic that moved Indian feminism to take up the issue of violence against women. The logic was both external and internal to the women's movement. On the one hand, the persistent if not necessarily increasing reliance on violence to bring ethnic, religious, and other group claims onto the political agenda in India made issues of violence a compelling "currency" in the quest for attention. On the other hand, the emergence of the more autonomous sectors of the movement allowed feminists to find their own voice, not simply around economic issues that were sanctioned as legitimate in the eyes of their leftist political patrons but also around issues of violence that were self-defined as important as women came to speak from their own experience.

The strategic approach of autonomous feminist organisations towards incidences of violence against women. Their political perspective can perhaps best be described as emerging from an ideology of radical pragmatism. Feminist groups have worked hard at retaining autonomy from philanthropic organisations and from the state. Moreover, through an insistence on nonbureaucratic structures and by their ready use of marches, street plays and political demonstrations, the autonomous organisations continue to emphasise mobilisational goals. At the same time, a certain pragmatism prompts feminist activists to work in support of legal and policy reforms and to use class connections and social contacts to elicit the cooperation of institutional authority on behalf of women victims of violence.

The achievements of this radical pragmatism are considerable. Feminist activism has led to important legal reforms. But the law is at best a clumsy tool to change patterns of behaviour within the family and between individuals. Thus the success with which feminist activism directed the attention of the media to the once invisible phenomena of dowry deaths, rape, and domestic violence has been critical to what Susie Tharu so aptly calls "the slow, creeping change in the mood of women."

Those who might wish to argue that the movement's priorities overplayed the importance of gender violence must be prepared to argue that other issues could have as effectively gained the attention of the public and of the state. Those that might argue that issues of violence are better subordinated to the prior concerns of economic livelihood and the amelioration of poverty might well heed Amartya Sen's comments in a different context. Writing in the aftermath of the Emergency, he asked, "Would not better feeding, clothing, and health for the Indian population compensate for the loss of liberty which after all effectively concerns only a minority?" "I believe," he continued, "this way of posing the choice is both banal and wrong. First, there is little evidence that matters of liberty do not concern most of the people, even in poor countries. Second, the choice posed is unreal." Sen's answer is no less convincing as an argument on behalf of the mobilisation by the Indian women's movement against gender violence.

REFERENCES

Basu, Amrita, "Grass Roots Movements and the State: Reflections on Radical Change in India," *Theory and Society,* vol. 16, 1987, pp. 647-74.

Caplan, Patricia, *Class and Gender in India: Women and their Organisations in a South Indian City,* New York: Methuen, 1986.

Chen, Marty, "Overview of Women's Program: 1980-86, India and Bangladesh," Oxfam America, October 1986 Program Paper, p. 8.

Christian Science Monitor, 22 June 1987, p. 23.

Desai, Neera, "From Articulation to Accommodation: Women's Movement in India" *Visibility and Power; Essays on Women in Society and Development,* ed. Leela Dube, Eleanor Leacock, and Shirley Ardener, Delhi: Oxford University Press, 1986.

Desai, Neera, *Woman in Modern India,* Bombay: Vora and Company Publishers, 1957.

Desai, Neera, and Maithreyi Krishnaraj, *Women and Society in India,* Delhi: Ajanta Publications, 1987, p. 275.

"Discussion Forum: From the Commission on the Status of Women in India to the End of the Women's Decade: Some Personal Reflections," *Samya Shakh,* vol. 2, no. 1, 1985, pp. 80-98.

Ferree, Myra Marx, "Equality and Autonomy: Feminist Politics in the United States and West Germany," *The Women's Movements of the United States and Western Europe; Consciousness, Political Opportunity, and Public Policy,* ed. Mary Fainsod Katzenstein and Carol McClurg Mueller, Philadelphia: Temple University Press, 1987.

Flavia, *My Story, Our Story; Rebuilding Broken Lives,* Bombay: Women's Centre Publication, November 1984.

Forbes, Geraldine, "The Indian Woman's Movement: A Struggle for Women's Rights or National Liberation," *The Extended Family, Women and Political Participation in India and Pakistan,* ed. Gail Minault, Columbia, Mo.: South Asia Books; Delhi: Chanakya, 1981.

Forbes, Geraldine, "The Politics of Respectability: Indian Women and the INC," in *A Hundred Years of the Indian National Congress,* ed. Anthony Low, New Delhi: Oxford University Press, 1988.

Gandhy, Nandita, "The Anti-Price Rise Movement in Maharashtra 1972-75," paper presented at the Third National Conference on Women's Studies, Chandigarh, 1986.

Haksar, Nandita, *Demystifitation of Law for Women,* New Delhi: Lancer Press, 1986.

Hardgrave, Robert, *India Under Pressure: Prospects (or Political Stability,* Boulder; Westview Press, 1984, p. 16.

Hariharan, Gita, "Women and Political Participation: An Emerging Perspective," mimeographed, no date but circa 1983 as quoted in Tharu, "Engendering Political Processes," fn. 5.

Institute of Social Studies, *Catalogue of Agencies Reaching Poorest Women in India,* Swedish International Development Authority, 1981.

Jain, Sharada, Nirja Misra and Kavita Srivastava, "Deorala Episode; Women's Protest in Rajasthan," *Economic and Political Weekly,* 7 November 1987, pp. 1891-94.

Kannabiran, Vasantha, "Commentary: Report from SSS, A Women's Group in Hyderabad, Andhra Pradesh, India," *Feminist Studies,* vol. 12, no. 3 (Fall 1986), pp. 601-12.

Mathew, P. M. and M.S. Nair, *Women's Organisations and Women's Interests,* New Delhi: Ashish Publishing House, 1986.

Mazumdar, Vina, "The First Six Years and Forward", New Delhi: Centre for Women's Development Studies, 1987.

Nandy, Ashis, "The Human Factor," *Illustrated Weekly of India,* 17 January 1988, pp. 20-23; *At the Edge of Psychology: Essays in Politics and Culture,* Delhi: Oxford University Press, 1980, and *The Intimate Enemy,* Delhi: Oxford University Press, 1983.

Omvedt, Gail, *We Will Smash This Prison,* London: Sed Press, 1980.

Palriwala, Rajni, "Women are Not for Burning; the Anti-Dowry Movement in Delhi," Paper prepared for Anthropological Perspectives on Women's Collective Actions, 1975-1985, Wenner-Gren Foundation for Anthropo-logical Research, an International Symposium, 9-17 November 1985.

Patel, Vibhuti, "Women's Liberation in India," *New Left Review,* vol. 153, Sept/Oct 1985, pp. 75-86.

Raj, Maitreyi Krishna, "Relevance of Research on Women," *Economic and Political Weekly,* 16 January 1988, p. 88.

Ray, Krishnendu and Satish Kumar Jha, "Assessing Shetkari Sanghatana," *Economic and Political Weekly,* 19 December 1987, p. 2229-30; "Reaching for Half the Sky: A Reader in the women's movement", Baroda: Antar Rashtriya Prakashan, 1985, pp. 18-19.

Sharma, Kumud, "Women in Struggle: A Case Study of the Chipko Movement," *Samya Shakti,* vol. 1, no. 2, 1984, pp. 55-63.

Swaminathan, Mina, "Who Cares? A Study of Child Care Facilities for Low Income Working Women in India", New Delhi: Centre for Women's Development Studies, 1985.

Weiner, Myron, "India's Minorities; Who are they? What do they Want?" in *India 2000;The Next Fifteen Years,* ed. James Roach, Riverdale: Riverdale Publishers, 1986, pp. 99-135.

4

RURAL DALIT WOMEN : A SOCIOLOGICAL PERSPECTIVE

Dalits are one of the most unfortunate groups in India which suffer from numerous kinds of exploitative and oppressive practices of Indian society. Hinduism has degraded them beyond imagination. Psychological, social and cultural proscriptions have unleashed tremendous amount of miseries and hardships to them. The term Dalit is chiefly used for those who are ex-untouchables in Indian (mainly Hindu) society, and are extremely poor, landless, illiterate and exploited. They are the products of highly discriminatory and inhuman nature of the functioning of Indian caste system. An entire segment of population was assigned 'unclean' occupations like scavenging, flaying, tanning etc. and converted into untouchables.

The attitude of higher caste people towards the untouchables even today has not changed much. In the recent past, several restrictions were imposed on them like not allowing them to wear shirts or vests, not to use ornaments, sandals and umbrellas, to use only earthenware vessels at homes, not to enter cities after sun-set and before sunrise, and keep a prescribed distance of steps from upper-caste Hindus. They were thus totally ostracised. The exploitation committed against them under the garb of untouchability by and large continue to exist even today. In spite of the welfare programmes and ameliorative measures taken by the State, there has been social sabotage side by side by the dark forces of Indian society who do not want their progress and believe in the principles of equity and justice.

Even after fifty nine years of Independence, Indian society has not been able to deliver justice and dignity to them. Astrocities against them are on increase. Every two hours, one Dalit is assaulted, everyday 3 Dalit women are raped, two Dalit are murdered and two Dalit houses are burnt. The increase in the number of crimes against them is evident from the fact that as against 180 cases registered with police in 1955, the number of cases increased to 18,336 in 1991, and to 32,990 in 1995. They are mostly exploited by usurping their lands, giving them low wages and using them as bonded labour. There have been reports particularly from the state of Bihar that Dalits have been massacred by higher caste gangsters and feudals who have formed their private armies. The reason of massacred was a long-standing tussle between upper caste landlords and landless Dalits formers of the area. The total lack of political will to tackle the menace has been the bane of Bihar.

Today, the percentage of Dalit population in India has substantially increased. According to the Census Report of 2001, they formed nearly 16.5 per cent or slightly more than 169 million population in India. One out of every six Indian belongs to Dalit Category. The important Dalit caste are Chamar, Dusadh, Regar, Musahar, Bhuiya, Dhobi, Pasi, Dom, Bhogta, Halalkhar, etc. in north India and Paraiyans, Pallans Chakkilis in Tamil Nadu, and Mehar, Belsi, Bauri, Meghwal, Rajhans, Mazhobhi Sikhs, etc. in other states. The highest number of Dalits are found in Uttar Pradesh (21%) where the present study has been conducted, followd by West Bengal (12%), Bihar (9%), Tamil Nadu (8%), Rajasthan (5.5%) and so on. (India: 1998). Thus, about two-third of these people are concentrated in six states. About 84 per cent of them live in villages and are working as cultivators, sharecroppers, marginal farmers, and agricultural labourers, etc. About 42 per cent of Dalits fall in the category of workers, of the total workers, 4 per cent work as scavengers, while the rest work as weavers (12%), fisherman(8%), toddy-tappers (7%), basket and rope makers(5%), washarmen (5%), art sans(1%), shoemakers (1%), and so on. Most of Dalits live below poverty line and are illiterate (India: 2001). The main socioeconomic problems affecting the bulk of Dalit population are—Chronic indebtness, landlessness/land alienation, lack of education, lack of productive assets, forced labour and prostitution, lack of 'minimum wages', child labour, social and religious discrimination, etc.

Because of the perpetual landlessness and only seasonal employment, chronic indebtness has been a concomitant problem with Dalits. The lot of Dalits in the rural areas (where most of them live) has been pitiable because their existence in characterised by all sorts of deprivation, exploitation, discrimination, injustice and violence against them (Mahar: 1998).

The Dalit Women

The situation of Dalit women in India is just unexplainable. They are one among the worst sufferers of socio-cultural, political and economic exploitation, injustice, oppression and violence. Their woes and miseries are boundless. They are the ones who form 'real' teeming millions in India, and are affected by all kinds of social and economic oppressions. They are mainly employed in unorganised sector of the Indian economy as daily wagers and marginal workers. The lack of adequate employment opportunities, limited skills and illiteracy have made their mobility extremely limited and prevent them from achieving independent status.

The persistent gap between consumption and expenditure leads them to perpetual indebtness. The proportion of Dalit women living below the poverty line is just enormous. They do not enjoy any social security, maternity benefits, pension schemes or any other kind of economic protection. With the adoption of policies of globalisation in India, their employment opportunities are likely to be further reduced as they will have to suffer from competition from foreign technology and modern methods of agriculture.

They are oppressed by the broader Hindu society, their own community's men and also their own husbands. Thus, they are triply disadvantageous. The issues of Dalit women are different from that of other Indian women. They have been deprived from all kinds of human rights, education, income, dignity, social status, religious rights, etc. They have to face outside world necessiated by economic deprivation, and an urgent need to earn for livelihood. Thus, their subjugation is more acute—being Dalit they are treated with great contempt by upper caste men and women alike, and their own menfolk.

Despite that they have hugely contributed to the development of India by their seer hardwork and labour. But, their contributions have never been recognised. Their voices and protests are almost invisible. In fact, when we talk of marginalisation of women in the development process, or feminisation of poverty or woman's contribution to the unorganised sector in India, we are referring to them without even being conscious about their specificity. It is regrettable to note that mainstream women's movement in India also ignored and neglected the pitiable condition of Dalit women. Very few literature on the life of Dalit women have been generated so far.

Violence Against Dalit Women

Violence against women in India has never been uncommon phenomenon. Women in the Indian society have been victims of humiliation, torture and harassment as long as one can observe from written records and newspaper reports. Dalit women have been the object of violence in greater degree from their own menfolk, and also from higher caste men. They have been subjected to rape, molestation, kidnapping, abduction, homicide, physical and mental torture, immoral traffic and sexual abuse. There is a tendency of increase in the cases of violence against Dalit women. According to the National Crime Statistics there were 2,824 reported cases of rape, 4,591 vases of serious injuries, 517 cases of murder, 2,261 cases of kidnapping and abduction, 8,527 cases of physical torture, 10,425 cases of eve-teasing, 3,588 cases of molestation and sexual harassment, 556 cases of importation of girls, and 4,452 cases under Immoral Tariff Act. Thus, there were 37,841 registered cases of violence against Dalit Women in the year 2001 alone.

It should be noted that in India about 90 per cent crimes against Dalit women are not reported to the police for the fear of social ostracism and threat to personal safety and security. Also the legal proceedings are so complicated, tardy, time consuming, costly and unfriendly to Dalits that usually they do not approach courts or other law enforcing agencies for their redressal. Besides, a huge number of Dalit women are dragged in the profession of flesh-trade and prostitution. Many of these unfortunate women are minor and innocent girls who are lured by unscrupulous touts and agents into this profession. The religious practices like Devadashi and Sevikas of the temples in south and western India also force them into this profession and are given religious colour.

Present Situation

Now, we turn our attention to a micro-empirical study which is based on 300 Dalit women belonging to four villages of Saidpur Development Block of Gazipur district of eastern Uttar Pradesh province of India. It should be noted that Gazipur district in easternmost part of U.P. bordering Bihar state and Ballia district on the eastern side, Varanasi on Western and Southern side Azamgarh and Mau districts in northern side. It is an extremely backward district where no industry or prosperous business exists. Only small shops and trading are found in the countryside and city. Agriculture is the main occupation of people, while some people have joined armed forces and police. The literacy rate is just 60.06 per cent (73.45% among males and 44.39% among female), while the same among Dalits is very low (35.95% among males and just 14.25% among females). The literacy rate among rural Dalit women is extremely low *i.e.* less than 10 per cent. Gazipur district has been known for its criminality, casteism, feudalism, oppression of Dalits and orthodoxy. The reason for selecting these villages for the study is that these villages have sieable population of Dalits, and are situated far away from the city centre, and thus, are less affected by the city culture and values. Most of the Dalits' families in these villages are landless and are engages as labourers in agricultural fields, construction sites, and in the small shops. Some of them are ricksaw/trolly/handcart pullers. A few lucky ones have migrated to neighbouring cities and engage themselves in some kind of manual work or vending. Some of them are also engaged in animal farming, piggery, poultry, fishing, small handicraft, etc. The general condition of Dalit famalies in these villages is very poor or rather appalling. They are on the extreme margin of the rural community who are not benefited by any developmental programmes of the government, and are most neglected, exploited and oppressed.

For the purpose of objectivity, a systematic list of all Dalit families living in these four village was prepared which constituted about 1547 families. From this list 300 households were selected through the random sampling method using Tippett's Random Number Table which was considered more suitable and appropriate in this case as the whole Dalit population under the study has homogenous socioeconomic characteristics though they are divided into several castes and sub-castes. From these selected households one Dalit women from each family between the age of 25-55 was picked-up who had agreed to become respondents for the study. A interview-schedule was earlier prepared and applied to obtain information from them. Besides, in a few cases indepth case-study and observational methods were also used for collecting data on real life-situation of the respondents. It should be noted that detailed analysis of the data is still going on.

(*a*) It was observed that most Dalit women covered under the present study are living under abject poverty and sub-human conditions. In most cases, they do not have proper houses to live in. The facilities of pure dinking water, sewage and toilet, etc. were just not available to them.

Most of them have to live in small hutments without proper sanitation, and hygiene. In fact, many of them live under trees or open sky.

(*b*) More than 90 per cent of Dalit women covered under the study are either illiterate or very scantly literate. They are not even able to recognise Hindi letters and words, and put their signatures in their own handwriting. They could hardly count numbers beyond nine or ten. Ironically, they do not seem to be much interested in receiving education through adult or non-formal channels. Neither they are interested in educating their children, particularly daughters as they think that it was of no use to them and in no way related to their real life situation, or fetch some meaningful work or employment for them.

(*c*) The health and nutritional status of the respondents are very poor. Most of these women suffer from various kinds of diseases like leucorrhea, respiratory diseases, tuberculosis, joint pains, general weakness, diarrhoea, etc. Even some of them are found to be suffering from some kind of mental disorders. Frequent pregnancies and abortions have further made them very weak. They are least aware of the methods of keeping good health and hygiene. Their daily diet is mainly the leftover of the family meals which are inadequate in quantity and inferior in nutritional quality. Thus, their health is perpetually poor resulting in premature death in many cases.

(*d*) Most of the Dalit women covered under the study are found neck-deep dipped into various kinds of beliefs in things like sorcery, spirit worship, magic, unhealthy customs and traditions, religious rituals and practices which often takes away their hard-earned money and resources, and further make them vulnerable to exploitation and false promises.

(*e*) Dalit women's husbands covered under the study are also ignorant lots. They are mostly suffering from false sense of superiority for being men and thus suffering from all kinds male chauvinism. Usually, they command the authority structure in the family putting Dalit women at the secondary or tertiary positions. They are often under the habits of liquor-consumption and gambling, and take away the wages earned by Dalit women and thus, leaving the whole family to starve. They also often beat their wives on the slightest pretext and protest. Thus, Dalit women's husbands are found to be their worst enemies.

(*f*) Dalit women covered under the study are often employed in agricultural farms owned by higher caste feudal landlords during tilling, sowing, irrigating, cutting and harvesting seasons, and are on their mercy for their bread and butter. They are always paid far less wages than prescribed by the rules and have to work for longer hours. During the course of their work in the fields they are often sexually exploited by their feudal landlords. They are hardly able to resist routine kind of the maltreatment and misbehaviour meted out to them. Not only that, many of them are kept as bonded labourers by their landlords and are not paid their legitimate wages at all. In such cases, they are given only some food and cloths. They do not even know how to seek legal help and redressal to overcome their bonded status.

(*g*) After the day-long hardwork at the field, when they return to their homes in the evening, another kinds of hardwork i.e. household work like cooking, cleaning of utensils, cloth-washing, cleaning of homes, mitching cattles, etc. await them. In most of the cases, their husbands do not help them in their household chores; instead often they take away their hard-earned wages for wasteful expenditures. Their young children remain unattended, half-fed and crying. Their husbands often show cruelty towards them and beat them mercilessly. Rape, violence and atrocities are in their destiny. They have very limited space in community and society at large.

(*h*) There are several schemes of upliftment of Dalit women by the State and the Central Governments. But, the benefits of such schemes and programmes rarely reach to them. Indian bureaucracy is hopelessly insensitive, inefficient and corrupt. It hardly cares for them and their plights. Whatever funds come for their improvement, are cornered by unscrupulous local politicians, government functionaries and petty bureaucrats. Thus, the funds which are earmarked by the government for their welfare, are hardly able to bring any noticeable change in their life. They remain hapless, ignorant, exploited and oppressed. They are the victims of worst kind of patriarchy, feudalism, casteism, corruption and insentivity of the Indian society. Their plights are endless, life is difficult and full of miseries.

In sum, rural Dalit women of India have been living in the culture of silence throughout the centuries. They have remained mute expectators to their exploitation, oppression and barbarity against them. They do not have any control over their own bodies, earnings and lives. The extreme expression of violence, exploitation and oppression against them is visible in forms of hunger, malnutrition, disease, physical and mental torture, rape; illiteracy, ill-health, unemployment, insecurity and inhuman treatment. The collective forces of feudalism, casteism, and patriarchy have made their lives just a hell. An overwhelming majority of them live under the most precarious conditions. In the present age of modernism and post-modernism, they are still living in darker age of savagery. Therefore, I most humbly, appeal to this august gathering to come-out to help them comeout of this miserable condition.

Thus, it is being felt that sincere and honest efforts for the improvement in rural Dalit women's status is urgently required with food-security, safety, housing, medical facilities, availability of pure dinking water, educational facility for their children, proper orientation and training for confidence building into them so that they may be able to gather some courage and self-confidence and protect their body, money and dignity. The delivery system of the governmental programmes also need to be streamlined and strict monitoring system should be evolve to ensure that funds and materials meant for them really reach them, and are not diverted elsewhere by corrupt officials and unscrupulous tauts, agents and middlemen. Here, the role of NGOs and other conscientised individuals including women activists and grassroot social-workers cannot be underestimated.

REFERENCES

Ahuja, Ram, *Social Problems in India,* Rawat, Jaipur, 2003.

Beteille, Andre, "Caste in South Indian Village" in *Social Inequality: Selected Readings,* Beteille A (ed.) Penguin, London, 1976.

Bhoite, U. and Boite, A., "The Dalit Sahitya Movement in Maharashtra: A sociological Analysis" in *Sociological Bulletin,* 27(2), 1977, pp. 60-75.

Issacs, Harold R., *India's Ex-untouchables,* John Day, New York, 1965.

Mahar, J. Michael, *The Untouchables in Contemporary India,* Rawat Publication, Jaipur, 1998.

Ramesh, Chandra, Mitra Sangh, *Dalit Identity in the New Millennium,* Commonwealth, New Delhi, 2003.

Rege, Shamila (ed.), "Sociology of Gender: Challenges of Feminist Sociological Knowledge" in S. Rege (ed.) *Themes in Indian Sociology*-Volume-1., Sage Publication, New Delhi, 2003.

Roy Burman, B.K., The Problems of Untouchables in Romesh Thaper (ed.) *Tribe, Caste and Religion in India,* Mc Millan, New Delhi, 1977.

Sharma, R.S., *Sudras in Ancient India,* Motilal Banarasidas, Varanasi, 1958.

Times of India, Editorial, October 17, 2005, New Delhi.

Verma, J.M.S. (ed.), *Gender Justice in India,* Spellbound, Rohtak, 1999.

Zelliot, Eleaner, *From Untouchables to Dalit,* Manohar, Bombay, 1992.

5

CASTE SYSTEM AND DALIT WOMEN IN MODERN INDIA

The aim is to highlight the harsh reality of the suppression, struggle and torture Dalit women face every day of their miserable lives. The hardships of Dalit women are not simply due to their poverty, economical status, or lack of education, but are a direct result of the severe exploitation and suppression by the upper classes, which is legitimised by Hindu religious scriptures. We see many examples of brave Dalit women who being quite aware of the horrifying truth and despite the heavy odds still strive to put an end to their suffering. In doing so they most certainly ensure a brighter future for the generations to come. Ruth Manorama, an active member of the National Campaign on Dalit Human Rights and the National Alliance of Women, once stated that in a male dominated society, "Dalit women face a triple burden of caste, class and gender" in which she sums up the plight of Dalit women, highlighting the fact that Dalit women are a distinct social group and cannot be masked under the general categories of "Women" or "Dalits."

Caste System in Ancient India

In Ancient India (3200-2500 B.C.), the caste system was non-existent since even the most learned men were good householders and had varied occupations. The women of ancient India were just as superior as men in learning, education and intellect. The choice for her mate was according to her own wishes and marriage was practiced after the coming of age. She attended parties, competitions, and religious functions as she wished. The remarriage of young widows was also a common practice.

The creation of a number of Hindu religious books including the *Manusmriti, Atharva Vedas, Vishnu smriti,* and many others like these and their strict compliance by the Brahmans (upper priestly hindu caste), led to a society in which equality between men and women was far from existent. Dr. B. R. Ambedkar, an architect of the Indian constitution, also makes it very clear in his article titled "The rise and fall of Hindu woman" that the root cause of suffering for women in India are these so-called Hindu religious books. Books like the *Manusmriti* divide people into a stratified caste system and promotes inequality between men and women. According to the *Manusmriti,* women have no right to education, independence, or wealth. It not only justifies the treatment of dalit women as a sex object and promotes child marriage, but also justifies a number of violent atrocities on women as can be seen in the following verses:

> A man, aged thirty years, shall marry a maiden of twelve who pleases him. Or, a man of twenty-four marry a girl of eight years of age. If (the performance of) his duties would otherwise be impeded, he must marry sooner.

By a girl, by a young woman, or even by an aged one, nothing must be done independently, even in her own house."

Her father protects (her) in childhood, her husband protects (her) in youth, and her sons protect (her) in old age; a woman is never fit for independence.

Women have no right to study the Vedas. That is why their *Sanskaras* are performed without *Veda Mantras*. Women have no knowledge of religion because they have no right to know the Vedas. The uttering of the *Veda Mantras* is useful for removing sin. As women cannot utter the *Veda Mantras,* they are as unclean as the untruth.

A Brahman, Kshatriya, or Vaishya man can sexually exploit any shudra woman. Even the killing of a dalit woman is explicitly justified as a minor offence for the Brahmins: equal to the killing of an animal *(Manusmitri).* If the killing of an untouchable was justified as a minor offence, you can imagine the treatment they received throughout their lives.

In a male dominated society, Dalit women suffered unimaginable oppression, not only through caste, but gender too, from which there was no escape. The laws in the *Manusmriti* and other Vedic scriptures close all economic, political, social, educational, and personal channels through which Dalit women could be uplifted. The horrendous Laws in the *Manusmriti* were incorporated into Hinduism because they were favourable only to the Upper castes, which form the majority of India. Even today, in modern times, we see the severe oppression and exploitation of Dalit women. The Laws of the Manusmriti have a devastating effect on the level of education reached by Dalit women.

According to the National Commission for Scheduled Castes and Scheduled Tribes 2000, approximately 75 per cent of the Dalit girls drop out of primary school despite the strict laws of the Government of India, which hold reservations for Dalit children *(National Commission* n.pag). Despite showing keen academic aptitude, reasons for this early drop out from the education system is poverty or to escape humiliation, bullying and isolation by classmates, society, and even their teachers.

There are large numbers of reported atrocities on Dalit women that can be found recorded in various newspaper articles, journals, and government reports in India many of which can be viewed on www.ambedkar.org. The majority of the stories we read and hear are of bright young Dalit girls who are punished by the upper caste teachers in rural area of India, for daring to score good grades. Feeling rejected most girls in this situations drop out of school and have nowhere to turn but towards manual scavenging and other repulsive jobs.

According to the National Commission for Scheduled Castes and Scheduled Tribes, the majority of the educated people are of the upper caste, many of which may practice caste-based discrimination. Therefore, Dalit girls feel discouraged to enter education and we see the lowest literacy rate for Dalit girls compared to the Total population of educated upper caste girls. The Annual Report of University Grant Commision for 1999-2000, shows that Dalits in general have very low participation rates in higher education.

The main reasons for the very low literacy rate among Dalit women could be some or all of the following:

- The Lack of educational resources especially in rural areas.
- Privatisation of schools and colleges.
- Extreme poverty, because of which they cannot afford the expensive fees for the private schools.
- The demand for an increase in the Dowry for educated girls.
- Humiliation and bullying by the high caste students and teachers.

Since only a small percentage of the total population of Dalit women are educated, the fate of the majority is very grim. According to India's Ministry of Labour, 85 per cent of the Dalit women have the most formidable occupations and work as agricultural laborers, scavengers, sweepers, and disposers of human waste. Many of these women work for minimal wages under the upper caste landlords, since it is proposed that by the National Commission for SC/ST that 85 per cent of the Dalits are landless *(News Archives)*. When the Dalit women refuse to work for ridiculously low wages or fail to follow their harsh orders it results open violence, humiliation, beatings, rape, and jail. There are also a number of cases where the houses of Dalit women have been burnt down. In one particular case, a four months pregnant agricultural labourer, from the southern part of India, was stripped naked and beaten, in front of the whole village and her family by the upper caste landlord. Later, she was retained in jail, where the police beat her. This resulted in the miscarriage of her baby. In another case, a school student in Gujarat made a mistake of joining the dancing in the main square of her village, in which most of the participants were of the upper caste. The upper caste boys pulled her out and threatened to rape her. For interfering, her mother was slapped. In the hope for justice, she forced her parents to file a complaint to the police against her assailants. Her mother was constantly threatened by the upper caste families for complaining to the police. Feeling deeply humiliated by no justice and rumors of rape, the girl committed suicide.

There are many cases like these, all of which cannot be discussed here. The worst exploitation of dalit women involves a lifetime of suffering, torture, and rape. Justified by the Vedic scriptures, the *Devdasi system* (also known as temple prostitution) was introduced by the High caste Hindus, and it still exists in some parts of India. According to the *Human Right Watch Report* in 1992, an estimated 50,000 girls were sold every year to Hindu organisations that are involved in the Devdasi system. These girls are called the "female servants of god" and are sexually exploited. After a lifetime of living as a prostitute and servant, the women in their later years are sold to brothels, where they are further tortured and often die of neglect or AIDS. The Devdasi system and Child marriage are also justified by Hindu Scriptures.

The 1992-93 Annual report from the Ministry of Welfare shows 1,236 reported cases of rape on Dalit women and the National Commission for SC/ST shows that approximately 10,000 cases of human right violations on Dalits are reported every month. But what is even more disturbing, is that only one out of ten of the cases are reported annually whilst, nine go unreported. In addition to this, according to the Human Right watch Report, approximately 115 million children are in slavery and 2.6 million children are held as bonded labourers. After sixty-two years of India's Independence and despite the excellent laws in place to protect Dalit women, they are still suffering unimaginable atrocities from the high caste Hindus. It is believed that thousands of these cases go unreported and unpublicised because the poor Dalits that live in rural areas, who are the worst victims, have no control on power, wealth, justice, police and the media. The only way these Dalit women can escape the viscous cycle of poverty, abuse and oppression is through education. Through education more Dalit women can come to know their basic human rights and they can then raise an even stronger voice against abuse and exploitation from the upper castes.

Emergence of Dalits Organisations

Many Dalit Non-Government Organisations (NGO's), both in India and abroad, have been involved in raising the plight of India's 250 million untouchables. One of the most important tasks of these Dalit NGO's is to bring the plight of Dalit people to the attention of the International community and to document and publicise human right violations. As the poorest of the poor, Dalit women lack the means and the opportunity to defend themselves at home or to make their problems known outside of rural India. Many Dalit women have formed NGO's through which they collectively fight against abuse from the upper classes. Such Dalit women abandon tears and embrace the shield of confidence in the hope of equality. The courage, struggle, and persistence of today's Dalit women against suppression, exploitation and torture has the power to ensure that the future generations will not have to face the bleak reality Dalits have faced for the past two thousand years. The caste system is truly a crippling disease to approximately 250 million Dalits in India today. Since its roots are embedded in the Hindu religious scriptures, it seems this disease has no cure, but "every voice raised against caste-based discrimination and suppression through Dalit Organisations will turn this from a losing battle to one of victory in which every Dalit will have equal rights, access to education, and a chance to succeed and prosper.

Many of the Dalit NGO's are involved in establishing schools, scholarships, and basic supplements to Dalits in the rural parts of India. NGO's such as the Ambedkar Centre for Peace and Justice and the National Campaign on Dalit Human Rights are involved in bringing the plight of the Dalit people to the attention of the international community and to document and publicise human rights abuse. The longterm objectives are to enfranchise Dalits as full citizens of their society and eliminate caste-based discriminations.

REFERENCES

Bhoite, U. and Boite, A., "The Dalit Sahitya Movement in Maharashtra: A sociological Analysis" in *Sociological Bulletin,* 27(2), 1977, pp. 60-75.

Issacs, Harold R., *India's Ex-untouchables,* John Day, New York, 1965.

Mahar, J. Michael, *The Untouchables in Contemporary India,* Rawat Publication, Jaipur, 1998.

Manu, *Manu Smriti: The laws of Manu with the Bhasya of Medhatithi.* Translated by Ganga Natha Jha, University of Calcutta, Calcutta, 1920.

Narula. S. *Broken People: Caste Violence Against India's "Untouchables."* London: Human Rights Watch, 1999.

Ramesh, Chandra, Mitra Sangh, *Dalit Identity in the New Millennium,* Commonwealth, New Delhi, 2003.

Sharma, R.S., *Sudras in Ancient India,* Motilal Banarasidas, Varanasi, 1958.

The National Commission for Scheduled Castes and Scheduled Tribes, Government of India.

The Annual Reports of University Grant Commision, Government of India.

Thind, G.S. *Our Indian Sub-Continent Heritage.* Crosstown Press, LTD. British Columbia, Canada.

Zelliot, Eleaner, *From Untouchables to Dalit,* Manohar, Bombay, 1992.

6
STRATEGIES OF THE INDIAN WOMEN'S MOVEMENT

The term *Indian women's movement* is highly contested. The appellation of "Indian," when used for the women's movement, implies a political and cultural singularity that obscures the movement's diversity, differences and conflicts. The problem is not simply one of disunities but rather has to do with intractable conflicts involving the word "women" that derive from the central position of gender in post-colonial Indian culture and politics. Indeed, processes of gender—the construction of identities, roles and relations based on sexual differences—played a key role in the historical formation of the Indian nation-state. But, gender cannot be separated from other, conflicting political identities, all of which play a crucial role in the life of the nation.

Key Gender Issues

Gender has been a central 'issue' in India since the colonial encounter. An overwhelming preoccupation with the "woman's question" arose from the 19th century social reform movement, crucially informed anti-colonial nationalism, and remains a point of crisis in India's cultural, social, and political space. The recognition of gender as an issue forms the basis for India's women's movement.

One prominent gender concern was status—that is, the rewards and benefits that accrued to women on India's journey to self-determination, statehood, democracy, progress, modernity, and development. In 1974, the Indian government published a report, *Towards Equality,* that put status of women forcefully on the national agenda by arguing that the position of Indian women had declined, not improved, since 1911 (Committee on the Status of Women 1974). As a consequence, development and progress became gender issues. Data on gender discrimination in employment, education, land distribution, inheritance, nutrition, and health became impossible to overlook.

At the same time, violence and atrocities against women was on the rise and widely reported in the media. There were rampant cases of rape in police custody, wife murder (usually called bride-burning or dowry deaths) on a large scale, and sexual harassment at the workplace and on the street too. Women's issues entered the fields of culture, religion, and law; of family and community structures; of the problems of and official responses to population, poverty, illiteracy, and labour; and of the new social movements of dalits, environmentalists, tribals, anti-dam activists, peasants, and trade unions. Rajeswari Sunder Rajan, taking stock of the 50th Independence celebrations, comments that in "all these discourses, disciplines and sites of action, gender began to figure as an 'issue' as well as a category of analysis."

Search for Cohesion

The recognition of gender as an issue powered the post-colonial women's movement, supported by feminist critiques and women's studies in academia. Women mobilised to protest against violence, legal discrimination, and rising prices and raised their voices for better living conditions through higher wages, the prohibition of liquor, and the provision of safe drinking water. These women represented a wide range of castes, classes, and communities—rural and urban.

But, differences among these women grew, fracturing not only the category of women but also solidarities among them. In 1986 the developing tensions were exposed and fueled by the Shah Bano case. Discrimination against women in personal law had been on the women's movement's agenda since the 1920s, but the Shah Bano case snowballed the issue into a crisis of national debate. The case intensified a process in which nationalist ideology, religious fundamentalism, communalism, and caste tensions were pitted on the site of gender. Thus embattled, women—and their movement—lost the fragile unity and broad identity in which their differences and diversities were contained in the first phase of their active political engagement.

Today, the women's movement in India is deeply cleaved. There is, nevertheless, a vigorous search for a viable feminist politics. To succeed, feminists must develop transformative politics, managing and (hopefully) transcending class, caste and community differences.

This chapter addresses this critical challenge. It seeks, through historical analysis, to understand the cleavages in the women's movement by examining the two most divisive issues before it: the Uniform Civil Code and the move tò reserve for women one-third of the seats 33 per cent in legislative bodies. But it also mines the promise of a transformative (feminist) politics. Today, there is not one women's movement in India, an overarching collective in which gender politics is articulated. Yet, the multiplicity of sites, disciplines and discourses makes for vibrant gender politics.

Although women often define and identify themselves through difference and conflict rather than through similarity or common belonging, this book uses the term *women's movement*. This approach is justified because analytical categories often must indulge in abstraction from the perceptions and definitions of social actors, so the term can be used to indicate a variety of campaigns around issues important to women. Moreover, I wish to affirm the possibility—and even necessity—for a women's movement to exist, to offer women the possibility of a space outside the structures, if not also the identities, of community.

Identity, Colonialism and Independence

The primary identity of an Indian, male or female, is citizenship whose basic definition offers a promise of equality and justice within the nation's democratic constitutional framework. Repeatedly, however, this promise is undermined by the masculinity of nationalist ideology, the fiction of citizenship, and the malleability of law. Instead of offering an alternative space, the nation often simply functions as an extension of family, caste, and community structures and defines women as belonging in the same way as their structures. This definition of belonging is contradictory, implying both "affiliated with" and "owned by." The first interpretation connotes voluntary, participatory membership; the second a secondary, functionalist, and symbolic status (Rajan 1999). And both are constantly overlooked because social and political order is defined through women's ownership by and place in structures of family and community.

This chapter began by positing the problem of gender within the matrix of the post-colonial nation-state. The four elements of this term are significant. We have already considered the role of the nation in understanding gender and vice versa. In that sense, India's colonial past is also critical. The colonial period is considered a watershed in gender relations. During that period modernity was set in motion through colonial and indigenous initiative. Modernity was accompanied by capitalism, which under colonialism transformed agriculture, commerce, and manufacturing.

In addition, the 19th century saw the emergence of anti-colonial nationalism, and in the early 20th century the contours of the nation-state evolved. These two political legacies led to the formation of the independent Indian state. Together these social, economic, and political trends defined and structured gender relations in contemporary India. A general acknowledgement of the importance of understanding how the situation of Indian women is embedded in these contexts was intrinsic to the new, self-consciously feminist women's movement that emerged in the late 1970 and early 1980s.

The significance of the nation-state lies as much in the second part of the term as in the first. The state—both the colonial state and the independent state after it—has a dual and paradoxical attitude toward the "woman's question." One the one hand the state plays a paternalistic role by "protecting" women and has, as a result, a remarkable range of pro-women legislation. But while such legislation is enacted, it has a poor record of implementation. The colonial state propitiated patriarchal interests through administrative pragmatism, and there continues to be systematic administrative and judicial dilution of women's given rights. In fact, the state plays a pivotal role in upholding and sustaining patriarchal institutions and instruments, both by omission and commission.

Moreover, the women's movement has an ambiguous relationship with the state. From its inception, the movement has placed a disproportionate emphasis on seeking solutions from the state, usually in the form of progressive legislation. In the colonial period such demands were constrained by the women's movement's alliance with the nationalist movement, which challenged the colonial state's Intervention in Indian social relations. For a few decades after independence, female leaders, drawn mostly from the urban elite, believed in the fiction of the state's neutrality and assumed the goodwill of the male nationalist leadership. The critique of the state came from leftist women—intellectuals and participants in mass movements—who placed an equally disproportionate emphasis on solutions emanating from the state and its agents as perpetrators of violence. There was less theorising and strategising on the family and violence in the private domain.

To emphasise the need to understand the processes outlined above over the long term, the structure of this book follows a chronological as well as a thematic logic. There are two parts. In the first part the historical background is sketched out in two brief sections. The first section focuses on the colonial period and zooms in on the role of the state and the indigenous male elite in determining tropes of modernity for

Indian women. This period has been viewed by historians as one in which a New Patriarchy was fashioned to meet the exigencies of colonial rule and the desire for modern progress. But soon "New Women" began to speak on their own behalf for a future different from that charted for them, and often against both the new and old patriarchy. These women are the focus of the second section, which examines the development of the women's movement in the colonial period. It also traces the shifts in the movement through Independence and the disenchantment with nationalism. The second part of the book focuses on the contemporary period and outlines the controversy over the Uniform Civil Code and the reservation of seats for women in legislative bodies. The discussion covers the origins of these debates, the different positions within the women's movement, and the political implications of each.

History of Indian Women

Four issues affecting the women's movement in India require careful consideration:

- The tensions and fractures in the movement.
- The way these fractures are related to women's relationship to the nation-state, which at least partly follows from women being "owned" by their families, communities, and even nation.
- The possibility of managing or transcending differences among women to create a political community to which women will belong by voluntary association rather than by ownership.
- The significance of women's agency in gender politics.

As noted, any discussion of these issues must be grounded in an understanding of the long-term historical processes in which gender relations and gender politics are articulated. Indeed, many of these issues have to be discussed with reference to India's colonial past, because that is when their terms were set.

"Woman's Question" and Men's Answers, 1820-1920

When James Mill wrote in his *History of India* in 1817 that the condition of women in a society is an index of that society's place in civilisation, he wrote women into the project of modernity and modern history-writing in India. In one fell swoop, "women," "modernity," and "nation" became essential and inseparable elements in a connected discourse of civilisation. The "woman's question" not only came to dominate public discourse for more than a century, it also became the touchstone of the colonial-nationalist encounter, inscribed with the trope of modernity and the legitimation of political power.

For colonial rulers, the atrocities practiced against Indian women became a confirmation of the rulers' modernity and the moral ground on which their "civilising" mission could be launched. As outsiders they could claim the role of protector of Indian women, interceding on their behalf against brutal patriarchal practices. And there were spectacular barbarities in the everyday customs of India, including *sati pratha* (burning of widows alive on the funeral pyres of their dead husbands), female infanticide (especially common in northwest and western India), enforcement of celibate and ascetic widowhood, and pre-pubertal marriages (especially in northern India). Colonial officialdom and missionary rhetoric singled out such practices to characterise the status of Indian women as especially low and Indian men as exceptionally violent.

Social Reform Movement

This was the mirror in which Indian men were invited to see themselves when colonial education began. The new urban elite, drawn mostly from the upper castes, imbibed the enlightenment philosophy of individualism and humanism. They perceived barbaric traditional practices against women as a civilisational lapse and as recognisable social evils. Thus emerged the social reform movement, an attempt on the part of the new elite to redress, sometimes with and sometimes without British help, the worst features of the old patriarchal order.

Women were torch-bearer on the agenda of the social reform movement. For reformers, women's emancipation was a prerequisite to national regeneration and an index of national achievement in the connected discourse of civilisation, progress, modernitys and nationalism. One strand in the movement concentrated on legislative remedy. A series of campaigns resulted in the abolition of sati in 1829 and the enabling of widow remarriage in 1856. Another strand was concerned with creating the female counterpart of the new male elite, "New Women", who would share the sensibilities of the men in the family and be able to sustain their new class roles. The chief instrument was formal education but the issue became inextricably linked with the gender segregation and seclusion *(purdah)* practiced by the upper castes and classes and, by extension, with a reworking of public-private gender roles.

Between the 1820s and 1850s reformers, who favoured both legislative interventions by the colonial state and a wider programme of female emancipation, set up organisations like the Brahmo Samaj in eastern India, the Prarthana Samaj in western India, the Arya Samaj in northern India, and the Theosophical Society in southern India.[1] Elite urban men led these movements and challenged many of the ritual and social restrictions to which upper-caste women were subjected. As

1. There is a rich historical literature on the social reform movement in India. The movement's focus on the condition of women has been widely noted and differently explained. There are at least three main schools of thought. The "modernising"' school, which dominated until the 1970s, argued that these reforms helped draw women out of seclusion and gave them opportunities for self-realisation. Since the 1970s there has been a scathing critique of the elite character of the movement and the limits of its vision with regard to women's emancipation. In recent feminist historiography, it has been pointed out that the reforms led to the formation of a new patriarchy.

fathers and husbands, the men were able to extend many benefits of modernity to a small but significant group of women. These women were drawn into the public spheres of formal education and eventually into employment, political participation and leadership.

These achievements are sometimes underestimated: "elite" has often been used to categorise—and dismiss—women who struggled to gain an education and a place in India's public life, neither of which flowed automatically or easily from their class or caste status. Women often earned "freedom" at the price of social ridicule, ostracism, and harassment. And while some women were aided by well-intentioned male relatives, others faced severe familial resistance. Still, the achievements were remarkable. Take the case of Rassundari Devi (born around 1809), who was entirely self-taught and wrote the first autobiography by an Indian woman:

> I was so immersed in a sea of housework that I was not conscious of what I was going through day and night. After some time, the desire to learn how to read properly grew very strong in me. I was angry with myself for wanting to read books. Girls did not read.... People used to despise women of learning.... In fact, older women used to show a great deal of displeasure if they saw a piece of paper in the hands of a woman. But somehow, I could not accept this.

From Rassundari Devi's painstaking efforts to trace her son's lessons in the seclusion of her bedchamber at night, Bengali women progressed rapidly. In 1883, Kadambini Basu and Chandramukhi Basu received B.A.s from Calcutta University, becoming the first female graduates of the British empire. Kadambini went on to train in medicine and practiced as a doctor in Calcutta in the 1880s. Other women became doctors, teachers, and educators. Women's education also proceeded apace in urban centres like Bombay, Poona, and Madras. Remarkable women like Pandita Ramabai, Anandibai Joshi, Tarabai Shinde, Haimavati Sen and Saraladevi, some privileged and some not, challenged patriarchal constraints, at least in their own lives, and some went on to participate in the emerging nationalist movement.

While the liberal section of the new elite demanded legal and administrative initiative from the colonial state in their reform project, more conservative Indian opinion resisted colonial intervention into traditional social relations. The debates between these two segments have often been seen as a battle between modernists and traditionalists. Lata Mani, however, argues that both groups were redefining tradition and, therefore, "Indianness." Women were "neither the subjects nor the objects" of this discourse, but merely the "site" on which the debates were conducted (Mani 1986, 1989). And even as this recast tradition came to occupy the core of modern Indian identity, gender as the exemplary site (or symbolic expression) became and remains central to political and cultural processes of identity formation.

Colonial and Nationalist Responses

These processes followed from the colonial state's characterisation of Indian society. The colonial discourse had assumed the existence of a "domestic" domain to demarcate what the colonisers found difficult to know but that without knowledge of which the colonial state would not be able to understand and master Indians. This domestic domain became, in colonial discourse, the repository of India's singularity, of Indianness (Sen 1993). Nationalism inherited this language. Thus nationalists, like earlier reformers, redefined the domestic space according to invented categories of tradition. The early articulation of nationalism focused on the domestic—the family, the home, and women in it—as the locus of Indianness and the politically disenfranchised male elite's only domain of autonomy. Nationalists thus resisted the subordination of the domestic to the civilising scrutiny of colonial missionaries and bureaucrats and the transformative will of modernity.

The demarcation of the domestic as the arena of nationalist resistance to colonial intervention involved, by the late 19th century, a significant break from reformism. Women had become the arena in which agreements and conflicts between the colonial bureaucracy and the colonised middle class was to be played out. The colonial state could no longer be given political legitimacy as a source of laws that impinged on the idealised space of the family. Early nationalists opposed colonial interventions in gender relations (especially in the constitution of family) on the grounds that these were anti-traditional and, therefore, anti-national.

The Age of Consent Controversy (1890-91), which followed from the colonial government's attempt to raise the age of marriage for Indian women, was a watershed in this regard. Nationalist resistance to reform took the form of a defense of tradition. The dominant ideology being shaped in this process relocated women from an index of social malady (as in the discourse of colonial missionary reformists) to an embodiment of moral order. The good woman, the chaste wife and mother empowered by spiritual strength, became the iconic representation of the nation.

This transformation of the symbolic meaning of women has had long-term consequences. First, their iconic stature renders irrelevant any criticism of or inquiry into women's actual social condition. Tradition severed from social reality finds fulfilment in an emotional and aesthetic imaging of a heroic mother-goddess. Second, the idealised opposition between domestic and public has located women firmly in the domestic realm, with housework and child care at their only legitimate concerns. The moral health of the community is felt to depend on the " different but equal" roles of men and women, and thus on established values of a gender-based division of labour. Third, the aesthetic, cultural, and emotional investment in the imaging of women has become the cornerstone of an ethnicised and oppositional entity. "Woman" has become the arena in which community, caste, and class battles are fought. In such a discursive space, the unity of nation, caste, class, or community requires the subordination of women. Hence women's aspirations for gender justice or gender equality sit uneasily with claims of justice or equality flowing from their other identities (such as being low caste or poor or a member of a minority community).

The ideological and symbolic location of women was buttressed by legal and administrative measures that laid the foundations for a new patriarchy. This too colonialism bequeathed to the "daughters of independence," and it is a legacy the ruling powers of the post-colonial nation-state have not discarded. The persistence of the new patriarchy was foreshadowed in the manner it was fashioned—with the complicity of the male Indian elite. Few women of the time voiced an understanding of these processes. Pandita Ramabai was perhaps of that era's most scathing critic of Hindu patriarchy and casteism. When Rukhmabai, married as a child, was tried and sentenced to prison for refusing to live with her husband, Ramabai wrote:

> Our only wonder is that a defenceless woman like Rukhmabai dared to raise her voice in the face of the powerful Hindu law, the mighty British Government, the 129,000,000 men, the 330,000,000 gods of the Hindus; all these have conspired together to crush her into nothingness. We cannot blame the English Government for not defending a helpless woman; it is only fulfilling its agreement made with the male population of India.

Ironically, while the "liberal "and "civilising" arm of the colonial state was disabled by indigenous opposition, the enhancement of male control over women happened relatively quietly, often at the initiative of the colonial state and without nationalist opposition. The colonial state inherited a highly coercive labour arrangement, based on the household, organised by gender and age and maintained through family roles. It was in the state's interest to maintain this arrangement to prop up the increasingly unviable small peasant economy that was the basis of the state's revenue calculations. Segments of the male Indian elite were demanding greater cohesion of the family and consolidation of patriarchal control over women (and children) against the incursions of capitalism and modern institutions. Especially in urban India, women's exclusive domesticity became the most effective marker of middle-class status (as in Victorian Britain). Besides, the increasing control over women—their sexuality and their power—underwrote indigenous elite men's claim to autonomy in the domestic domain. The question of women's labour was enmeshed in elite ideologies of domesticity, while control of sexuality (and labour) was increasingly effected through the legal and ideological manipulation of marriage systems.

The marriage system was the key to men's control over women. The interests of the colonial state and (male) nationalist sentiment converged in the desire for a more draconian marriage regime. The promotion of marriage as the upper castes and middle classes understood it and the defining of the husband and father as the undisputed head of the family were important colonial and nationalist enterprises. It prompted efforts to reconstrue a 'Hindu' and a 'Muslim' law, assumed to be fully formed and 'out there', which would rigidify gender hierarchies and elevate the authority of the paterfamilias to an unassailable position. The process was twofold, involving a move toward a more rigid definition of marriage loaded in favour of male control and a universalisation of upper-caste (or class) norms that sought to eliminate regional, caste, and class variations in marriage practices.

The social reform movement had initiated these processes. The movement had addressed, selectively, issues that affected high-caste and upper-class women and had invoked change under the broad definition of Hindu. This became possible because the legal and institutional innovations of the colonial state empowered elite men to speak on behalf of Hindus in their widest definition. Moreover, elite men were encouraged to represent a "tradition" constructed from selective appropriation of variable and contradictory Hindu texts *(sashtras* and *smritis)* representing idealised brahminic norms. As a result low-caste peasants, laborers, and artisans were coopted as participants in upholding a putative Hindu ideal of womanhood and a ritual and legal brahminisation of marriage. In the only accepted brahminical view, marriage was a sacrament (as opposed to the contractual nature of marriage in Islamic law) and, therefore, irrevocable.

The brahminisation of marriage had a disastrous effect on the customary rights and marriage practices of low-caste women. The law of divorce is a telling example. Colonial officialdom, on the basis of scriptural prescription and upper-caste custom, understood the absence of divorce to be the most significant feature of the Hindu marriage system (as opposed to the Muslim system). They ignored, despite overwhelming evidence furnished by their own officials to the contrary, the fact that all but the very high castes routinely allowed divorce. In the 1860s, a series of High Court judgments ruled that there was no divorce in Hindu law and that Hindu women, because they were not allowed polygamous marriages, could not marry a second time (Anderson 1993).

As a result, many poor and low-caste women became criminally liable under the penal law against bigamy. Hindu men were allowed polygamous marriages and had no liability to maintain discarded wives; thus the outlawing of divorce had no material effect on them. Hindu women were legally empowered to remarry only after their husband's death, as dictated by the Hindu Widow Remarriage Act (1856). Yet this apparently enabling act became the means through which orthodoxy was reinforced, because the act stipulated that a Hindu woman who remarried forfeited all claims to the property of her first (dead) husband. Criminal laws, migration regulations, and other legal and administrative innovations enhanced such restrictions.

Thus a small group of elite women became the crucial beneficiaries of colonial modernity and were able to negotiate patriarchal (and class) spaces to access education and employment and to aspire to political leadership. Yet, the recasting of patriarchy in the image of high-caste and upper-class norms meant that most women were left out of the benefits of modernity and deprived of their traditional rights and freedoms. There was not only increasing divergence in the trajectories of upper caste/middle class urban women and the 'others', the very process that underlay the 'moderisation' of the first group became the foundation for further disempowering the poor, low caste and minority women. Thus the new patriarchy was no less draconian or barbarous than the system it sought to civilise and replace.

The "New Women" began to speak in the 1880s, questioning elements of their subordination. They found a voice in writing about their lives and the condition of women. In 1881 Vijayalakshmi, a young Brahmin child-widow, was sentenced to death for killing her illegitimate child. Tarabai Shinde, a young woman, responded with a harsh critique of Brahminical patriarchy, *Stri-purush tulana* (A Comparison between Men and Women): "So is it true that only women's bodies are home to all the different kinds of recklessness and vice? Or have men got just the same faults as we find in women?" (O'Hanlon 1991: 93). In the 1920s, the second generation of "New Women" became more active. They articulated the needs of women, critiqued their society and foreign rulers, started associations, developed institutions, and sought to consolidate women's interests.

Women Question and Seek Answers, 1920-70

During 1920-70, Indian feminists focused on gaining equality through two main channels: by forming associations and becoming active in politics.

Associations

Saraladevi Chaudhurani, perhaps the most remarkable of the "New Women", was both a feminist and a nationalist, an active participant in both the social reform and nationalist movements. She was one of the first women to see the need for and start an association for women. She argued that women's issues could not be addressed adequately as an adjunct of the National Social Conference (set up by the Indian National Congress in 1887) or by men who "advertise themselves as champions of the weaker sex, equal opportunities for women, female education and female emancipation.... their pet subjects of oratory at the annual show" (Saraladevi 1911: 345) but who actually lived in the "shade of Manu," unwilling to allow women independent action (Bagal 1964: 24). Saraladevi founded the Bharat Stree Mahamandal (Great Group of Indian Women) in Allahabad in 1910.

Saraladevi's efforts came on the heels of several women's clubs, groups, and associations initiated by men. These included the Bharat Ashram (Indian Hermitage) in Bengal, formed by Keshab Chunder Sen (of Brahmo Samaj) in the 1870s; Arya Mahila Samaj (The Aryan Women's Association) in Bombay, formed by Pandita Ramabai and Justice Ranade in the 1880s; Bharat Mahila Parishad (Ladies' Social Conference), formed as part of the National Social Conference in 1905; and Anjuman-e-Khawatin-e-Islam (The Muslim Women's Association) in Punjab, formed by Amir-un-Nisa of the Mian family.

These associations, initiated or inspired by men, were critical training grounds for women, allowing them access to education and their first experience with public work. But they also tried to impose traditional gender roles and values. Their limits became evident when women attempted to define the "woman's question" in their own ways. As a result women followed in Saraladevi's footsteps to organise women-only associations (mostly called *Mahila Samitis*) in the early decades of the 20th century. These were mostly city-based, sometimes neighborhood-based, small, limited, and dispersed. Some taught basic subjects like mathematics and geography. Some focused on classes on health, hygiene, nutrition, and child care. Some were class-oriented and taught new social skills such as polite conversation in English, tea serving, or public speaking. And many concentrated on livelihood solutions such as skill training (sewing and embroidery) or handicrafts (weaving and pottery; Forbes 1996 and Southard 1995).

These local associations laid the ground for national associations of women. During the early spurt of nationalist agitation the Women's Indian Association was launched in 1917, followed by the National Council of Indian Women (1925) and the All-India Women's Conference (1927). The Women's Indian Association defined itself as including and representing women of all races, cultures and religions. It opened branches in different parts of southern India but remained connected to the Madras Theosophical Society. Its political debut was immediate. In 1917, a delegation met Secretary of State Sir Edward Montagu to argue for female franchise. But the Women's Indian Association remained highly limited in class and caste composition and failed to spread outside the Madras presidency.

The National Council of Indian Women was even more elitist. It was set up as a national branch of the International Council of Women and was influenced by Lady Tata and other women from wealthy industrialist families of Bombay. Many of these women saw charity as the council's main purpose, providing a scope for "enlightened" activity based on the model offered by British middle-class women. Still, the council had committees on labour, legislation, and the press. The legislation committee, under the guidance of Mithan Tata Lam, was the most active.

Both the Women's Indian Association and the National Council of Indian Women claimed to represent all Indian women, but they were cut-of from the masses of women whom they confidently sought to benefit. They targeted the government for solutions and advice on what they considered problems. They concentrated on "petition politics" because such activity best suited their stations and purposes. Their contacts, through family, marriage, and social interaction, gave them far more credibility than was warranted by their numbers or experience.

The All-India Women's Conference, the third of these organisations, was much more successful in offering a national representation of women and in its alliance with the Indian National Congress. Within 10 years the conference included subcommittees on labour, rural reconstruction, industry, textbooks, opium, and child marriage legislation. It was through the campaign for the Hindu Child Marriage Bill (1927; introduced by Harbilas Sarda and known as the Sarda Bill) that the All-India Women's Conference came of age.

Child marriage and the age of consent (for sexual intercourse) had been controversial issues since 1891. Women's organisations actively organised in support of the Sarda Bill because from the beginning they had identified child marriage as a major impediment to women's progress that "crushed..... [women's] individuality and denied them opportunities for education and development of mind and body." The government argued, based on a petition demanding that Muslims not be subject to the bill, that the Muslim community was against the measure. Muslim women tried to combat this move. Sharifah Hamid Ali said that two of her daughters had been "victims of this custom" and favoured 18 as the minimum age for marriage. Muslim members of the Women's Indian Association submitted a special petition:

> We speak also on behalf of the Muslim women of India, assert that it is only a small section of Mussalman men who have been approaching your excellency and demanding exemption from the Act. This Act affects girls and women far more than it affects men and we deny their right to speak on our behalf.

In the end, the Child Marriage Restraint Act that was passed included Muslims but compromised on everything else. The minimum age of marriage for women was set at 14, and for men at 18. The age of consent was not mentioned.

The Child Marriage Bill was a consensus issue for the women's movement—perhaps the last. In the course of the campaign, women's organisations acquired a national profile and gained legitimacy and credibility in representing Indian women. By the early 1930s women's organisations emerged as a consolidated force and were able to respond to national and international issues. They participated in every committee and planning group set up to discuss India's future. Women, it almost seemed, had been accepted as an equal partner in the nation-to-be. But their hegemony wasephemeral. As the momentum of the movement for freedom paced, priorities changed and overtook the fragile alliances and narrow base on which the women's movement was founded.

Politics

From the 1920s onwards, the Indian National Congress INS began to forge linkages with peasant, worker, and women's organisations to demonstrate mass support. Women's political participation was socially legitimised, completely altering equations within the women's movement. Some women were already engaged in a variety of political activity. From 1889 every meeting of the Indian National Congress included some women, a few delegates and many observers. Their participation was often token and symbolic, but the women were educated and politically knowledgeable and were seeking (or being given) new public roles. The Partition of Bengal (1905) and the Swadeshi movement attracted common masses, larger numbers, including uneducated rural women.

Different Forms of Participation

Geraldine Forbes argues that a new kind of feminine political role was fashioned in the course of this movement:

> Where private and public roles were sharply divided by both ideology and physical arrangements, women's political acts were hidden from British authorities. Women hid weapons, sheltered fugitives, and encouraged the men, their domestic roles providing the cover for these subversive and revolutionary acts... [These activities] were quite different from their representative roles in the [Indian National Congress]. There the delegates appeared as equals of men, but their true significance was symbolic. They sang in praise of Mother India and posed as regenerated Indian womanhood. [In the Swadeshi movement] women did not do the same things as men. Instead, they used their traditional roles to mask a range of political activities. While the public and the private continued to exist as distinct categories, usual definitions of appropriate behaviour in each sphere were redefined and given political meaning.

This distinction between two kinds of political activity undertaken by different groups of women continued within the nationalist movement through independence and beyond and existed in many other political formations (such as the left-led peasant and worker movements). As a result, while a small group of women were able to aspire to public and leadership roles on equal terms as men, most were restricted to "feminine" modes of participation. The latter were functionally significant and amenable to valorisation in terms of "feminine" virtue. But for these very reasons, such activities were easily subsumed within traditional gender structures.

Mahatma Gandhi extended the logic of "feminine" modes of protest to the whole of the nationalist movement. It is argued, credibly, that Gandhi "feminised" nationalist politics by emphasising *satyagraha* and passive resistance and creating a special space for women. He drew to the nationalist movement groups and numbers of women as never before. The Bengal women showed the way during the non-cooperation movement of 1921. Basanti Debi, Urmila Debi, and Suniti Debi (members of C.R. Das's family) joined picketing lines, courted arrest, and precipitated a broadening of the movement. They were:

> joined by numerous lady volunteers, especially Sikh ladies. Calcutta students came out in hundreds, joined the prohibited volunteer corps and marched out with *khaddar* on, seeking imprisonment.

Gandhi appreciated the value of female picketeers and continually sought to draw more women into such activities. These efforts bore fruit in the civil disobedience movements of the 1930s. In various parts of the country, masses of women took to the streets and joined picketing lines.

Women's participation legitimised the Indian National Congress and Gandhian politics. It bolstered claims of Indian unity against foreign rule. It also undermined the "civilising" mission of the British and the government's claim to be a protector of women. Police violence toward and sexual abuse of female political activists helped prove the illegitimacy of colonial rule. The movement for women's rights was furthered as well. The leadership of the Indian National Congress, for instance, became committed to the civil rights programme of women's associations. Middle-class women in particular gained many social benefits. By breaching the public domain, female activists facilitated their daughters' entry into the world of formal education, professions, employment, and politics. Within the moral framework of the nationalist movement, they were able to redefine gender roles.

Female demonstrators and nationalist leaders claimed the participation of all Indian women, but upper- and middle-class Hindus dominated the movement. This limitation was implicit in Gandhi's political idiom. He invoked India's sacred legends—all Hindu—to appeal to women. Icons like Sita, Savitri, and Damayanti resonated with Hindu women, even the most poor, low caste, and uneducated, because for them these were living legends. But they excluded Muslim women, who were uncomfortable with such invocations. But Gandhi's idiom was successful because it drew on traditional gender ideology, which not only appealed to women but also reassured men.

Some women who joined the revolutionary movement transgressed stereotypical gender roles, but they were few and exceptional. Their political achievements were valorised, but society did not consider them respectable or representative. Pritilata Waddedar, the most celebrated female martyr of the freedom movement, asked an impassioned question that could not be answered within the dominant gender ideology of nationalism:

> I wonder why there should be any distinction between males and females in a fight for the cause of the country's freedom? If our brothers can join a fight for the cause of the motherland why can't the sisters?.... The pages of history are replete with high admiration for the historic exploits of.... distinguished ladies. Then why should we, the modern Indian women, be

> deprived of joining this noble fight to redeem our country from foreign domination? If sisters can stand side by side with the brothers in a Satyagraha movement, why are they not so entitled in a revolutionary movement?

The radicalism of revolutionary women was seen again in the 1940s among early communist women (many of whom came from the ranks of earlier terrorist-revolutionaries). Many of these women questioned social restrictions on women's mobility, the values of segregation, and the discriminatory sexual morality imposed on women. From their ranks came bold social statements like intercaste and intercommunal marriages, and some questioned the institution of marriage. But like the revolutionaries, they were a small group and outside the mainstream. Only these small groups asked radical gender questions. Congress-led nationalism, which had already cast itself in the image of a reinvented patriarchal tradition, found it easier to jettison even the little commitment it had to social reform. Most nationalist women accepted the social and cultural idiom of "Indianness"—values of segregation and male guardianship—in which their participation was sought. Nationalist activism did not lay any straight road to feminist consciousness.

Not all women accepted male inscriptions on nationalism, however. Saraladevi, Muthulakshmi Reddy, Amrit Kaur, and others were committed to Gandhi and his non-cooperation and civil disobedience, but they did not abandon the struggle for civil rights. Women leaders who remained active in demands for social reform or in the franchise movement were aware that the agenda for women and that for the nation diverged. In 1931 Saraladevi, by then a veteran leader, led a move for a separate women's Congress. Indeed, Saraladevi's vision were ahead of her time. The current Congress, she said, "assigned to women the position of law-breakers only and not law-makers," and had to be forced to address women's demands. Her initiative was frittered away.

Divisions

The contradictions within the women's movement became increasingly apparent. On the one hand, by the 1940s the All-India Women's Conference was establishing itself as the premier organisation representing women. Indeed, it could rightfully claim that after the Indian National Congress it was the second most representative body in India. On the other hand, differences were emerging within its ranks. By 1942, activist women were so engrossed in the struggle for Independence that they ignored gender issues or, like Sucheta Kripalani, deliberately put them aside. The franchise movement demonstrated the dilemma of the women's movement—there was danger in both British collaboration and nationalist alliance.

Gandhi had set the script in his first article on women in *Young India,* where he said that women should take their proper place beside men, but not with a "votes for women" campaign that would only detract from the fight for freedom. Women, he argued, should use their energy "helping their men against the common foe." During the 1930 Round Table Conference, organised women rejected Begum Shah Nawaz's recommendation to accept special reservation as an interim measure. They remained loyal to the nationalist position not to cooperate without a firm commitment to the end of British rule. Similarly, when the Rau Committee (1941) was examining the possibilities of reforming Hindu law, women leaders who had worked hard and long to secure legal reform were hesitant to join Congress's boycott. Gandhi dismissed the Rau Committee as a government ploy to divert attention, and Mridula Sarabhai insisted that women put nationalist issues first. In this complicated and compelling situation, few women leaders were able to balance their commitments to nationalism and feminism.

By the mid-1940s, the hegemony of all-India women's organisations had eroded. For two decades, they had spoken for all Indian women, placing their demands within the framework of social feminism, which constructed women as socially and psychologically different from men. But their ideology was too Hindu, too middle-class, and too urban to appeal to or adequately represent all Indian women. The 1940s were a tumultuous decade for India. Growing communalism led to partition and one of the largest known population displacements in human history. There was war and famine. And the Quit India movement go hand-in-hand with more radical movements for socioeconomic justice. Women were a significant part of all the major events of this time, and their involvement helped shatter the constructions of "Indian woman" from which, in different ways, the women's and nationalist movements drew.

Already, organised women's commitment to a comprehensive legal bill had alienated some Muslim members—foreshadowing a deep cleavage to be unleashed in the elections of 1937. Women's organisations' attempts to attract lower-class rural and urban women failed for want of programmes with mass appeal. There was significant participation of peasant and working-class women in class-based action and nationalist movements under the leadership of a variety of leftist (primarily communist) leadership.

Examples include the Tebhaga movement in North Bengal, the Telengana movement in Andhra Pradesh, and the cotton textile workers' movements in western India. But the women's movement—autonomous women's organisations—was not able to articulate its campaigns on women's issues with this mass upsurge of women.

The left created women's organisations of its own—like the Mahila Atmaraksha Samiti (Women's Self-Defense League) in Bengal—that did significant relief work in times of famine, war, and later partition. But these movements did not coalesce into any significant mass mobilisation of women on gender issues. Agitation over women's issues remained limited to urban elite women, while poor women were mobilised for class or nationalist causes. The questioning of gender roles and relations that had characterised early communist groups soon dissipated. In its "mass face" the Communist Party found itself questioned on its patriarchal leanings. To the now famous question of a peasant woman, "Why should my comrade beat me at home?" (referring to her husband), the party had no answer.

These disjunctures became more acute after independence in 1947. There were far-reaching changes in the legal-judicial domain and with the extension of universal franchise. Women's education was expanding, and more middle-class women entered services and professions. Many "women's" activities returned to the house, but some found berths in the welfare arms of the new government. Large all-India women's organisations became institutionalised and more clearly welfarist. Upper- and middle-class women were clearly going to be the beneficiaries of the new nation-state, and they agreed with the government that economic growth was the first priority.

Leftist women were the least satisfied with constitutional guarantees and promises of prosperity. Under the leadership of women from the Communist Party, in 1954 they formed the National Federation of Indian Women.[2] Peasant and working-class women remained politically active to fight the class wars of the new nation-in-the-making. The Telengana movement continued into the 1950s, and industrial workers' wage and unionisation struggles peaked in the 1950s and 1960s.

Women who were active participants began to challenge the leftist leadership for ignoring women's specific grievances (such as domestic violence). But these were as yet small rumblings. There was no women's platform in which such issues could be articulated, mobilised, or fought.

---

2. Vidya Munshi was a founding member of the National Federation of Indian Women and today is a member of the National Council of the Communist Party of India.

Genesis of Feminism

The 1920s and 1930s witnessed the peak of the so-called first feminist movement. This was the period when women began to organise and mobilise on issues of social reform and civil and political rights. It was a phase of remarkable unity, albeit one achieved at the cost of major social and ideological exclusions. The focus of the movement dissipated in the 1940s: the urgency of the nationalist struggle overrode the priorities of the feminist agenda, and the variety and range of activities in which women began to participate shattered unity. As with many other political forces in India, widening and inclusion inevitably undermined the claim of a few to represent the many.

The second feminist movement inherited many of the legacies of these developments. Issues of family law "nationalised" both the first and second feminist movements. But while child marriage legislation unified the women's movement in the 1930s, the second feminist movement's unity foundered on marriage law reform in the 1980s. The Uniform Civil Code controversy had begun to expose fault lines in the women's movement in the 1940s; in the 1980s these developed into deep and unbridgeable fissures.

At first one question seemed to have been laid to rest. The franchise movement and campaigns for civil and political rights seemed to have been won when the constitution of the new nation-state assured fundamental rights of equality and universal adult franchise. Twenty years later, however, women realised how hollow these provisions were and how little representation they had gained in political establishments and higher reaches of power. Political and social disenfranchisement powered the rise of the second feminist movement, but when in the 1990s the government proposed a bill reserving for women seats in legislative bodies, the women's movement was too fractured to unite in its support. The next section discusses the rise of the second feminist movement and two issues of contention within it: the Uniform Civil Code controversy and the debate over reserving for women seats in legislative bodies.

Contemporary Women's Movement: Solidarity and Schism, 1970-99

Among the early all-India women's organisations, the All-India Women's Conference had the closest links with the Indian National Congress. But all the organisations were to some extent committed to a "harmonious alliance" with the male nationalist leadership. As a result (and because the Congress espoused many women's causes), these organisations accepted the Independent Indian state as an ally. In their critique of patriarchy, identification of oppressive male agency was muted. The enemy was the system, not men. This political position meshed well with the organisations' welfare orientation and charitable work. The position was also consistent with the broad framework of the social feminism—in which claims to equality were based on the importance and value of women's traditional roles—that continued to dominate women's organisations until the 1960s.

From the 1940s, however, women began broadening their scope far beyond women's organisations to the freedom struggle and peasant, worker, and trade union movements. Women's organisations lost their hegemonic claims to represent all Indian women, female activists lost their privileged position when their numbers in political parties and movements increased. As a result the "harmonious alliance" with Congress faced new stresses and strains. Women began to articulate a more diverse, radical, and nuanced critique of patriarchy, reaching toward a new and more politicised gender identity.

New Women's Movement

The turning point came in 1970s, when several events—some within and some outside India—gave a radical turn to the women's movement. The "new feminism" in developed Western countries led in 1971 to the international year and then decade of women. The focus was on development. In the

1950s the India state had bypassed Gandhi's vision of an alternative path to progress, opting instead for conventional models of development: industrialisation, central planning, expansion of science and technology. It was assumed this model would deliver the same results as elsewhere in the developed world—that is, raising aggregate well-being would deliver benefits to all.

But, this prediction foundered on the "hard rock" of Indian patriarchy. This outcome became evident when, at the urging of the United Nations, the Indian government appointed a Committee on the Status of Women. The committee's 1974 report confirmed the worst fears of skeptics. According to the report, since 1911 the condition of Indian women (especially poor women) had worsened in a variety of conventional measures of well-being. Gender disparities had widened in employment, health, education and political participation. The new generation of middle-class women in the public world who encountered isolation and other disabilities brought a new eye to bear on the "woman's question."

The mid-1970s were also a watershed in Indian politics. Congress, under the leadership of Indira Gandhi, inaugurated a new era of populist politics, and there was a gradual broadening of the democratic base of mainstream political institutions. At the same time, the Indian left fractured, giving rise to a new body of leftist thought. A series of locally organised and intense popular struggles broke out. This was the beginning of new social movements, within which popular women's voices found their first platform.

The first of these was the Shahada movement in the Dhulia district of Maharashtra, initiated by Bhil (tribal) landless labourers. In 1972, with help from activists of the new left, the labourers formed Shramik Sangathana, which initiated a vigorous campaign against domestic violence. In the same year, Gandhian socialists broke away from the Textile Labour Association to form the Self-Employed Women's Association under the leadership of Ela Bhatt. In 1973 Mrinal Gore from the Socialist Party joined women from the Communist Party of India (Marxist) to form the United Women's Anti-Price Rise Front, which turned into a mass movement of women seeking consumer protection. A student movement against price rises in Gujarat developed along the same lines to form Nav Nirman (1974), led by middle-class women.

A beginning was made in this period toward the formation of women's organisations along lines completely different from pre-independence ones. There was no effort to form all-India organisations. New organisations were local and tightly knit, with focused agendas. In 1973-74 Maoist women formed the Progressive Organisation of Women, initiating a self-consciously feminist critique of radical leftist politics along with an overarching analysis of gender oppression. This led to other Maoist women's organisations in Pune and Bombay, culminating in the first major celebration of March 8 as International Women's Day in 1975.

Although the New Women's movement gathered momentum, the declaration of emergency by Indira Gandhi in 1975 drove many radical leftist women underground, and their networks fragmented. After the emergency, however, new forces emerged. From around 1978, city-based women's groups were founded, some of which had strong roots in leftist politics. These autonomous organisations focused on raising consciousness about gender issues (Patel 1985). There were also localised struggles—such as the Chipko movement (seen as the precursor of eco-feminism) and the Bodhgaya movement.

The autonomous urban groups drew their visible leadership from the elite, who were able to draw on their horizontal links with state agencies and the intelligentsia (such as the pre-Independence groups). But the groundswell of popular movements also gave these groups vertical links and a mobilisation potential far beyond precedent. Thus the second feminist movement developed, national in scope and with mass connections.

This was a phase of self-conscious commitment to feminist politics. The national character of this movement is usually ascribed to the countrywide protests (led by women) on a case of custodial rape (rape perpetrated by agents of the state on women in official custody, such as police lock-up), the Mathura rape case.[3] Also of considerable importance in the early days were dowry deaths,[4] cases where wives were murdered by their husbands or his relatives for not meeting demands to transfer more cash, goods, or assets from their natal to their conjugal family.[5] In the first case, the demand was for the state to take responsibility for crimes committed by its agents and led to a wider movement for the amendment of the rape law. In the second case, the agitation focused on legislative and administrative remedies, resulting in a provision in the penal code giving the police wide powers in arresting perpetrators of domestic violence.

The government's prompt response with fairly radical legislation on both counts led some women's groups to

---

3. The incidence of rape can be culled from figures published by the Bureau of Police every year. The statistics from Delhi and Calcutta (1995-96) show that the largest number of rapes occur inside the home and are committed by persons known to the victim, often relatives. However, both the women's movement and the media tend to focus on rapes committed in police custody or in public spaces.
4. In 1979 in Delhi, of 358 such deaths, fewer than 50 were suicides, 23 were classified as dowry burnings, and the others were recorded as accidental. The number of accidental burnings increased to 466 in 1981 and 537 in 1982. Feminist groups agitated for the state to recognise these deaths as murders, not accidents. These data were obtained from Saheli, a Delhi-based women's group.
5. A dowry includes money and other consumables, as well as assets like shares or real estate, given by the bride's family to the groom's family at the time of marriage. Traditionally an upper-caste Hindu custom, the practice has widened to all classes and castes since the beginning of the century. In recent years it has also become common among non-Hindus.

question the efficacy of public campaigns for changes in law—because the more the law changed, the more things remained the same. Without political will or an enhancement in women's ability to claim and assert legal rights, laws existed only on paper; they were rarely enforced. From the mid- to late 1980s, women's groups concentrated on providing services to individual women to enable them to gain advantages already given in law. This case was significantly different from the welfare dispensed by earlier women's groups. The earlier groups sought amelioration; the new groups sought recognition and realisation of rights.

In the mid-1980s, the movement encountered severe challenges. The Shah Bano case catapulted the demand for a Uniform Civil Code into the cauldron of communal politics. The Deorala sati incident (1987) initiated a critique of feminism, highly sophisticated but bearing a striking resemblance to earlier dismissals on grounds of elitism, modernism, and Westernism. This backlash was complicated by rising majority fundamentalism, which spawned its own women's organisations and its own "feminist" language. These challenges fragmented the broad perceptions of unity that had underwritten notions of sisterhood and political alliances with low castes and the poor. They demonstrated how fragile was the collectivity based on gender politics and how vulnerable it was to challenges of community, class, and caste interests.

The politics of community acquired a special edge in the women's movement from the Shah Bano case, but the grounds for it had been laid in the 1930s with demands for a comprehensive legal code in place of separate codes based on different religions. Most scholars and activists have tried to understand the Uniform Civil Code debate in the context of heightened communal tensions in the 1980s. The following section examines why family laws are such a flashpoint for communal tensions.

Uniform Civil Code Controversy

In India family, laws are called personal laws. The laws are personal in that they relate to the sphere of personal relations but also in that they are person-specific. The specificity flows primarily from religious affiliation, though local custom is also important. As a result family laws are hived off from the main body of civil law, codified separately for four communities—Hindus, Muslims, Christians and Parsis—based on their religious prescriptions. In reality the four codes are a mix of scriptural sanctions, heterogeneous customs and practices, and, most important, precepts forwarded and established through the political mano-euverings of powerful spokespersons from these communities. Thus the laws necessarily reflect patterns of social and political dominance based on region, caste, class, and gender.

Personal laws define the relationship between men and women within the family and control and direct marriage, divorce, maintenance, guardianship of children, adoption, succession, and inheritance. All four codes concern women intimately, and all treat women as subordinate to and dependent on male kin. The male is considered to be the head of the family, and women do not have equivalent rights, especially to property.

Personal laws are codified separately for the four religious communities—that is, they are not just customary (or common) law, but also statutory law based on religion. As a secular nation-state, India maintains these religious laws alongside secular laws, civil and criminal, all of which are administered by the same legal-judicial apparatus.

Since the 1930s, these contradictions have given rise to demands for a Uniform Civil Code based on secular and egalitarian principles to replace personal laws. But there has also been considerable public opinion in favour of retaining the different personal laws, with great resistance to state interference in the religious communities the laws affect. This debate has plagued the Indian state and fueled communal politics and, in recent years, evoked bitter conflicts within the women's movement.

The Development of Personal Laws

The history of personal laws helps explain the politically charged nature of the debate. The duality of law was a product of colonial imperatives in 18th century Bengal, and part of the process of private-public delineation discussed above. A profound misunderstanding of the pre-colonial system led the British to believe that religious and scriptural tradition was the basis of all custom, morality, and jurisprudence. Accordingly, from the 1770s the British concentrated on codifying Hindu and Islamic laws (drawing on scriptures) and administering these in court with the aid *of pundits* and *maulavis* (Hindu and Muslim scholars and priests).

The codification constituted a herculean feat of selection, appropriation, and reinvention of scriptural texts that were many, varied, and contradictory. Moreover, the pundits and maulavis imprinted on the implementation of these laws their own class and caste interests. British Indian government officials disregarded evidence that many of these precepts and practices were specific to upper classes and castes. This codified and ossified family law was designated in 1860-61 as the domain of personal law, to be drawn and developed from religious principles and kept separate from the secular civil and criminal legal system, based on English law, being developed in British India (Mani 1989; Nair 1996). In the end, British personal laws were substantively different from those of pre-colonial legal and judicial systems.

The new personal laws were the bedrock of the new patriarchy. The colonial state and elite Indian men were concerned with legally buttressing familial authority (see above). Personal laws and a "flexible" approach to customary law were used to that end. To enhance patriarchal control over property and labor, the family was consigned to the amorphous domain of religion, community, and custom (rather than of a law that admitted some measure of individualisation)—all three of which could be manipulated at many levels.

The rise of nationalism and the politicisation of the private family domain placed personal laws at the center of colonial-nationalist conflict. While personal laws were being codified and administered with the active intervention of the East India Company and then officers of the British Raj, the argument that the laws were based on Indian religion, custom, and practice helped make them less alien. The family, to which these laws pertained, was the arena in which the subjects claimed sovereignty and sought, therefore, grounds for political mobilisation against the Raj. This inevitably led to a politicisation of personal laws, which helped displace concerns of gender (central to family law) into other domains of politics— nationalism, to start with. Indian resistance to British attempts at legislative intervention in marriage and succession was based on nationalism—the right of subjects to self-determination in personal and family affairs.

By extension, community and later communal politics became deeply implicated in the politicisation of personal laws. Because religion formed the basis of the laws, communities were predefined by religious affiliation. In British India such communities were also inscribed in the political system through separate electorates and other formal devices. These were removed after Independence, but fundamental rights protected the right of minorities to practice their religions. Since personal laws became the main formal arena of religious difference, they came to be the quintessential symbol of the Indian state's commitment to minority rights. Already charged as the repository of cultural identity, personal laws became the critical marker of the political identity of the community and provided a potent ground for communal mobilisation.

Efforts at and Debates on Reform

While the 1891, Age of Consent Bill witnessed the first major nationalist mobilisation around the question of family law, the Sarda Bill controversy (1927-30) witnessed the first major communal mobilisation. As noted, women's organisations—under the leadership of the Women's Indian Association, All-India Women's Conference, and National Council of Indian Women—united Hindu and Muslim women in favour of the Sarda Bill and against communal leaders. But this was a fragile moment of unity.

Throughout the 1930s, Bills were introduced to remove women's legal disabilities. As these bills were discussed (and defeated), it became apparent to women that their male political allies were opposed to even the most moderate reform of family and property arrangements. Blocked in their efforts at piecemeal reform, women's organisations sought a more comprehensive secular legal code, alienating Muslim women supporters. In the absence of sensitive consideration for the communally charged atmosphere of the period, the move for a secular code was doomed before it got off the ground. In the end the National Planning Committee,' women's subcommittee endorsed a common code but deemed it more feasible to have an optional code that would gradually replace the personal laws. In the meanwhile, the subcommittee recommended reforms within each personal law. The All-India Women's Conference continued its campaign, but in its charter of demands just before independence, it abandoned the demand for a common code in favour of reform of personal laws.

The question of personal law reform came to the fore during the Rau committee (1941-46), which was formulating a code of Hindu law. All women's organisations helped collect evidence for the committee, which recommended a rationalisation of Hindu law for the consideration of the Constituent Assembly, established in 1945. In the debates and discussions on legal reform, the meaning of the common code had become increasingly identified with citizenship in a united nation-state. In the Constituent Assembly the common code became more firmly thus inscribed. These meanings then became imprinted on the term itself: Uniform Civil Code.

The Uniform Civil Code became especially contentious as an instrument of national unity (rather than for securing women's rights). One group in the Constituent Assembly favoured including a provision for the Uniform Civil Code as a fundamental right for breaking down barriers of community. Another group opposed it. The compromise was to include it among the noncontestable directive principles. But several questions remained. First, the right to religion, especially of minorities, was protected as a fundamental right against state intervention, but it was not clear whether personal laws were included in "religion." Second, protection against sexual discrimination was included as a fundamental right, but it was not clear how gender equality could be squared against discrimination in personal laws. Third, an anomalous relationship among women's status, personal laws, minority rights, and citizenship rights was set up.

In the first Congress government of Independent India, first Prime Minister J.L. Nehru and then Law Minister B.R. Ambedkar favoured the Uniform Civil Code as an instrument of modernisation, secularisation, and national unity. But given the immediate political context, they concentrated on reforming Hindu personal law first and proposed a comprehensive Hindu Civil Code. In the course of debate in the 1950s, both sides invoked the Uniform Civil Code[6] (Everett 1981; Parashar 1992). Opponents of the Hindu Civil Code argued that it was unfair to target one community for reform and that a Uniform Civil Code was the only legitimate instrument of reform. The aim was to derail the Hindu Civil Code, but in the process personal laws (especially for Muslims) became marked as an area of minority privilege. "Minority privilege" necessarily implied minority male privilege. As in British India, men were the spokespersons of the community, and the interests of the community were identified with male

6. The Hindu Civil Code had to be scaled down in the face of virulent opposition and passed as four successive acts with major compromises on women's rights.

interests. Many proponents of a Hindu Civil Code, especially women, saw it as a step toward a Uniform Civil Code, heightening minority fears that the uniform code would be an instrument of homogenisation.

While issues of national integration dominated the debate on the Hindu Civil Code, its implications for gender relations within the family also attracted attention. Many opponents saw the code as a radical experiment of "equality run mad" that would imperil "the purity of family, the great ideal of chastity and the great ideal of Indian womanhood" (Pandit Thakur Das). The Hindu Civil Code was an instrument of both modernisation and gender equity, and it was so perceived by opponents and proponents. In fact, the longest and most bitter debates were over women's property rights, and these rights were the most compromised in the legislation that finally passed.

Thus, during the period of nation formation—the latter days of the freedom struggle and the early years of the independent state—the Uniform Civil Code acquired many layers of meanings. It signified women's rights as citizens of a modern secular state but against the threat of particularistic and traditional values of religion, culture, and family. It came to represent the unity and secularity of the nation and a means of modernising pre-modern customs. But politicised religious identities perceived it as a threat to their particularity. Most important, Hindu personal law reform helped create a majority that was seen as being subjected to the discipline of citizenship and a minority that the state granted the indulgence of community authority. This last argument became a ticking time bomb in the hands of the Hindu right with the rise of aggressive majoritarianism in the 1980s.

In the 1970s, the New Women's movement attempted to revive the Uniform Civil Code within the framework of gender politics. But women's rights became articulated within a state-led reform agenda, reinscribing the concerns of national integrity, modernity, and progress. The female activists perhaps believed that this approach would serve as better propaganda for the male political establishment, but it did little to allay fears of majority hegemony. In 1974, the report of the Committee on the Status of Women raised the question of the Uniform Civil Code, appealing to earlier arguments but also squarely in the context of gender equity and justice:

> The absence of the [Uniform Civil Code] in the last quarter of the twentieth century, twenty-seven years after independence, is an incongruity that cannot be justified with all the emphasis that is placed on secularism, science and modernism. *The continuance of various personal laws which accept discrimination between men and women violate the fundamental rights.*

In fact, personal laws became the primary site of a constitutional and structural opposition between the fundamental rights of minorities (to religion) and of women. This opposition was settled in favour of religion by the judiciary in the early years of independence. In the 1950s, the Supreme Court upheld a decree of the Bombay High Court that Article 14 of the fundamental rights (the sex equality clause) could not be invoked to challenge personal laws by virtue of Article 15 (minority rights). This became a binding precedent, pitting women's rights against community rights and giving precedence to the latter. But the judiciary was playing an ambiguous role. From the 1950s, in several judgments, both the apex court and lower courts suggested that state should work toward a Uniform Civil Code, especially with reference to anomalies in the Muslim legal system. The judiciary thereby reinforced minority fears that the reformed Hindu system, which was being posited as rationalised and modern, would override their laws.

The Shah Bano Case and its Aftermath

In 1985, Chief Justice C. J. Chandrachud (of the Supreme Court) delivered a favourable judgment in the case of a divorced Muslim woman, Shah Bano, who had sued her husband for financial support. Her husband claimed that he had done all that was required under Muslim law, but the court granted Bano support under a provision in secular criminal law (section 125). This judgment provoked furious Muslim opposition and precipitated a national crisis. Chandrachud had been careful to quote the Shariat to prove that the right he was granting was in keeping with Muslim personal law. But he emphasised the need for a Uniform Civil Code:

> It is... a matter of deep regret that Article 44 of our Constitution [about the Uniform Civil Code] has remained a dead letter.... A belief seems to have gained ground that it is for the Muslim community to take the lead in the matter of reforms in their personal law. A common civil code will help the cause of national integration by removing the disparate loyalties to law which have conflicting ideologies. No community is likely to bell the cat by making gratuitous concessions.... We understand the difficulties.... But, a beginning has to be made if the Constitution is to have any meaning. Inevitably, the role of the reformer has to be assumed by the courts..... Piecemeal attempts at courts.... cannot take the place of a common civil code. Justice to all is far more satisfactory way of dispensing justice that justice from case to case.

The judgment in favour of Shah Bano was also a judgment against Muslim personal law. Thus a woman's issue became a communal issue. Muslims challenged the right of courts to interfere in their law and constructed the judgment as an attack on their identity as a religious minority. The violation of personal law became a rallying point for Muslim political identity. Feminists, liberals, and orthodox Hindus denounced the Muslim reaction and argued, by implication, that Muslim law was especially harsh to women. The judgment had indicated that it was Muslim personal law from which the courts (or the state) would have to protect oppressed Muslim women. Meanwhile, Rajiv Gandhi's Congress government, already troubled by a loss of Muslim support, rushed through the Muslim Women (Protection of Right in Divorce) Act in 1986 along the lines demanded by Muslim leaders, ignoring other voices in the community.

The issue of personal laws and the Uniform Civil Code was now firmly embedded in conflictual communal politics. The 1980s were a period of growing crisis in India. The secular consensus had broken down and communal conflicts were escalating, with both majority and minority fundamentalism on the rise (Upadhyay 1992). The Supreme Court's emphasis on the Uniform Civil Code raised old fears that it would be an instrument for imposing Hindu hegemony. The meteoric rise of the Bharatiya Janata Party and its espousal of a Uniform Civil Code on grounds of a singular and homogeneous national identity confirmed these fears. The Bharatiya Janata Party, most believe, will extend the reformed Hindu code under the guise of a Uniform Civil Code.

Feminists initially responded to the Shah Bano case and the Muslim Women (Protection of Right in Divorce) Act as women's rights issues. Most leftist and liberal feminists still support a Uniform Civil Code as necessary to promote unity and uniformity and to ensure women's rights. Others have argued that the way to rescue the agenda for women's rights is to focus on gender equality, rather than personal laws as such (Indira Jaysingh, *The Lawyer*, 1986). Many have argued in favour of a common code provided that its framing involves human rights and women's groups.

The Mumbai-based Forum against Oppression of Women has suggested gender-just legislation in areas such as marriage, inheritance, and social security. Some have argued for a gender-just code to cover not only family but also economic, workplace, and livelihood rights—the whole gamut of law (Nari Nirjatana Protirodha Mancha, UCC and Personal Laws, 1996). The Delhi-based Working Group of Women's Rights (supported by the Human Rights Law Network) has proposed a new national secular civil code that would be optional. It has also suggested a "reverse optionality"—that is, all citizens would be born under the national code but could later opt into personal laws.[7] These positions favour one-time

7. This mechanism is not clear. In a dispute between two codes, which would prevail?

legislation. A national conference met in Mumbai in May 1996 to deliberate the possibility of such legislation.

Maitrayee Mukhopadhyay, a feminist researcher, argues that with the passage of the Muslim Women (Protection of Right in Divorce) Act, "the [Uniform Civil Code] as a motor generating political contention seemed to have run out of steam." Flavia Agnes (1991), a feminist lawyer, argues that the rise of majority communalism makes it impossible to view the Uniform Civil Code as non-sexist. A resolution passed at the 1991 Indian Association of Women's Studies Conference acknowledges that appealing to equal citizenship for women is impossible when its meaning translates into contests between politicised religious identities seeking hegemony in the state.

Indira Jaysingh (1996), however, argues that there is never a "right" political moment for a demand like the Uniform Civil Code, not only because of communally charged politics but also because the demand for women's equal status is bound to be contentious. She points out that the issue of women's rights is always displaced by dominant political concerns—class or community—and that it is always deferred in the expectation of a more propitious political climate. There is an urgent need, she argues, for the women's movement to take control of and inscribe its concerns on the agenda (see also Kavita Punjabi, *The Telegraph*, 11 August 1996).

Issues not Highlighted

The highly contentious debate over the Uniform Civil Code has tended to marginalize urgent questions of women's rights to inheritance and maintenance. In the post-independence period the large-scale public distribution of agricultural land—the country's main asset and source of livelihood—proceeded without any regard for women's rights (Agarwal 1994a). This issue remains beyond the scope of personal laws.[8]

---

8. First, land distribution is regulated by state governments. Second, its cannot be challenged on constitutional grounds because of its placement in the ninth schedule. The fear of further fragmentation

Personal laws grant women varying property rights.[9] The reformed Hindu law, perceived as revolutionary in giving women equitable rights and entitlements, made only two basic changes: daughters gained equal rights to self-acquired or intestate property (excluding the family estate), and widows' circumscribed enjoyment of marital property became an "absolute" right.[10] But marriage remains the primary form of women's property. Women still depend on (and prefer) the dubious path of marriage as a source of access to property. This setup creates enormous vulnerability for married women. The two popular notions of women's acquisition of property are through dowry (which deflects inheritance) and through "enjoyment" of marriage property (which bypasses ownership). Two alternative ways of acquiring property are as rewards for elder care or in sonless families. Thus the fundamental male entitlement is affirmed by constructing women as surrogate, secondary, and temporary owners in place of male heirs.

Marriage is an issue of central concern to most Hindu women. Women's entitlements are largely defined by marriage. Yet, in Hindu personal law, marriage is ephemeral, a legal fiction progressively unprotected by case law. Flavia Agnes points out how Hindu law is the worst in this respect and

---

of holding has undercut progressive personal law reform and led to a complete obscuring of women's rights. And though the question of fragmentation has been greatly debated, women's rights have not been addressed within these. As a result in both "ceiling laws" and allotment policy (which regulate public land distribution), the formal definition of family explicitly excludes the rights of women—as wives or daughters.

9. Parsi law stands as the most gender equitable. Muslim law recognises women's rights (as widows and daughters) but on an unequal basis. Christian law, governed by an antiquated statute, gives wives no real property rights.

10. In some states, like Tamil Nadu (1990) and Karnataka (1994), there have also been attempts to give women rights to the family estate.

would be a weak peg on which to hang a gender-just civil code. Higher courts, sympathetic to the deprivation of polygamy rights of Hindu men, have consistently rescued errant husbands by prescribing instead of strict monogamy a strict standard of proof for marriage.[11] The Hindu marriage has become an illusive and constantly suspect legal occurrence. The emphasis on the "sacramental" nature of marriage has prevented compulsory registration provisions. Courts have upheld ancient brahminical norms derogatory to women against more egalitarian traditions within Hinduism. Hindu personal law is, in fact, based on the forced uniformity of varied and heterogeneous practices in the image of the most orthodox of its traditions, rendering it ambiguous and often unenforceable.

Uniformity and Diversity

Since such forced uniformity undergirds personal laws, the argument that a Uniform Civil Code will destroy the pluralism and diversity of Indian society seems weak. Anveshi, a Hyderabad-based women's centre, takes the argument in favour of pluralism much further. It argues that the modern legal system uses homogeneity and a singular notion of justice "to organise relationships of power within its boundaries." The multiplicity of personal laws by itself should not hinder women's access to justice. The important issue is to recognise a "whole new generation of claims to equality and justice that are emerging."

---

11. The courts have imposed an absurd standard of (ceremonial and ritual) uniformity based on a specific upper-caste tradition, which few marriages satisfy. They have emphasized the performance of valid ceremonies but decreed that they cannot be inferred by leading evidence of the officiating priest, also insisting that custom to the contrary can be relied on only if proved by legal text (which is absurd and ossifies dynamic and changing customs). Even admission by the husband (or a second and subsequent wife) in matrimonial proceedings is not considered proof of bigamy.

The issue of pluralism in relation to the debate on the Uniform Civil Code versus personal laws must be addressed with reference to the historical constitution of these laws. The diversity of personal laws is based on community rights, which are the property of pre-formed, sealed religious communities, transgenerationally beyond the scope of change or choice. A principle of social plurality must include the rights to change, make, break, segment, and reform communities. Otherwise we are talking of a principle of fixation, not plurality. The question of cultural diversity cannot be reduced (as is often done by post-colonial or post-modern critiques) to limiting the horizon of non-Western women's self-definition to their "own culture," and then further to that of religious communities.

Religious communities as represented in personal laws are a product of homogenisation and suppression of plurality and diversity. The Muslim personal law (1936-38) was reformed during colonial rule through two acts: the Muslim Personal Law (Shariat) Application Bill (1937) and the Dissolution of Muslim Marriages Bill (1938). The first gave women property rights as decreed by Islam, contravening custom to the contrary. It was through women's rights that Muslims sought to assert their right to be a collectivity, to remove differences within them and to speak with one voice. From this close association between women's rights and community, women lost the space to discuss their rights from the point of view of gender equality but found questions of their rights displaced into questions of community identity.

The second bill was intended to prevent Muslim women from converting to other religions to gain grounds for divorce, which was otherwise denied them. In Anglo-Muhammedan law, previously, only the husband could initiate divorce. While the incidence of such conversion (to obtain divorce) is unknown, the issue had acquired political importance for the Muslim leadership, who sought to prevent a "weakening of the community." Together these bills made women's marital status of crucial significance in the definition of Muslim distinctiveness: both through the distancing from "customary corruptions of Islam" and the imposition of a singular "Islamic" homogeneity at odds with the diverse schools of Islamic law.

Hindu personal law reforms (1955-56) produced a tendentious legal definition of "Hindu" as a residual category (including, for example, Sikhs, Buddhists, and Jains) that took away the freedom of legal self-determination and self-designation from individuals born in so-called Hindu families. The new definition represented an erratic mix of the religious and the secular, an arbitrary homogenisation of diverse schools of Hindu law premised on the northern upper-caste model. It was an attempt to homogenise Hindu patriarchy by suppressing other more egalitarian or secular traditions in what was defined as Hindu. The inconsistent break with upper-caste and *sashtric* (textual) origins made it even more difficult to absorb lower-caste practices.

Thus politicised religious communities encompass diverse voices. In questions of personal laws and the "reform from within" agenda, the question that arises is whose interests the laws represent and who are the spokespersons for reform. This question raises several issues. First, these communities are hierarchical, and "consensus" usually represents the voice of the dominant and powerful. Personal laws are necessarily patriarchal, and within the logic of predefined and primordial religious communities, they cannot be effectively challenged. It must be remembered that the reproduction of community identity is premised on the subordination of women. Besides, in the context of politicised religious communities, the spokespersons are those recognised by the state. Thus, there is collusion between state and community patriarchal forces (the male elite) who hold power of negotiation in both arenas.

The assumption that primordial communities are the only basis of diversity precludes the possibility of secular political communities that are joined by choice and not ascription and that offer the best arena for feminist agency. The most insightful statement about the way in which women's rights (as equal citizens) are pitted against minority rights in this debate comes from Kumkum Sangari. She argues that the opposition between Uniform Civil Code and personal laws is "manichean and politically peremptory." The possibility of gender equality, democratic rights, and full access to equitable laws cannot be recuperated without changing the terms of the debate. The question is not whether women should come under the patriarchal jurisdiction of the state or that of the community. Such a formulation ignores feminist agency. The stake should not be the state or the community but gender justice as a principle and a social horizon.

A theoretical "horizon" provides a major difference between the state and the community. If women can claim a direct relationship with the state unmediated by the community, as citizens with full democratic rights, then they can potentially challenge divisions based on denominations, on public and private, and on legal categorisation, and seek, if they wish, secular collectivities.

Against this vision, is a new view set forward, most comprehensively by Anveshi (Mukhopadhyay, 1998). Anveshi poses an important question: how does the women's movement finds itself on the same side as the Hindu right on issues from anti-obscenity laws to the Uniform Civil Code? Is it accurate to argue that the Bharatiya Janata Party is coopting women's rights issues? The answer, according to Anveshi, lies in the discourse of citizenship and human rights. The issue of women's equal citizenship is posited through the human rights discourse, which assumes that "human" remains prior to and outside structuring of gender, class, caste, or community. The discourse of citizenship treats caste and community as backward and pre-modern, so political mobilisation around these identities creates discomfort for the women's movement.

Anveshi also points out the problem in eliding "gender" and "women." Underlying the demand for a Uniform Civil Code is a universalistic understanding of women's identity (the basis of which can only be biological difference). The perception of women as a universal category has been bolstered by the globalisation of women's rights, which has promoted a static and singular conception of justice. A singular conception of (pure) gender justice cannot accommodate the different notions of justice emerging from caste-, class-, or community-based movements. To recognise this is not to surrender to relativism but to question the dominant meanings of terms like *secularism* and *rights*, which are leading us into a political impasse.

The Law and the State

There is an equally important question of law itself and of the Indian women's movement's relationship with the state and legislation. It was been noted that India has a remarkable range of pro-women legislation. The 1980s, especially, saw extraordinary legislation. But these laws ultimately created despair because they meant so little in practice. As Flavia Agnes points out:

> If oppression could be tackled by passing laws, then this decade would have be adjudged a golden period for Indian women.... .Almost every single campaign against violence on women resulted in new legislation. (Agnes 1992)

Srimati Basu has pointed out, moreover, that women fare quite well within the legal process—especially women who have sufficient financial assets to take on court battles. But to invoke law is to invoke the state. Furthermore, law alone cannot effect changes in cultural practices without widespread state intervention.

There is, some argue, a trap in the debate over the Uniform Civil Code. The code is a political question, and to try to settle it in terms of law is to invoke the law in the service of the state. It is also to bypass the patriarchal nature of citizenship and the patriarchal (and upper-caste Hindu) culture of law and adjudication (Agnes 1995). Women's rights should not be collapsed into the question of law and legislation on the assumption that the legal system is secular or gender (or caste, class, or community) neutral. The law is not the only or even the principal site where issues of justice can be articulated or where feminist intervention can take place. The legal system itself establishes this equation between gender justice and law (arrogating to itself the role of social reformer) to legitimize the domination of the judiciary.

Thus, the judiciary often echoes concerns of the Hindu right in the way it promotes the Uniform Civil Code. A landmark in this regard is the Sarla Mudgal case (1995), which highlighted instances of Hindu men embracing to Islam to commit polygamy. The judgment invalidated such polygamous marriages and invoked the need for a Uniform Civil Code to plug such loopholes, contributing to the belief that the provision for polygamy in Muslim personal law constituted a male privilege and victimised Muslim women. It also obscured loopholes in Hindu law and courtroom practice that have systematically condoned Hindu polygamy. In fact, the incidence of polygamy is higher among Hindus (5.1 per cent) than among Muslims.

These are troubling questions. It has been argued that when the state gives women property rights, women are empowered (Agarwal 1994a). There is in a small measure a redistribution of state power. But demand for legislative change breeds elite modes of agitation (such a lobbying), whereas mass politics can also be a vehicle for women to realize the critical significance of property rights (as evidenced in popular movements that begin with a radical critique of multiple systems of power). Property often emerges as the cornerstone of women's self-empowerment to challenge numerous oppressors: the state, contractors, landlords, husbands, and parents.

The question of whether law initiates or reflects social change is an old one in feminist movements worldwide. Some have argued the symbolic role of progressive law in altering roles and entitlements in the family. Besides, law is not a unitary category that only serves the interests of men. It operates at multiple levels depending on the location of the person invoking it and can be used effectively by women. The state and the law do not speak with one voice and do not represent simple instruments of class, caste, or gender power. While the state should not be seen as the prime "protector," it should not be demonised. It represents itself as at once the protector of religious freedom and the reformer of injustices based on religion. Women can use these paradoxes in the rhetoric of the state purposively and subversively. Because the state is the guarantor of rights, moreover, the history of state intervention is itself partly a history of struggles against patriarchal relations institutionalised through the state.

Whatever consensus may have remained in the early 1990s in favour of a Uniform Civil Code has broken down. The fear remains that the Bharatiya Janata Party will attempt to impose a Hindu code in the guise of a Uniform Civil Code, though the hold of any one party on power at the center is too tenuous to allow a homogenising drive of this kind. At the present political juncture, the impossibility of a Uniform Civil Code or a gender-just code renders its desirability an academic question. The women's movement is too divided to adopt any forceful agenda for reform of family laws. Meanwhile, the movement's focus has shifted from demanding legislation from the state to increasing women's participation in the processes of the state, in legislative and other political decisionmaking. Still, the unity achieved in the early 1980s has not been revived over these "political" issues. The move to reserve seats for women in legislative assemblies found the movement no less divided than over the question of family law reform.

Reserving Seats for Women in Legislative Bodies

In September 1996 the United Front government introduced the Constitution (Eighty-first) Amendment Bill, which sought to reserve for women one-third of the seats in Lok Sabha and state assemblies. In the preceding elections almost all political parties had promised such reservation in their manifestos. The bill was referred to a joint select committee under the chairpersonship of Gita Mukherjee, a veteran Member of Parliament MP from the Communist Party of India. The resubmitted bill was hotly debated in the House in 1997 and 1998. Since then the bill has been stalled. It remains on the agenda in each parliamentary session, but with current political instability, no party is willing to take on such a controversial issue.

Empowerment and Political Representation

Empowerment was the buzzword of the 1990s. But, there is little consensus on the definition and use of the term. Indeed, most of the time it seems to be transparent, and so not in need of definition. According to Bina Agarwal, empowerment is a "process that enhances the ability of disadvantaged (powerless) individuals and groups to challenge and change (in their favour) existing power relationships that place them in subordinate economic, social and political positions." In a general way, the emphasis on power is a response to post-feminist (and feminist) critiques of the earlier focus on victimisation. But, indiscriminate application of the term is likely to trivialize it and defuse its potential.

Devaki Jain rightly points out that "to say inputs of education, better health facilities or toilets are empowering.... is misusing the word and misleading policy." Toilets by themselves cannot be empowering, but the exercise of power by certain groups may lead to a situation where most people are denied basic facilities, like toilets, and the goal should be to empower underprivileged groups so that they can claim such facilities. Empowerment is about power—and politics is the field where power is negotiated. Achieving empowerment requires the women's movement to operate in the field of politics, not only in the manner in which it redefines the field (the personal is the political) but also in the arena where power is brokered—the public world of formal, institutionalised politics.

In India, the demand for reserved seats in legislative bodies did not arise from the women's movement, but the alacrity with which a section of the movement picked it up reflects a political understanding of empowerment and shifts in the women's movement. A crucial step has been taken since the 1980s, from protest politics toward the political mainstream, in order to actualize the movement's claims of playing a transformative role in society and politics. In addition, there is growing awareness that since governments matter, women must be part of them. This awareness was reflected in the platform for action developed at the 1995 Fourth World Conference on Women in Beijing China, one of the goals of which was to increase women's participation in political institutions. In fact, the government claimed the reservation bill to be a fulfilment of the pledge made at Beijing. But despite their best intentions, non-governmental organisations (NGOs) cannot claim true and authentic representation of a tenuously defined "people" relative to democratically elected governments.

Indian women have had little representation in institutional politics since Independence. The largest share of women in Parliament occurred in 1985, when the women's movement was at its peak. Since then women's representation has fallen. The women's constituency is fragmenting rather than consolidating. There is an urgent need for political intervention. The issue of reservation is meaningful for women's leadership; feminist arguments and advocacy now have to deepen into validating claims about the quality of leadership. Leadership is essential because feminist claims on the political arena are not just to share power but to change the nature of power; not just to govern but to change the nature of governance. Women have many ways of enhancing, transforming, and expanding the notion of power and politics, and giving full meaning to the concept of representation.

All this requires us to address the broader field of power and politics. Action at the local level can be useful. But, such action inevitably remains at the margins and has limited transformative potential. Only a strong political content can make empowerment a reality. Similarly, empowerment can be made meaningful for women only by enhancing the political-ideological content of development. The definition of "political" has to reach out to the widest arena of power. Moreover, to be effective players in the distribution of power and resources, women have to stake a claim not only on the state's munificence, but also on state power.

The issue of reservation did not emanate from the women's movement. Nor has the debate been confined to the movement. The possibility of such a large claim by women is of major significance to established and entrenched interests. Passions have risen to a fever pitch, both in Parliament and outside, especially in the visual and print media. Notably, the public ascribes authorship of the measure to feminists.[12]

Many feminists have welcomed the Bill and the political vicissitudes through which it is passing. Male Members of Parliament who oppose the bill have indulged in aggression and violence on the floor of the House; and there has been explicit male collusion to block the bill.[13] The "male plot," says Jain, has actually done women a service by uniting women parliamentarians across party lines as never before. Yet, the Indian women's movement is bitterly divided on the issue. One section, led by leftist females Members of Parliament, has vociferously campaigned in its favour. But an equal number of activists have been hesitant, doubtful, indifferent, and even hostile to the proposed measure.

Background of the Debate

The Indian women's movement has never been favourably disposed toward reservation. High-profile women leaders have

---

12. The Sangh Parivar (Mumbai) called it "state-sponsored feminism" in a statement reported in *The Telegraph*, 9 December 1996.

13. The day after the bill was introduced (13 September 1996), less than half the members turned up at the Lok Sabha. Congress members protested to their president, and leftist leaders were in a quandary because each member feared that he would be the one to suffer from "rotation."

interpreted "equality" in a literal sense and seen in positive discrimination measures a threat to the full recognition of their achievements. Their faith in the political establishment reinforces their meritocratic leanings. In the Constituent Assembly, even female members argued that the provision of equality and universal suffrage was enough and rejected the proposal for reservation. But, the Assembly had 16 women among 150 members, foreshadowing women's political marginality in Independent India.

The limited participation of women in political institutions was noted again during the deliberations of the Committee on the Status of Women. Its 1974 report recommended that seats be reserved for women in municipalities and proposed measures to ensure that committees, commissions, and *panchayats* (rural local government units) include women; that political parties decide on a minimum per centage of female candidates for assemblies and Parliament; and that all-women panchayats be set-up. Some committee members who objected to these measures set out their views in minutes of dissent. Phulrenu Guha, a veteran movement activist, argued that:

> Women are an integral part of society. The provision of reservation... will only serve to reinforce the separate identity of women rather than promote their representation and integration with the rest of society.

Maniben Kara, a veteran trade unionist, radical socialist, and humanist, supported her:

> I am generally opposed to the system of reservation of seats in Legislatures and other elected bodies.... Larger representation of women is essential in their own interests as well as in the interests of the society, but they should secure it by awakening women to their rights and responsibilities, and by creating public opinion in its favour.

Many of these arguments reappear in contemporary debates. So do arguments laid out in other minutes of dissent favouring a larger reservation. Even today these arguments remain the most powerful in favour of reservation. Lotika Sarkar and Vina Mazumdar argued that:

> When one applies the principle of democracy to a society characterised by tremendous inequalities, such special protections are only spearheads to pierce through the barriers of inequality. An unattainable goal is as meaningless as a right that cannot be exercised. Equality of opportunities cannot be achieved in the face of the tremendous disabilities and obstacles which the social system imposes on all those sections whom traditional India treated as second class.... citizens.... *The application of the theoretical principle of equality in the context of unequal situations only intensifies inequalities, because equality in such situations merely means privileges for those who have them already and not for those who need them.*

The committee recommended, in effect, that seats be reserved for women in local government.

Progress and Problems

Women's participation in local governance had already been discussed in the context of Panchayat Raj, introduced in 1957. The solution at that time was a provision for co-opting two women who were interested in work among women and children (Balwantrai Mehta Committee Report). The 1961 Maharashtra Zilla Parishad and Panchayat Samiti Act provided for the nomination of one or two women if they were not elected, and the 1973 West Bengal Panchayat Act provided for coopting two women.

The major breakthrough came in 1983, when a law was passed in the southern state of Karnataka to reserve for women 25 per cent of seats in local councils. In 1987, the first elections were held. The impetus came not from the women's movement but from Janata Dal, whose ideology was a mix of democratic socialism and Gandhian politics, and as part of a pro-people agenda.

This initiative was adopted nationally 10 years later, in April 1993, when the Constitution Act 1992 and The Constitution (Seventy-fourth Amendment) Act 1992 were passed. The first related to panchayats and the second to municipalities. In all panchayats and municipalities one-third of seats were reserved for women. One-third of the offices of chairpersons of panchayats and municipalities were also reserved for women. The full effects of this radical step have yet to be realised. However, in 1987-92 Karnataka had 14,000 women in its development councils. In 1991, in Orissa, 22,000 women were elected to panchayats. In Kerala, 30 per cent of seats were reserved, but women won 35 per cent. In 1994 in the Madhya Pradesh panchayati polls, 33 per cent of seats were reserved, but women won 43 per cent. In West Bengal in the same year, the all-women Kultikori panchayat took office with 11 members. In just two to three years, from about 1 per cent elected women and 4-5 per cent total women in local government bodies, there were more than 350,000 women (Jain 1997b). This figure is expected to rise to about 1 million.

The panchayati reservations were passed in a sudden move that generated little debate and no opposition. Male Parliament members "gave" women one-third of the seats in the lowest elected bodies in the country. This measure had (or still has) the potential of revolutionising not only the common lot of village women but also India's political culture. Immediately after the first round of elections, there was a great deal of skepticism. Studies in West Bengal showed that in many areas, women's inexperience allowed their marginalisation; that given the limited power and resources of the panchayats, women's roles were highly circumscribed; and that political parties included women for panchayati representation without allowing them voice in party decisionmaking (Sachetena 1995; Rural Development Consortium 1995).[14] A second round of elected women are now in office, and activists and scholars argue that there have been many benefits. True, many of the women elected had little or no political experience, but they have gained self-confidence. These women have questioned priorities in panchayat programmes and stressed "domestic"

14. Two other problems have been pointed out. There is considerable suspicion about devolving power and resources from centres of (male) power to the periphery where women have gained a voice; and the prioritization of departmental segregation over area-based activism hampers the workings of panchayats.

issues like fuel, water, schools, and the proximity of services. Women have been less committed to party interests and been able to build broad alliances among themselves (Jain 1996b). Some argue that the success of the panchayati reservations has been an eye-opener. The backlash has hardened male opposition to women's inclusion in higher decision-making bodies (Jain 1997a). Nevertheless, the 81st Amendment Bill was proposed. Its provisions were similar to the 73rd and 74th amendments: one-third of seats in Lok Sabha and state assemblies were to be reserved for women along with the existing provisions for SC/ST (Scheduled Castes/Scheduled Tribes). The justification given was that since independence, women's participation in Parliament has been quite limited (table 1).[15] And in 1995 women accounted for just 3.9 per cent of the members of state assembles.

Table 1 : Women Representatives in Lok Sabha

Year	*(per cent)*
1962-67	6.7
1967-71	5.9
1971-76	4.2
1977-80	3.4
1980-84	5.1
1985-90	8.1
1990-91	5.3
1991-96	7.1
1996-98	6.3

15. Statistics from the past few elections indicate that women vote in about the same proportions as men. Some analysts argue that they follow the lead of male family members on who to vote for, but there is equal evidence that many vote independently. Moreover, the proportion of female parliamentarians is not low by international standards—until recently it compared favourably with levels in the United Kingdom and United States. French women have been fighting for parity for years. Only Scandinavian countries have achieved more than 30 per cent representation of women.

Current Arguments

The issue of quotas for women in Parliament and state assemblies has inspired sharp debate. Many problems that appear to be about practical details or procedural formalities are in fact locked into fundamental questions of politics. Reservation has made strange bedfellows. It is typically a liberal feminist demand but is championed by Marxist women. It has drawn fundamentalist and rightist women to the side of leftist parties, and opposition has created equally curious alliances among men. I organise the arguments around three principles: democracy, equality, and representation.

Democracy

Democracy has been invoked to both defend and oppose the bill. The rationale of the bill is an affirmation of democracy, grounded in the belief that democracy has to be made more meaningful and representative. Opponents argue that quotas are anti-democratic. SC/ST quotas are in place for schools, colleges, jobs, and legislative bodies. Among the upper-caste elite, there is growing meritocratic opposition to these quotas. But many accept social justice arguments in favour of such quotas. Many elites are indifferent to women's quotas at the panchayati level. Ela Bhatt (of Self-Employed Women's Association), for instance, is in favour of SC/ST quotas and the panchayati reservations for women, but she considers women's quotas at the upper reaches of the legislature to be undemocratic.

It is argued that the paucity of women in politics and public life will be eased by wives and daughters participating in democratic institutions. But these women will not be democratic representatives, properly speaking. Moreover, the women will remain mere mouthpieces for their male kin. A "*biwi* [wife] brigade" will come to power (Mahdu Kishwar, *Sunday Times of India,* 22 September 1996). There are enough examples to support this argument (Katzenstein 1978).[16]

16. Katzenstein calls the prominence of Indian women in politics the "Indira Gandhi anomaly." Women's participation in the

But, it is also possible that wives and daughters will build coalitions and gain power. The "family" idiom is longstanding in Indian politics. Nepotism is not just a dominant practice, it is normalised behaviour, since kin-based patronage networks form the bedrock of politics. Such networks are usually pressed for male relatives—almost all the sons of political leaders inherit some of their fathers' political capital. Wives and daughters usually benefit materially and derive status and authority, but they do not qualify for political patronage except in the absence of suitable sons. But, once a woman acquires power, will she remain docile? The panchayat example seems to indicate the contrary. Once a woman has power, she may question family structures, which exclude her from resources and authority through marriage and inheritance practices. One can hope that women will be able to use the family to access political power and then use that power to transform the institution of the family.

It is, nevertheless, true that the family (or dynastic) system helps reproduce elite domination. There is understandably a great deal of hesitation in accepting gender discrimination as grounds for affirmative action because in a deeply hierarchical society like India, the highly visible minority of successful middle-class women cannot be easily conceived as discriminated against relative to the large majority of underprivileged men.

Equality

The desire for equality drives the demand for reservation. Since Independence, women have not had more than 8 per cent representation in legislative bodies. The enormous social and economic obstacles to women's entry into these arenas make quotas a political means of achieving social change.

Equality also provides an argument against quotas. If women are equal, why do they need quotas? There is confusion

---

freedom struggle and the importance of kinship networks have given women scope to acquire leadership positions. But this is not effective for the mobilisation of women's interests.

here, as pointed out by Lotika Sarkar and Vina Mazumdar (1974), between "theoretical equality" and "unequal situations," between intrinsic equality and potential equality, between equality of individuals and of members of a collectivity. Women are equal in that individual women are as capable as individual men and have equal rights. But women as women face social discrimination, which continues to limit their capabilities and opportunities.

But, the equality argument becomes problematic when extended to "more than equal" arguments. There is an interesting continuity from the women's suffrage movement led by the Bangiya Nari Samaj (Association of Bengali Women) in the 1920s. Women's suffrage was promoted through social feminist arguments grounded in the "equal but different" slogan. The struggle for rights was based on a celebration of women's traditional roles and an acceptance of traditional definitions of womanhood. Thus women's entry into the public world was justified by their biological and psychological uniqueness. Only women, it was argued, can bring certain knowledge and skills from the private domain into public life. It was commonplace in the 1920s to argue that women's skills at managing the household budget could profitably be extended to public finance. A "good for society" argument is always easier to sell. Proponents highlight the need for women's special perspectives in public life for the benefit of society as a whole.[17] The emphasis is on constructing political activity around the uniqueness of women's experience—for instance, their mothering and nurturing activities are supposed to give them a special affinity for peace and environment movements.

One of the most common defenses of the reservation bill rests on women's supposed moral superiority. Some offer visions of honest and virtuous women sweeping clean the

17. Najma Heptullah, then deputy chairman of Rajya Sabha, made this statement on 10 September 1996, along with a demand that the provision be extended to Rajya Sabha.

parliamentary stables of sleaze and corruption. Women, untainted by cut-throat political competition, will restore harmony and cooperation to Indian politics.[18] Some offer a muted hope that women, being new players in the game of parliamentary politics, will be less manipulative.

Paternalist sympathisers are usually comfortable with assertions of women's moral superiority because these reconfirm notions of difference. Such assertions promise continuity in gender relations since they identify women with precisely that domain already prescribed for them in dominant patriarchal discourse. Moreover, these are weak assertions which, when inconvenient, are easily refuted by examples of corrupt or aggressive women politicans like Indira Gandhi, Mayawati, or Jayalalitha.

The current feminist dilemma is to chart a safe path through the minefield of these biological and social feminist defenses. Without doubt, the question of a women's quota is locked into an assertion of biological identity. It may be, as has been stressed, that biology is inescapable in developing country feminism because women continue to fight for formal rights from which they are excluded on the basis of biology. But basing demands on biology and social feminism has long-term implications. Gains today are offset by the reinforcement of the idioms and images that restrict women. Thus it is important to choose one's argument with care.

Issue of Dabate

Representation is obviously the key issue in the reservation debate. The proposed bill assumes that women are a political collectivity who requires fair representation, which can only be achieved through separate representation, guaranteed by quota. This contention is reinforced by the fact that Indian women fall behind men in all social and economic indexes. Only women, it is argued, will promote the interests of women

18. T. N. Seshan, then chief election commissioner, made this statement on 13 July 1996.

in the process of national growth and development. The inference is that men cannot (for social or political reasons) or do not (to protect patriarchal authority) represent women's true interests. Women have to do their own representing.

But then, who are women? Other Backward Castes (OBCs) members of Parliament have effectively mobilised around the demand for a "sub-reservation" for OBC women. Gita Mukherjee has set out her objections to the sub-reservation: there is no precedent or move for a general OBCs reservation in legislative bodies or panchayats, and the problem can be solved without reservation if OBCs women are put up in OBCs-dominated constituencies. The demand, however, has been made on the basis that OBCs men will be replaced by upper-caste urban elite women. Mukherjee offered a solution: that OBCs women be nominated in areas dominated by these castes. But this alternative is also not acceptable because OBC men not only fear losing their seats to non-OBCs women but also to OBCs women. They fear the fracturing of community solidarity; they certainly do not want to lose the monopoly to speak for "their" women; and they object to the empowerment of women in the community over which male leaders have so far had undisputed authority.

The demand for an OBCs sub-reservation has been followed by similar demands from minorities. These demands have fractured the category of "women" by introducing the two most powerful forces in Indian politics—caste and community. Thus the notion of the individual as the bearer of rights is in tension with various definitions of collectivities. If men cannot represent women, can women uniformly represent each other? Once again the hoary and impossible to settle question is raised of the relationship between gender and caste, class, and community. Who has the better ability (or right) to represent OBCs women— OBCs men or upper-caste (or non-OBCs) women?

The question of who legitimately represents who is tied to the nature of the political collectivity that seeks representation.

One of the most common criticisms of the bill is that reserving seats for women is pointless because women are not a homogeneous group. This truism is rarely applied to caste or community, which are also characterised by divisions of (at least) class and gender. But the problem goes deeper in the case of women.

The claim to reservation for women is based on the distinctive character of collectivities based on gender. Caste and community are already both social and political collectivities. These collectivities are knit by the institution of the family, which ensures their reproduction; and are underwritten by political institutions like protection and reservation, already framed in the constitution of India. Women are not as clearly framed constitutionally, except in negative terms by prohibition of "discrimination by sex." Indeed, identities based on caste and community (and rights flowing from them) have been given precedence in many cases over the fundamental right of "equality by sex"—as in the judicial decision to uphold the "protection of minorities" clause over the "equality" clause in matters of personal law.

It follows that in social terms too women are not a collectivity. Rather, they are the opposite. Social institutions like the family and political instruments like caste and community fracture gender. Thus the insistent litany of apologists of patriarchy: "women are women's worst enemy." One of the first lessons a feminist learns is that every social institution actively divides women. Moreover, the isolation of one or two women in the family (and home) provides them with few opportunities to form the primary collectives from which they can aspire for a political identity. The demands for sub-reservations have made this an urgent issue. Political collectives like caste and community are constituted by and through the family and women's isolation, and are therefore male communities predicated on the exclusion of the large majority of the women for whom they (illegitimately) seek to speak.

Women do not yet exist as an effective political collectivity (or even simply a vote bank). That remains a vision of the women's movement. The reservation bill may not have intended the creation of such a collectivity, but it is an implicit and necessary corollary. That is, the bill is not an expression of an extant political community but an aspiration toward a political collective. This political collective is not a political extension of a biological category (any more than caste or community) but must be a product of political mobilisation. The formation of such a collective will be a political act, an exercise of political will.

Women, Power and Politics

The bid for reservation has been troubled within the women's movement because feminism has been ambiguous about power. The long and systematic exclusion from formal politics has inhered in the very definition of femininity. When women are associated with power in traditional construc-tions, the emphasis is on moral power.[19] Feminisms that have drawn on traditional feminine imagery face a double bind. One the one hand, women must not seek power because it corrupts. On the other hand, women need power to fight corruption. The possibility of women's large-scale induction into the hurly-burly of electoral politics throws this duality into sharp focus. Will electoral politics corrupt women, divide them in self and party interests? Ors will women make power pure?

Such questions are impossible to answer. But, it must be emphasised that the reservation Bill is not a revolutionary manifesto. No one believes that reserving seats for women in Parliament will solve all the problems of all women. The bill is and must remain one tool among many deployed to alleviate some of the grossest forms of inequality and injustice to which women are subject. It is a means to an end. It will, hopefully, serve as a "shock treatment" to the political system.

---

19. Introducing the Bill (on 12 September 1996), then Law Minister Ramakant Khalap said that it was incomplete but reflected the spirit of Indian culture, where women are worshipped.

Moreover, the Bill is unlikely to have immediate, far-ranging consequences, such as promoting the moral transformation of India's political culture. Women cannot hope to keep their hands clean. That is, having more women in power may lengthen the Mayawati-Jayalalitha list. And there can be little doubt that some women will benefit more and, especially in the short term, many women will not benefit at all. But, such is already the case (for men and women). The reservation bill cannot seek to change all the inequities of the political system. It merely seeks to ensure that significant numbers of women enter the arena of political decision-making.

Reservation must and will work through the multiparty system. Parties will be prodded to put up women for election. The fear is that such women will toe the party line at the cost of representing women's interests (Bhaswati Chakravorty, *The Telegraph*, 23 March 1997). In the case of panchayats, inducting women at the lowest levels of the party—thereby ensuring that they remain marginal in decision-making— has satisfied reservation provisions. But state or national elections cannot be handled on that basis. Political parties have been unwilling to admit women, allow them a voice in policy formation, or give them opportunities for leadership positions.

Ironically, leftist and self-styled progressive parties, the most insistent champions of reservation, have the worst record in this regard. Brinda Karat resigned last year from the politburo of the Communist Party of India (Marxist) in protest over this issue. In this scenario, the Indian National Congress leads the way, with further changes recently initiated by Sonia Gandhi. The Bharatiya Janata Party BJP is the next best. Thus, women's participation has not been a good sign of "progressive" politics. But the need to field significant numbers of women candidates is bound to fundamentally change the gender equations within parties. There will not only be 180 women in Parliament and more than a thousand in state assemblies, but losers in elections and others seeking elections.

The intention, which is to draw large numbers of women into the political arena, will be served, and neither male relatives nor party bosses can hope to ensure that so many women will speak only their words. A party line is not immutable; it depends on its members and decision-makers. Women members will, like male members, follow the party line. But, if present in large enough numbers in the party, they are also bound to influence the line. Thus, while we fear divisions among women, we can also look forward to crucial coalition of interests.

Women are hoping to break into the political mainstream through reservation. There will be no handouts *(The Telegraph,* 2 March 1997). Women will not be "given" reservation. A long and hard battle has prepared the ground for this demand. A difficult campaign is now under way, with thousands of letters, petitions, demonstrations, and meetings across the country. Mukherjee (1997) wrote, "never in my life have I seen so many postcards written in blood by women from different walks of life." The outcome is uncertain.

CONCLUSION

In 1974, Indira Gandhi, India's Prime Minister, told reporters: "I do not regard myself as a woman. I am a person with a job to do" *(The Asian Student,* 23 November 1974). A year before, a popular magazine for "modern" women released a special Independence Day issue with Indira Gandhi portrayed as Goddess Durga on the cover. It said, "to be a woman—a wife, a mother, an individual—in India means many things. It means that you are the storehouse of tradition and culture and, in contrast, a volcano of seething energy, of strength and power that can motivate a whole generation to change its values, its aspirations, its very concept of civilised life." Women in Indian politics have always negotiated these two extreme poles: as the unsexed equal or the highly feminised goddess or queen. Such negotiation has allowed a small but significant group of women to aspire for high offices within the political establishment. But, women on the whole have attained little democratic representation, either in numbers or in terms of their specific gender interests.

Since the 1920s, a few women have been on a quest for a feminist politics outside the political mainstream. In the 1920s and 1930s, in the first wave of a feminist movement, women's organisations were able to draw both on the benefits of modernity (from colonial rulers and male Indian reformers) and from the idiom of "Indianness" constructed in the nationalist discourse. Female segregation and seclusion offered opportunities to build women's collectives that rejected male tutelage but accepted traditional patriarchal gender roles. This social feminism allowed a remarkable hegemony of elite women to speak for "all Indian women" from a united platform. The involvement of many of these women in the freedom struggle tied their demand for women's rights to nationalist movements to produce a uniquely Indian feminist nationalism with that had three important consequences. First, nationalism implicated female activists in a singular cultural Indian identity based on a new patriarchy. Second, the cause of women's rights was advanced but hitched to a state-led nation-building discourse in Independent India. And third, women became vulnerable to the many competing discourses that constituted the nation-state.

During the 1940s, the growing involvement of women in diverse social and political movements broke down the essentialist construction of "Indian women." Neither women's organisations nor nationalists could continue to speak of (or for) "Indian women." The loss of hegemony hindered women's organisations' quest for equality but helped many other women seek new gender identities beyond narrow caste or class constituencies and the limitations of social feminism. The "petition politics" of the 1930s had outlived its efficacy by the 1940s. After independence, female activists were marginalised because they avoided the political arena for behind-the-scenes activities. At the same time, the ideas that replaced social feminism had nothing to offer activist women—none of them even had an agenda against patriarchy. Thus women's concerns and ideas were not incorporated into the various struggles they joined, either against the Raj or for social and economic justice before and after Independence.

The second wave of feminism emerged in the late 1970s and early 1980s. Women's organisations set up at this time did not make a bid for hegemony. These were autonomous groups, joined not through the structure of formal association but through informal networking, local leaderships, an emerging feminist press, and an intensification of multivoiced exchanges. This panoply of organisations represented women from all classes, castes, communities, and locales defined by, if anything, a common commitment and a language that is more leftist than liberal—a situation not very different from that in most European feminist movements. This movement can make no singular claim to represent all Indian women, but it has, collectively, a national profile and presence. The various All-India campaigns launched by women engendered a cultural radicalism in which a broad range of issues and a multiplicity of voices could be articulated. This is an Indian women's movement with a difference.

The common commitment and language of this movement grew out of an engagement with violence against women. Violence was, of course, not new in India. But earlier issues of violence had been articulated within the mainstream political agenda: sati as an issue of tradition, and the age of consent as one of Indian fitness to rule. In these discourses women's bodies were the site on which men fought their battles. In the 1980s, feminists drew attention to the facts and consequences of violence against women themselves.

Even as feminist intervention has expanded our perception of the field in which violence is perpetrated against women, intractable differences have emerged within feminist ranks on the place of the women's movement and feminist politics in India. The controversy over the Uniform Civil Code is, at one level, a battle between (Hindu and Muslim) men who relish their rights in the family and the community based on their "ownership" of women. At another level, female activists are no longer on a universal trajectory of "rights" and are uncertain about the possibilities of the women's movement offering a secular space outside the structures of community. The exigencies of the political situation—fundamentalism and ethnic conflict—preclude concentrating only on issues of interest to women or a feminist perspective on all issues of importance.

To be viable, many argue, feminist politics must address the many competing class, caste, community, and ethnic struggles for justice and equality. The fissures within the women's movement sit uneasily with the move by the state to reserve seats for women in the legislature. Women, properly speaking, no longer exist as a constituency. Perhaps that is why the move to reserve seats came from the government rather than from the women's movement. And yet, while many feminists have written against reservation in the popular media, effective opposition to the bill has come from male parliamentarians and on the demand of separate representation (sub-reservation) for OBCs and minority women.

The debates over personal laws and reservation of seats for women, the latter more clearly than the former, represent competing claims to speak for women. But communities (of caste, community, or ethnicity) are inescapably gendered in their occupation and location even as they assert their presence within and against the nation. The nation-state and the discourse of citizenship, on the contrary, allow women to figure as unmarked subjects and to invoke their rights and entitlements. The women's movement alone can expose the "gender markings" of the woman in the process of invoking her rights and entitlements, and building an emancipatory politics on that basis.

Thus, there is an urgent need to redefine feminist political agency—to allow for the possibility of secular political collectives to which women can belong not by ascription, but by voluntary participation. In other words, to rebuild the fragmented constituency of women. But the solution may not lie in a revitalised national women's movement, particularly in the current context of economic fragility and political instability. There is already the contours of a women's movement, actual or potential, in the impressive networking capacities of autonomous groups and the mobilising potential of left-led women's groups. We need to recognize the importance of women's associations at the local and regional levels without retreating into the irreducibly local. The developing and strengthening of local institutions is also necessary, and seems to dominate women's movements in the late 1990s. The question is how to mobilize these institutions for a transformative feminist politics—that is, to ensure that these localised struggles face and accommodate the challenges posed by community and caste politics without allowing them to displace gender concerns.

REFERENCES

Agarwal, Bina, *A Field of One's Own: Gender and Land Rights in South Asia,* Cambridge University Press, Cambridge, 1994a.

Agnes, Flavia, Presentation at Indian Association of Women's Studies Conference, Calcutta, 1991.

—, "Protecting Women Against Violence? Review of a Decade of Legislation, 1980-1989", *Economic and Political Weekly,* 27, 17 (April 5), 1992, pp. 19-33.

—, "Hindu Men, Monogamy and Uniform Civil Code", *Economic and Political Weekly,* 30, 50, (16 December), 1995.

Anderson, M.R., "Work Construed: Ideological Origin of Labour Law in British India to 1918" in Peter Robb (ed.) *Dalit Movements and the Meanings of Labour in India,* Oxford University Press, New Delhi, 1993, pp. 87-120.

Ansari, Iqbal A., "Muslim Women's Rights; Goals and Strategy of Reform", *Economic and Political Weekly,* 26, 17, 27 April, 1991.

Anveshi, "Is Gender Justice Only a Legal Issue? Political Stakes in UCC Debate", *Economic and Political Weekly,* 1 March, 1997.

Bagal, J.C., "Sarala Devi Chaudhurani", *Sahitya Sadhak Charitmala,* 99, Bangiya Sahitya Parishad, Calcutta, 1964.

Banerjee, Nirmala, "Working Women in Colonial Bengal: Modernisation and Marginalisation" in Kumkum Sangari and and Sudesh Vaid, *Recasting Women: Essays in Colonial History,* Kali for Women, New Delhi, 1989.

—, Abstract of presentation in "The Eighty-First Amendment Bill 1996: A Report", IAWS, School of Women's Studies, Jadavpur University, Calcutta, 1997.

Basu, Srimati, *She Came to Take Her Rights. Indian Women, Property and Propriety,* State University of New York Press, 1999.

Bhatt, Ela, Abstract of presentation in "The Eighty-First Amendment Bill 1996: A Report", IAWS, School of Women's Studies, Jadavpur University, Calcutta, 1997.

Borthwick, Meredith, *The Chaging Role of Women in Bengal, 1849-1905,* Princeton University Press, 1984.

Bose, Saugata, *Peasant Labour and Colonial Capital. Rural Bengal since 1770,* New Cambridge History of India, III-2, Cambridge University Press, Cambridge, 1993.

Carroll, Lucy, "Law, Custom and Statutory Social Reform: the Hindu Widows' Remarriage Act of 1856" in J. Krishnamurty (ed.) *Women in Colonial India, Essays on Survival, Work and the State,* Indian Economic and Social History Review, Oxford University Press, New Delhi, 1989, pp. 1-26.

Chakrabarty, Renu, *Communists in Indian Women's Movement, 1940-50* , People's Publishing House, New Delhi, 1980.

Chakravarti, Uma, *Rewriting History. The Life and Times ofPandita Ramabai,* Kali for Women, New Delhi, 1998.

Chatterjee, Partha, "The Nationalist Resolution of the Women's Question" in Kumkum Sangari and Sudesh Vaid (ed.), *Recasting Women. Essays in Colonial History,* Kali for Women, New Delhi, 1989, pp. 233-253.

Cooper, Adrienne, *Share Cropping and Share Croppers' Struggle in Bengal, 1930-1950,* K.P. Bagchi, Calcutta, 1988.

Custers, Peter, *Women in the Tebhaga Uprising,* Naya Prakash, Calcutta. Dasgupta, Kaberi, 1998.

De Haan, Arjan, "Towards a Single Male Earner: the Decline of Child and Female Employment in an Indian Industry" in *Economic and Social History of the Netherlands,* 6, 1994.

Engels, Dagmar, *Beyond Purdah? Women in Bengal, 1849-1905,* Oxford University Press, New Delhi, 1996.

Everett, J.M., *Women and Social Change in India,* Heritage, Delhi, 1981.

Forbes, Geraldine, "Medical Careers and Health Care for Indian Women: patterns of control", *Women's History Review,* 3, 4, 1994.

—, *Women in Modern India, New Cambridge History of India,* Cambridge University Press, Cambridge, 1996.

Gandhi, M.K., "Women and the Vote", *Young India,* 24 November 1920.

Gandhi, Nandita and Nandita Shah, *The Issues at Stake. Theory and Practice in the Contemporrary Women's Movement in India,* Kali for Women, New Delhi, 1991.

Joshi, V. C. (ed.), *Rammohun and the Process of Modernisation in India,* Vikas Publications, Delhi, 1975.

Karlekar, Malavika, *Voices from Within: Early Personal Narratives of Bengali Women,* Oxford University Press, New Delhi, 1991.

Kumar, Radha, "From Chipko to Sati: The Contemporary Indian Women's Movement" in Amrita Basu (ed.) *The Challenge of Local Feminisms. Women 's Movement in Global Perspective,* (Westview, 1995) Indian ed. Kali for Women, New Delhi, 1999.

Liddle, Joanna and Rama Joshi, *Daughters of Independence. Gender, Caste and Class in India,* Sed Books and Kali for Women, London and New Delhi, 1986.

Mandal, Tirtha, *Women Revolutionaries of Bengal, 1905-1939,* Minerva, Calcutta, 1991.

Mani, Lata, "The production of an official discourse on Sati in Early Nineteenth Century Bengal, *Economic and Political Weekly,* 26 April 1986, pp. 32-40.

—, "Contentious Traditions: The Debate on Sati in Colonial India" in Kumkum Sangari and Sudesh Vaid, *Recasting Women: Essays in Colonial History,* Kali for Women, New Delhi, 1989.

Mukherjee, Gita, Unite in Support of One-third Reservation for Women, National Federation of Indian Women, Calcutta, 1997.

Mukhopadhyay, Maitrayee, *Legally Dispossessed. Gender, Identity and the Process of Law,* Stree, Calcutta, 1998.

Murshid, Ghulam, *Reluctant Debutante: Response of Bengali Women to Modernisation, 1849-1905,* Rajshahi, 1952.

Nair, Janaki, *Women and Law in Colonial India,* Kali for Women, New Delhi, 1996.

O'Hanlon, Rosalind, "Issues of Widowhood: Gender and Resistance in Colonial Western India", Douglas Haynes and Gyan Prakash (eds) *Contesting Power. Resistance and Everyday Social Relations in South Asia,* Oxford University Press, New Delhi, 1991.

—, *For the Honour of My Sister Countrywomen: Tarabai Shinde and the Critique of Gender Relations in Colonial India,* Oxford University Press, Oxford, 1994.

Omvedt, Gail, *We Will Smash This Prison.* Zed Books, London, 1980.

Parashar, A., *Women and Family Law Reform in India: Uniform Civil Code and Gender Equality,* Sage, Delhi, 1992.

Sangari, Kumkum, "Politics of Diversity. Religious Communities and Multiple Patriarchies", *Economic and Political Weekly,* 23 and 30 December, 1995.

Saraladevi, "A Women's Movement", *Modern Review,* October, 1911.

Sen, Samita, "Motherhood and Mothercraft: Gender and Nationalism in Bengal" in *Gender and History,* 5, 2, Summer, 1993.

—, "Gendered Exclusion: Domesticity and Dependence in Bengal", *International Review of Social History,* 42, 1997.

—, "In Hope and Fear: Reservation of Seats for Women in Legilsative Bodies", INSPARC, Kalyani,1998.

—, "CITU Changes Tack. But Slogans Rule not Sober Analysis. *The Statesmen,* Calcutta, 1999a.

Shah, A.B. (ed.)., *Letters and Correspondence ofPandita Ramabai* (compiled by Sister Geraldine), Maharashtra State Board of Literature and Culture, Bombay, 1977.

Shiva, Vandana, *Staying Alive: Women, Ecology and Survival in India,* Kali for India, New Delhi, 1986.

Sinha, Mrinalini, *Colonial Masculinity. The 'manly Englishman' and the 'effeminate Bengali' in the late nineteenth century.* Manchester University Press, Manchester, 1995.

Smart, Carol, *Law, Crime and Sexuality: Essays in Feminism,* Sage, London, 1995.

Southard, Barbara, *The Women's Movement and Colonial Politics in Bengal, 1921-1936,* Manohar, New Delhi, 1995.

Stridharma, "Srimati Saraladevi Chaudhurani's Speech at the Bengal Women's Congress", *Stridharma,* 14, August, 1931.

7

POLITICS OF DALITISM

The attempt by some of activists of Dalit movement in India to internationalise the issue at World Conference against an impression that there is something basically wrong in the ideological orientation of the movement. The word "Dalit" was coined in post-colonial India by the disciples of Ambedkar. They did not accept the word Harijan (Men of God) used by Gandhi for the untouchables in Hindu social order because of their aversion against him. The word Dalit therefore, became the vernacular terminology for the oppressed classes, with a wider connotation for electoral sociology in the democratic polity of the country.

Mahatma Gandhi and Dr. Ambedkar

If we look into the history of Dalit movement, it is as old as the birth of the concept of untouchability, which was the darkest spot in Hindu social structure. Though, Hindu reformists tried their best to fight against this social evil right from the days untouchability was born, the real concern over it came to surface during the freedom struggle, when Mahatma Gandhi and Dr. B.R.Ambedkar fought against it in their own way. While Gandhi wanted complete eradication of untouchability for emotional integration of Hindu society, Ambedkar was for abolition of Varnashram structure of the Hindu social order.

The conceptual difference between the two messiahs of untouchables continues to affect the Dalit movement even after their death. While the disciples rejected Mahatma Gandhi for the sake of power and fulfilment of their personal ambitions, Ambedkar became a symbol of Dalit movement. A clue to understanding Ambedkar lies in his hatred of Gandhi. The activists of Dalit movement adopted the same philosophy against the upper castes and are still found boiling in the anger generated by their messiah Ambedkar. Taking advantage of the violent landscape, which started emerging since the closing decades of twentieth century, the followers of Ambedkar adopted the sole agenda to create social disorder and capture powerby hook or crook. In both the situations, the process of social transformation in Hindu society, which took off in positive direction just after Independence got disturbed.

Difference between Gandhi and Ambedkar on Gender Questions

To understand the multi dimensional direction of the Dalit movement, we may briefly look into the difference between Gandhi and Ambedkar on this issue. During the first Round Table Conference, when Ambedkar favoured the move of the British Government to provide separate electorate for the oppressed classes, Gandhi strongly opposed it on the ground that the move would disintegrate the Hindu society. He went for an indefinite hunger strike from September 20, 1932 against the decision of the then British Prime Minister J.Ramsay MacDonald granting communal award to the depressed classes in the constitution for governance of British India.

In view of the mass upsurge generated in the country to save the life of Gandhi, Ambedkar was compelled to soften his stand. A compromise between the leaders of caste Hindu and the depressed classes was reached on September 24,1932, popularly known as Poona Pact. The resolution announced in a public meeting on September 25 in Bombay confirmed -" henceforth, amongst Hindus no one shall be regarded as an untouchable by reason of his birth and they will have the same rights in all the social institutions as the other Hindus have". This landmark resolution in the history of the Dalit movement in India subsequently formed the basis for giving due share to Dalits in the political empowerment of Indian people in a democratic Indian polity.

Even though Ambedkar was a party to Poona Pact, he was never reconciled to it. His contempt against Gandhi, which continued even after his assassination on January 30,1948. On the death of Gandhi he expressed, "My real enemy has gone, thank goodness the eclipse is over." He equated the assassination of Gandhi with that of Julius Caesar and the remark of Cicero to the messenger—"Tell the Romans, your hour of liberty has come". He further remarked, "While one regrets the assassination of Mahatma Gandhi, one cannot help finding in his heart the echo of the sentiments expressed by Cicero on the assassination of Caesar". Considering Gandhi as a "positive danger to this country", he quoted from Bible that "sometime good cometh out of evil, so also I think good will come out of the death of Mr. Gandhi" (Gandhi and Ambedkar - *Saviours of Untouchables* by Sheshrao Chavan.

The reaction of Ambedkar over the death of Gandhi may be viewed as a politics of negation for vengeance against the caste Hindus and also for political power for Dalits. He felt, "the problem of depressed classes will never be solved unless they get political power in their own hand" (Thus spoke Ambedkar by Bhagwan Das). He however, did not clarify as to how in a democratic polity of pluralistic society, Dalits would be the sole custodians of power.

Post Ambedkar Dalit Movement: The post-Gandhian and post-Ambedkar Dalit activists re-invented the direction of their movement, which was by and large focussed towards developing the pessimistic ideas in a dark room. They are yet to take the next step to focus their negatives in light for positive prints. In the absence of a scientific endeavour, their movement lags in its march towards social reform, as it has more or less become a platform for the political empowerment of some individuals for their personal ambitions and vested interests. This is not only against the concept of equalitarian Hindu sociology of Vedic India but also against the concept of democracy.

The present clash for Dalit leadership has confirmed the theory of C., Rajagopalachari that many Dalit leaders are interested for continuance of the undesirable status of Dalits for the fulfillment of their personal ambitions. Disagreeing with Ambedkar on Dalits issue he said, "...This is material explanation for the violent dislike of Gandhiji exhibited by Dr. Ambedkar, who looks upon this great and inspired reformer as the enemy of the untouchables, meaning thereby of the educated and ambitious among them who find that the depressed status furnishes short cut to position."

It may be partially true that political empowerment is key to social and economic empowerment as suggested by Ambedkar but this cannot be the sole criteria for the social equality of Dalits. The representatives (122-76 SC and 46 ST in parliament against its strength of 543 and 1085 -556 SC and 529 ST in state assemblies against their strength of 4370) of Dalits in parliament and state assemblies in sizeable strength have been sharing political power for last fifty years. But if they have failed to bring a desired social change and economic upliftment of Dalits, there is something wrong in the movement, which is yet to be identified. The students of the constituting history have therefore, a right to know from Dalit activists the reason behind the failure of their representatives sharing political power.

One may be amused to understand that how only160 Dalit delegates under the umbrella of National Campaign on Dalit Human Rights in WCAR would have fought for the cause of Dalits in India if the representatives of Dalits sharing political power could not assert and agitate for the cause of their community? An objective analysis of the prevailing social condition and sentiments in India may corroborate the theory of C. Rajagopalachari that Dalit movement has become a vehicle to promote the personal interest of some individuals or groups.

The, Dalits despite empowerment are not a political force – why?: In the absence of an All India mind with a cohesive and unified perspective, Dalit movement has also failed to emerge as a strong political force. Dalits are divided and sub-divided into hundreds of castes and sub-castes. About 56 per cent of Dalit population belong to about 20 dominant castes among them. These dominant castes are presently grabbing all the privileges provided to the Dalits constitutionally. Even Dr. Ambedkar failed to give an intellectual explanation to unify them together, as a result, his political influence during his life time also remained confined to only Mahar caste of his community in the Maharashtra region.

Dalit activists, due to lack of actual ideological direction are not clear whether they are interested to ensure the material prosperity of Dalits or equal status in Hindu social order. Untouchability has almost disappeared, as touch of Dalit is no more considered to have any polluting affect on caste Hindus. However, so long the Dalits enjoy the benefits of quota in Government jobs and educational institutions, they may have to bear the stigma of being considered unequal in merit to the caste Hindus. The objective of Dalit movements should be therefore, to erase such stigma, which is possible only if Dalits get a chance for their proper education befitting to the standard required for competitions.

Vested interests in Command : Contrary to the objective of the movement discussed above, the managers of Dalit movement due to their vested interest do not want their people to be cleansed from the stigma of reservation and the agony of their past humiliation of being treated as untouchables. In stead of fighting for transformation of the Hindu social order, they are found more interested to promote themselves as Esperanto of United Nations politics. With weapon of hate, they are neither able to fight against the social inequality and injustice effectively nor in a position to contribute any significant social change.

Instead of looking on the growing consciousness among the educated caste Hindus against the social evil of caste discrimination against Dalits and appreciating this positive change, the Dalit activists ignore and understate the development. Their sole aim was now pointed towards personal ambitions at the cost of their community. This had created a new class of Brahmins among the Dalits, who are then exploiting the actual Dalits by grabbing the benefits meant for the latter. This may look like a paradox, but it is the hard reality. The ongoing Dalit movement is gradually losing its track. Its multi-dimensional character based on the philosophy of love and hate is unfortunately turned into political theocracy, which is contrary to the basic concept of the total transformation of Hindu social order. Inciting the Dalits against the caste Hindus for historical agony without any honest effort for their emotional integration with rest of the Hindu social order is neither in the interest of this disadvantaged section of population nor in the interest of the nation.

The shrinking influence of the so-called Brahminsm in electoral politics, social transformation, spiritual movement, or even other public affairs are enough indications of gradual changes in Hindu sociology. Dalit movements with a view to create social disorder by promoting caste hatred against the upper castes of ancient Varnashram system will simply halt the process of the ongoing social transformation. With their political empowerment by occupying the prestigious post of President, Union Cabinet ministers, Chief ministers, and bureaucrats, Dalits are gradually getting more opportunities for achieving social empowerment under democratic process. By gaining more confidence, Dalits are now found to be quite assertive of their rights. This however, does not mean that they have been acceptable in community dining or intercaste marriage, which is not even prevalent within the various Dalit castes.

The objective of any social reform movement is to ensure a peaceful, decent and dignified life for every body without any social confrontation. But, unfortunately the Dalit activists are so obsessed and possessive in their approach towards the historical agony of their community that they have made the latter as prisoners of Dalitism, which hardly has any constructive plan for creation of a just social order. Their slogan for abolition of Varnashram (professional units) system and total abolition of caste is an utopian concept, which will never take root in the diverse and pluralistic Indian society.

Casteism is the bane of Indian society but the Indian people accept caste as a hard reality. Even the Christians and Muslims boast themselves of their upper caste heritage. In South India too Christians are maintaining a distance from the Dalit Chritians as the latter continue to have separate church, separate burial ground and even separate places for social interactions. Similarly, even Muslims in India and Pakistan there is no intercaste marriage among the Sheiks, Syed, Pathan and others because of their upper caste heritage before conversion.

Dalits groups and their separate agenda: As far as the present Dalit movement is concerned, it is in the hands of three vested interest groups of Dalit politicians, Dalit writers and Chrisian missionaries. Dalit political leaders like late Kansi Ram and Ms Mayawati of Bahujan Samaj Party and Ram Vilas Paswan of Lok Jana Shakti are having their influence exclusively among the members of their own community. They can never come to power on their own due to their limited influence among the voters. For coming to power they are compelled to join some other parties dominated by caste Hindus. They are therefore, hardly in a position to bring any social change.

The second group, which claims to be the champion for the cause of Dalits is of Dalit writers. Their personal ambition and ego have kept them away from the common Dalits, who are illiterate and poor. They are more interested in their self-promotion than serving the cause of their community. Their possessiveness is often mistaken as love for Dalits. Since they do not get enough space in media to spit venom against the caste Hindus and are hardly in a position to play an effective role in electoral politics, they are always in search of the forces through which they could get national and international recognition. They have therefore, joined hand with forces (third group) determined to disintegrate the Hindu society.

The interest of the third group in Dalit movement is to de-Hinduise the Dalits and promote their proselytisational endeavour. The argument of this group that Christian society does not have any caste discrimination is not based on ground reality. The Dalit Christians are facing the problem of caste discrimination even in Christian society. Such discrimination is prevalent in Kerala even after the death of Dalit Christians, whose corpses do not find any place in the cemetery meant for upper caste convert Christians. T.V. Rajshekhar, a Dalit writer, while speaking in a seminar (Church and Dalit) organised by Christian leaders in Madras on June 14, 1986 said that Dalit Christians form about 80 per cent Christian population in India but contrary to what Jesus Christ preached, the Dalit Christians are also the victim of caste discrimination as they have separate burial ground, separate churches and separate dwelling places.

Ever since the promulgation of presidential order No 19 of 1950 debarring the Dalits of non-Hindu and non-Sikh community to be included in the list of Scheduled castes, the Christian missionaries have been facing difficulty in alluring the Hindu Dalits for their conversion. For this, they have already launched a movement for constitutional privileges for Dalit Christians. If they succeed in alienating the Dalits from Hindu social order, the entire Dalit community will get the benefit of constitutional provisions and it will help them in their mission for proselytisation.

In the backdrop of the dialectics of Dalit movements, it appears that the Dalits have now become the victims of the politics of Dalitism being played by various groups. Instead of fighting the evils of caste discrimination in Hindu society, the Dalit movement has given birth to neo Dalitism, which hardly has any difference with the polluted Brahmanism.

The movement, which does not have the ingredients to bring about reconciliation among conflicting social groups and fails to accelerate the process of social harmony and human dignity, is bound to lose real direction. Dalits should therefore be very careful about the politics of Dalitism being played by vested interests not only at the cost of the disadvantaged community but also at the cost of social harmony, which is more dangerous for the nation.

Dalit Activism

In recent years, the political radicalism of the Dalits has come to be defined in terms of two major modes. One is that they have shown a remarkable consistency in opposing both in elections and in the streets the Hindutva forces. Two, their politics is considered radical because of their constant efforts at empowering themselves by sharing power with others. It is particularly true in the case of the Dalits of Maharashtra, Uttar Pradesh and the southern States that they have been consistent in taking an uncompromising positions against the Hindutva forces. The anti-Hindutva feeling among the Dalits is so strong that they do not tolerate their own leaders who hobnob with these forces either directly or indirectly. Such leaders who took an ambiguous position *vis-a-vis* the Sena-BJP Government in Maharashtra and remained quite callous about the killing of the Dalits in police firing in Mumbai in July last year were assaulted.

The political radicalism is also being defined in terms of the Dalits' bargaining power that no political party can ignore in parliamentary politics in the country. This is true in Maharashtra and Uttar Pradesh where the Dalits seem politically organised outside the influence of the mainstream parties. Thus political autonomy is treated as another dimension of this radicalism by certain Dalit political leaders from these two States.

The scenario might be true in a sense, but this kind of reading of the Dalits' activism offers a narrow and uni-dimensional notion of their political radicalism. For it does not tackle the structures of oppression and discrimination that exist within the Dalit situation. For example, Dalits activism in Maharashtra is politically blind to the social practices such as Dalit patriarchy, which seeks to oppress, torture, humiliate and marginalise its womenfolk. This patriarchy in Maharashtra, and even in the entire country, reproduces the upper caste tradition of dowry which commodifies women even from landless Dalit families. The dowry system, which was almost non-existent among the Dalits two decades ago, has now become a serious problem particularly in Maharashtra. Poor parents who cannot afford to give dowry are reported to be "selling" their girls outside the State, and those who cannot be sold or married off are ultimately left to be tortured by parents and by the Dalit community, which arrogates to itself the right to ensure the chastity and fidelity of its women. Interestingly, this issue did not find prominence in the recently-held Dalit women's conferences in the State.

Apart from the gender insensitivity among common Dalits, their leaders and even Dalit feminists in Maharashtra, the notion of purity and pollution has deeply divided the community both vertically and horizontally. Vertically, for example, this notion has made the Charmakar (leather worker) despise the Mahar-Buddhists who, in turn, despise the Matangs who are treated as inferior in the social hierarchy not only in Maharashtra but also elsewhere. At the horizontal level, the Buddhists are socially divided among themselves. And the social division prevails in protecting the kinship boundaries. The kinship network that maintains the social distance among the Buddhists operates through marriage practices and other rituals in Maharashtra. But the Buddhists, who are socio-culturally divided, are politically united against the Hindutva forces.

The question one has to raise is why the Dalit leaders avoid addressing themselves to the question of internal critique. How does one understand such incoherent behaviour among the Dalits? In other words, why does this bizarre consciousness which represents their intellectual crisis waver between the conservative and radical modes? There are several reasons that help us understand this. The first and foremost is the threat of the Shiv Sena-BJP dominating their thought and action. This political immediacy dominates the cognitive map of Dalit politics, thus leaving out the question of confronting the oppressive patriarchy.

Moreover, the common Dalits do not undertake the painful exercise of internal critique as it undermines their power of patriarchy. This logical incoherence conforms to the political expectations of the Dalit leaders, who deliberately insulate the private sphere of the common Dalit from public criticism so that they can fill the common Dalit consciousness with emotion and manipulate the community. Their effort to maintain the distinction between the private or social and the political life of the Dalits, in effect, denies the common Dalit consciousness the critical edge that seeks to interrogate both the internal structures of manipulation and the external structures of domination. It is due to this compulsion that the common Dalits refuse to find a new political alternative and choose to pursue their recalcitrant leaders.

It is this curious relationship between the leaders that explains the limits of Dalit politics in Maharashtra. Thus it is "faith" rather than reason that determines Dalit politics. It makes the common Dalits more dependent on their leaders and prevents them from launching any decisive attack on erring leaders. In such kind of politics where faith dominates reason, any kind of argument against the leaders becomes futile.

In fact, the leaders and their cadre take extra care to create the "community of the faithful" among the Dalits by reinvoking the importance of hero worship and the myth of charismatic qualities of particular Dali leaders. The common Dalits feel that they cannot provide a more competent and sophisticated argument than what their leaders do. The leaders perpetuate this servile attitude by deliberately using an abstract language. This construction of an elite image works everywhere in Tamil Nadu, Maharashtra and Uttar Pradesh and creates a rather degrading dependence, which necessarily denies both dignity and critical faculty to the thinking of the Dalits.

This lack of enlightenment among the Dalits leads to the legitimisation of Dalit politics which has become self-limiting as it eludes the question of Dalit emancipation. It also makes the Dalits willing partners in supporting their political leaders who lack an ability to offer an alternative vision of politics.

In this regard, it is important to offer a critical comment on the contemporary Dalit feminism in Maharashtra. The Dalit leaders in the State fail to articulate gender equality and are in no mood to confront the Dalit patriarchy.

The Dalit feminist confidence in such a leadership appears misplaced, if not misleading. However, a few feminists have maintained their distance from such leadership.

How can the Dalit leaders feel empowered when they feed on the political passivity of their common people on the issue of internal critique? The lack of internal critique also robs Dalit politics of its universal character of reaching out independently to other oppressed sections which are also in need of a fresh grass roots initiative entailing a new vision of the world based on the concept of truth.

Contemporary Dalit politics, therefore, seeks a definite political departure from Ambedkar, not realising or deliberately avoiding the need for an internal critique. Ambedkar, on the one hand, criticised the communists and the Congress leadership for their sociological blindness to an internal critique of the Hindu social order and, on the other, condemned the Hindu nationalists, who ridiculed and then opposed the need for any internal critique.

This kind of externally-looking Dailt politics, instead of providing a creative context for activism, becomes supplementary to the politics of hegemonic faces in one way or the other.

CASTE IN THE PERIPHERY

Much of the 'classical' literature on caste, untouchability or even dalit politics has emanated from the western and southern Indian experiences. It was relatively recently, after the rise of bahujan politics in Uttar Pradesh and the frequent news of bloody caste-wars from Bihar, that caste began to be seen as an important actor in northern India as well.

The peripheral regions of India, *viz.* Punjab, Kashmir or the North East where the majority populations are non-Hindu, are still not seen to be of much significance for the understanding of caste or its politics. The anthropologist and sociologist working on India would, for good enough reasons, have viewed these regions as being 'different' from the mainstream Indian/Hindu civilisation. Though one can find the presence of some elements of caste everywhere in South Asia, its discriminatory practice was, after all, ideologically supported only in the Hindu religion.

While ideological or ideational aspects of caste were certainly important for a theoretical understanding of the system, it was its practice on the ground that determined the nature of caste politics. Furthermore, during the post-Mandal period or, to use M.N. Srinivas's expression, in its late 20th century avatar (Srinivas 1996), the question of caste has come up 'from below' primarily as a question of politics. Thus, while it may have been important for anthropological theorisations of caste to focus on where it could be seen in its 'purest' forms, the question of caste will perhaps need to be raised and theorised differently when the primary concern is political, *viz.* how to fight caste oppression.

The recent debate on caste and race provides a good example of this prolepsis. For those involved with dalit politics, equating caste with race was only a step forward in exposing the oppressive side of caste. The old anthropological discourses on caste remained marginal to their concerns. The professional social anthropologist's insistence that it was after a considerable amount of scientific research that they were able to establish the fact that caste was not race did not really matter to the activists. Even Ambedkar's arguments on the subject were ignored. The question for them was not of discovering or understanding the 'essentials' of caste, but rather about how best the fight could be taken forward.

Viewed from this perspective, it may be useful to look at caste and caste politics from the experience of a peripheral region where, though the brahminical ideology has not been so strong, the practice of caste still exists. Contemporary Punjab is an interesting case for such an exercise. A view of caste from the 'periphery' can also be a relevant point of a comparison with, what can be called, the 'brahmincentric' notion of caste, emanating from India's 'centres'.

Apart from being an interesting case for understanding caste in the periphery, Punjab is important because among all the states of India it has the highest proportion of scheduled castes in its total population. The scheduled castes accounted for 28.3 per cent of the total population of state in 1991, much higher than the all-India average of 16.32 per cent. Another important feature of the state is that the 'low-caste' Sikhs of Punjab are the only dalits from a non-Hindu religious community listed among the scheduled castes. Their counterparts in other 'minority' communities were not granted such a status, with even the Buddhist converts enumerated as scheduled castes only from the 1991 census.

Historically-speaking, despite its differences in social composition, Punjab has been an important centre of anti-caste politics. It was in Punjab that B.R. Ambedkar, on an invitation from the Jat Pat Todak Mandal, was to deliver his famous lecture on the annihilation of caste (which he eventually could not because the invitation was withdrawn by the organizers). Apart from the reformist movements of the Hindus and Sikhs, colonial Punjab also witnessed the emergence of an important autonomous dalit movement. The famous Ad Dharam movement initiated by Mangoo Ram during the 1920s has been among the most successful of dalit mobilisations in the history of modern India. The Ad Dharam movement not only successfully mobilised a large majority of the chamars from the Doaba region, it also played an important role in transforming the social identity of dalits in the region.

During the post-Independence period, Punjab has been in the forefront of agricultural development. Though a lot has been written on the green revolution, there has been little commentary on its impact on caste relations in the agrarian society of Punjab.

Despite the presence of the Bahujan Samaj Party in some pockets of the state and its occasional electoral success, Punjab has not seen many dalit mobilisations during the recent decades. Thus, there is a need, while talking about caste in the periphery, to not merely establish the fact that caste and caste conflicts do exist in Punjab, though different in nature, but equally to uncover reasons for the lack of a creative response from the local middle class dalit elite. Towards this end one needs to examine the social and economic changes experienced in the region and the ways in which they have empowered or disempowered dalits.

Given that Sikhism doctrinally does not support the practice of caste, it may be interesting to see how the dalits of Punjab have made use of this available 'cultural resource' while trying to negotiate their identities with the dominant communities in their immediate social context. Such an understanding may help us unravel the nature of dalits politics in Punjab today.

Much before the enunciation of modern dalit politics, the legitimacy of caste hierarchy was vehemently questioned by the Sikh gurus. Though all the ten Sikh gurus came from upper caste khatri families, their crusade against brahminical ritualism was genuine. This is perhaps most clearly reflected in the fact that along with their own writings, Sikh gurus included the writings of several of their contemporaries who had dalit origins while compiling the Sikh holy scripture, the *Adi Granth*. The most prominent among them were Ravidas, Namdev and Kabir. The new institutions initiated by the Sikh gurus, such as sangat (congregation) and langar (community kitchen or the practice of cooking and eating together, sitting in a row irrespective of caste distinctions), were radical statements against the brahminical system of caste hierarchy.

However, despite the crusade of the Sikh gurus against the idea of ritual hierarchy, the institution of caste did not disappear from the region. Even among the followers of the guru, the practice of caste based distinctions has continued. In a sense, even the idea of 'pollution' continued to be practiced, though not as strongly as in other parts of the subcontinent.

Though the institution of caste has survived in the region, the frameworks of caste hierarchy developed elsewhere do not always help us understand its functioning or dynamics in a region like Punjab. Perhaps, the most striking aspect of the practice of caste in rural Punjab/Sikh society is that it functions without the presence of, what is considered as the most important actor in the system, *viz.* the brahmins. Though brahmins as a caste community do exist in Punjab, they are ritually important only for the urban upper caste Hindus, who numerically constitute a small proportion of the population of the state.

The marginal status of brahmins in the region is perhaps not entirely a result of the Sikh movement. The predominance of Islam in Punjab until 1947 too would have played its role. However, it was not only among the followers of Islam and Sikhism that brahmins did not matter, even the Hindus of Punjab did not seem to revere them the way they did elsewhere. Writing on the social life in the late colonial Punjab, Prakash Tandon, an upper caste Hindu khatri, comments in his celebrated autobiographical *Punjabi Century* that the brahmins of Punjab lived a 'frugal life' and it was rare to find 'an affluent brahmin' in the region (Tondon 1961:77). Most brahmins in his native village were treated as members of the menial castes. Like other menials, they too were mostly dependent upon the food they collected from their *jajmans.*

Giving a vivid description of their social status, he writes: 'With us brahmins were an underprivileged class and exercised little or no influence on the community. Perhaps Muslims had so discouraged temples and external worship that the brahmins had no place left from where to exercise their authority.

'Our brahmins did not as a rule even have the role of teachers, because until the British opened regular schools, teaching was done by Muslim mullahs in the mosques or by Sikh granthis in the gurudwaras. Our brahmins were rarely erudite; in fact many of them were barely literate, possessing only a perfunctory knowledge of rituals and knowing just the necessary mantras by heart.'

Similarly, commenting on the lack of respect for brahmins in Punjab, Saberwal quotes Chanana: 'In Punjabi, the word pandat (pandit) denotes a brahmin and may connote some respect for the latter. But the word bahman (brahmin) almost always carries a little contempt.'

However, despite the insignificant position of brahmins and the marginal influence of brahminical ideology, the classical form of jajmani relations did exist in rural Punjab. In other words, a marginal position of brahmins did not necessarily mean the absence of all kinds of disabilities for dalits in rural Punjab.

Caste has remained an important parameter of social inequality in the region. While Khatris/Aroras enjoyed both power and status in urban Punjab, the landowning jats and rajputs dominated village society.

Punjab dalits, however, were employed not only in their traditional occupations but also worked on land. Writing about the chuhras and chamars of Punjab in the late 19th century, G.

W. Briggs mentions that they 'were little more than serfs; they were the hired labourers who followed the plough, drove the bullocks and sowed the seeds of both the tenants and the landlords... [they] performed most of the menial offices of the village.'

As elsewhere in the subcontinent, the establishment of British colonial rule in the region in the middle of the 19th century had far reaching implications for social and economic life. From a caste/dalit perspective, the immediate effect of colonial rule was that it opened up new avenues of employment. A sudden increase in demand for leather goods, such as boots and shoes from the newly set up military cantonment in Jallandhar, brought prosperity to enterprising chamars of the area. Dalits were also recruited into the colonial army. Along with the jats, they travelled across the globe, and some even migrated to western countries in search of better jobs. Mangoo Ram, who later became the leader of the Ad Dharam movement, had, for example, worked in the United States before returning to Punjab in 1925.

Along with the British rulers came Christian missionaries to spread the message of the Church. Not surprisingly, the first to find the appeal of the Church attractive were the members of untouchable castes. The first conversion is reported to have taken place in 1873, when a man named Ditt was baptized in Sialkot. 'To the surprise of the missionaries, Ditt was followed by hundreds of thousands of others from lower castes, and Punjab Christianity became a *de facto* movement' (Juergensmeyer 1988: 181). By 1890, there were 10, 171 Christians living in 525 villages of Punjab; by 1911 their number had gone up to 1,63,994 and by 1921 to over 3,00,000. Most of them came from a particular untouchable caste, the chuhras (scavengers) and mainly hailed from rural areas. Given the nature of the rural power structure, 'conversion to Christianity for these highly vulnerable people was a very risky act of rebellion.' The landholders were offended and tried to dissuade them through various means.

Conversions also sent 'a tremor of fear through the upper caste Hindu and Sikh elite.' The reform movements like Arya Samaj and Singh Sabhas began to compete for winning the untouchables over to their side. The introduction of the Census made the 'religious communities' sensitive to numbers. 'Numbers were equated with strength.'

The militant assertion of Hindutva identity by the Arya Samaj had already sparked off a debate on the question of Sikh identity. Sikhs began to assert that theirs was a separate religion and objected to being clubbed with the Hindus (Oberoi 1994). The practice of untouchability or discrimination against the low castes among the Sikhs was attributed to the continued influence of Hinduism on the community by the new reformist Sikh leadership. Thus, the struggle against caste and untouchability that were seen as core Hindu values, became implicated in the movement for a separate religious identity for the Sikhs.

The Singh Sabha movement for the liberation of Sikh gurudwaras from the 'Hindu mahants' launched during the 1920s also became a movement for de-Hinduisation of the Sikh religion. One of the main demands of the movement was 'unquestioned entrance to Sikh places of worship' for all. Some members of the Sikh Khalsa Diwan tried to create their own 'depressed class movements' to encourage scheduled caste support.

The movement was not confined to the liberation of historic Sikh gurudwaras; its impact went further. I.P. Singh, in his study of a village in Amritsar district, reported that the decline of brahmins in the village began around the time these reform movements were launched, *i.e.,* 1922-26. It was after these movements that a low caste Sikh was appointed a priest in the local gurudwara who began to give equal treatment to members of all castes in the village (I.P. Singh 1977: 81-82).

This process continued during the post-Independence period as well. The introduction of a new Constitution strengthened those mobilising against caste. Reporting on his village, I.P. Singh writes: The modern preachers of equality of castes like the sarpanch and his young friends point out that what the new law demands is just what the gurus had preached. It is in keeping with the percepts of Sikh religion. There lies the major difference of caste structure between a Sikh village and a Hindu village. While in a Hindu village, caste hierarchy and differences have religious sanction behind them, there are no such sanctions in the Sikh religion. Thus it becomes easier to propagate and instil equality of caste relations in a Sikh village.

While Sikh reformers attacked caste, the leadership, aware of the significance of numbers, did not deny its existence among Sikhs, or that the low castes among Sikhs did not face any disabilities due to their birth. The Sikh leadership, in fact, had to lobby hard with the national leadership that along with the Hindus, certain Sikh castes should be included in the list of scheduled castes for the provision of special benefits and reservations. They were obviously worried that if the reservation benefits were not extended to Sikhs, the low castes among them would declare their religion as Hinduism. Nayar reports that this 'concession was achieved in return for an agreement by Sikh leaders that no further political demands would be made in the future on behalf of the Sikh community.'

Apart from the competition among Christians, Arya Samaj Hindus and Sikhs during the colonial period, Punjab also witnessed autonomous mobilisations by local dalits. The most important of these was the Ad Dharm movement. In the favourable atmosphere created by social reformers, by the early 1920s some of the chamars began to think of their own organisation. Most of the early leadership of the Ad Dharm movement had grown under the influence of Arya Samaj, but felt uncomfortable with its overall ideology.

The Ad Dharam movement took off with the arrival of Mangoo Ram on the scene. Though the son of a rich chamar, his family had to bear the stigma of untouchability. He spent much of his early life in the United States where he got involved with the Gadar movement. On his return to Punjab in 1925, he set up a school for lower caste children with the help of the Arya Samaj, but soon distanced himself from the Samaj and took over the Ad Dharm movement.

The Ad Dharam movement saw itself as a new religious movement. It advocated that, "Untouchables were a qaum, a distinct religious community similar to those of Muslims, Hindus, and Sikhs, and that their qaum had existed from time immemorial." During the 1931 Census, the Ad Dharmis insisted on being listed as a separate religious community, distinct from the Hindus.

Their demand was accepted despite stiff opposition from the local Hindu leadership. In the 1931 Punjab Census, 4,18,789 persons reported themselves as Ad Dharmis, nearly equal to the Christian population of the province. They accounted for about 1.5 per cent of the total population and around a-tenth of the total low caste population of Punjab. Nearly 80 per cent of the low castes of Jalandhar and Hoshiarpur districts reported themselves as Ad Dharmis.

In other parts of the state, however, locally dominant groups were able to thwart the Ad Dharmi drive rather effectively. After the Census, the Ad Dharm movement was absorbed in Ambedkar's Scheduled Castes Federation that was later transformed into the Republican Party of India. While Ambedkar enjoyed a great deal of influence, particularly among the Ad Dharmis, and made several visits to the province (Ahir 1992), few among them followed his strategy of converting to Buddhism for social mobility in the Punjab.

After Independence, though the Ad Dharmis are listed among the Hindu scheduled castes of the Punjab, they do not follow Hindu rituals. In fact, over the years they have moved closer to Sikhism, a point that I shall come back to in the concluding section.

While new opportunities that opened up with the establishment of colonial rule and through social reform movements benefited dalits, the colonial policy of agricultural development worked against their interests. The passing of the Punjab Alienation of Land Act in 1901 clubbed dalits along with the 'non-agriculturists' castes. Consequently, they were legally denied access to landholding. The act was obviously passed exclusively keeping in view the interests of the dominant land owning castes. Even though a large majority of dalits worked on land as labourers, and in some cases as tenants and owner—cultivators, they were excluded from the right to own land in Punjab.

This had far reaching implications for the dalits of Punjab. The proportion of landholdings owned/cultivated by them in the state is one of the lowest in the India and clearly reflected in the available official statistics. For example, as against the all India average of 25.44 per cent, only 4.80 per cent of the main workers among the scheduled castes in Punjab were employed as cultivators. This percentage was as high as 42.63 per cent for Uttar Pradesh and 67.67 per cent for Himachal Pradesh. Similarly, only 0.40 per cent of all landholdings in Punjab were held by the scheduled castes in 1991. The corresponding figure for Uttar Pradesh was 24.50 per cent and for Bihar 12.11 per cent.

The most important development in the region during the post-independence period was the agrarian transformation experienced in the state with the successful application of the green revolution technology. Apart from an increase in agricultural productivity brought about by the growing use of new seeds, chemical fertilisers and machines, the green revolution also transformed the social structure of agriculture. As elsewhere, it led to the development of capitalist social relations of production. It transformed the old structures and ties between land-owners and landless. Even when the forms of relationships remained the same, their contents changed.

The commercialisation of agriculture led to a near complete disintegration of the *jajmani* ties and many of those employed in their traditional caste occupations moved to agricultural labour. The old system of keeping *siris* (attached labour) also changed into a formalised system of employing *naukars* (sometimes still called as *siris*) on monthly or annual wages. Those working as tenants too were asked to vacate lands by the land-owners. The new technology had made agriculture a different kind of enterprise. The growing intensification of cultivation and increasing popularity of crops like paddy increased the demand for labour as well.

It is quite true that much of the agricultural labour in the state was provided by dalits. Some of the tenants too were dalits. They, however, could not meet all the additional demand for labour. It was around this time that the poor from other less developed pockets of northern India, such as eastern Uttar Pradesh and later Bihar, began to migrate to Punjab.

The increased supply of labour had a direct implication on the bargaining power of local labour. Since only a small number of dalits owned agricultural land, their benefits from green revolution could have only been through increased wage rates. Though agricultural wages in Punjab did go up, it was not enough to transform their lives in a significant way.

While the landless dalits gained little from the green revolution, it further strengthened their immediate adversary, the landowning dominant castes. It was not only at the village level that the new agrarian technology made them stronger, the jats emerged as the most powerful community at the regional level too. Punjab, over the years, came to be identified with agriculture, which was not just an occupation of the dominant community but also came to be seen as a way of life. When looked at from the standpoint of power relations, the triumph of agrarianism was evidence of the growing hegemony of the dominant land owning community of the jats and, in a way, further weakened the dalit in the agrarian setting of Punjab.

The social reform movements initiated during the colonial period indeed had far reaching implications for the dalits and their politics in Punjab. The competitive reformism and autonomous movements further weakened the already marginalised brahmins in the social life of the state. A direct implication of this was that the ideas of pollution and untouchability began to loose their hold not only in urban Punjab but also in much of rural Punjab.

Though conversions to Christianity did not become a popular movement there, the dalits, over the years have systematically distanced themselves from Hinduism. While a large section of the chuhras converted to Sikhism, mostly during the 20th century, the chamars of Doaba, who were influenced by the Ad Dharam movement, too have moved closer to Sikhism (though many of them may still be reporting themselves as Hindus in the Census enumerations). Almost every village of the Doaba region has a separate gurudwara of Ad Dharmis where, along with the *Guru Granth*, they keep a picture of Guru Ravi Das, who was a chamar by caste and whose writings are included in the *Guru Granth*.

Why did they need to build separate gurudwaras when most of the villages already had one? The village gurudwara is the gurudwara of the jats. 'We can surely go there but we have to do so on their terms,' is the typical answer that comes from the Ad Dharmis. Building their own gurudwaras was a statement of autonomy, a question of pride and a form of local level resistance for the dalits.

This sense of autonomy among the dalits of Doaba sub-region of Punjab can be attributed to several factors. First, the social reform movements in the region made them politically conscious and many among them took to higher education. Second, over the years, they occupationally diversified themselves so significantly that only a small proportion remains dependent on agricultural labour. Some of them also have their family members working abroad; while jats go to the West, dalits send their children to the countries of the Gulf.

A large majority of dalits in the Malwa and Majha sub-regions of Punjab, as also a significant proportion in Doaba, however, are economically weak and continue to be dependent upon the landowning dominant castes. Here too, the question for the dalits is primarily one of social and economic dependency rather than that of untouchability and pollution. For dalit political organisations and NGOs in Punjab the problem is of oppression by land-owners and the practice of unfree/bonded labour rather than about the hegemony of the brahmin. Caste in Punjab can perhaps be understood better in the framework of 'agrarianism', rather than through the more popular notion of brahminism.

REFERENCES

Abbi, B. L. and Kesar Singh, *Post-Green Revolution Rural Punjab: Profile of Economic and Socio-Cultural Change (1965-95).* Centre for Research in Rural and Industrial Development, Chandigarh, 1997.

Ahir, D. C., *Dr. Ambedkar and Punjab.* B.R. Publishing Corporation, Delhi, 1992.

Grewal, J. S., *The Sikhs of Punjab.* Cambridge University Press, Cambridge, Indian edition by Foundation Books, New Delhi, 1994.

Jodhka, S. S., 'Prejudice Without Pollution? Scheduled Castes in Contemporary Punjab', *Journal of Indian School of Political Economy* 12(3-4), 2000, pp. 381-404.

John C.B., Webster, 'Leadership in Rural Dalit Conversion Movement', in Joseph T. O'Connell (ed.), *Organisational and Institutional Aspects of Indian Religious Movements.* Indian Institute of Advanced Studies, Shimla, 1999.

Judge, P. S., 'Emerging Trends in the Caste Structure of Punjab', *The Administrator* XLII, January-March, 1997, pp. 55-65.

Juergensmeyer, M., *Religious Rebels in the Punjab: The Social Vision of Untouchables.* Ajanta Publications, Delhi, 1988.

Nayar, B. R., *Minority Politics in the Punjab.* Princeton University Press, New Jersey, 1966.

Oberoi, H., *The Construction of Religious Boundaries: Culture, Identity and Diversity in the Sikh Tradition.* Oxford University Press, Delhi, 1994.

Prasad, V., *Untouchable Freedom: A Social History of a Dalit Community*. Oxford University Press, Delhi, 2000.

Saberwal, S., 'Receding Pollution: Intercaste Relations in Urban Punjab', *Sociological Bulletin* 22(2), 1973, pp. 234-59.

Sharma, S.K., *Social Movements and Social Change: A Study of Arya Samaj and Untouchables in Punjab*. B.R. Publishing Corporation, Delhi, 1985.

Singh, H., 'Caste Ranking in Two Sikh Villages', in H. Singh (ed.), *Caste Among Non-Hindus in India*. National Publishing House, New Delhi, 1977.

Singh, I.P., 'Caste in a Sikh Village', in H. Singh (ed.), *Caste Among Non-Hindus in India*. National Publishing House, New Delhi, 1977.

Srinivas, M.N. ed., *Caste: Its Twentieth Century Avatar*. Penguin Books, New Delhi, 1996.

8

CHANGING POLITICS OF DALIT

The Dalits adeptly used the open space to protest against casteism, denial of human rights, and the debilitating effects of privatisation upon the state. Clearly evident was a global-local pattern of interaction by Dalit organisations attempting to publicise their cause in a global venue, albeit one staged in a particular place and time. The Dalit interventions at the WSF were an excellent reminder of the dynamic between the global and the local, space and place. While the global matters so does place and history and both have left their imprint on the social movements of India, the Dalits being one example. One cannot understand why the Dalits have moved to global venues unless one knows more about where they come from.

This study attempts to understand the local contexts which underlie the Dalit movement and its decision to create advocacy networks beyond the borders of India. However, it does not centre on the WSF and the Dalits, but rather on their earlier efforts to publicise and promote their struggle against caste discrimination at various United Nations venues including a global venue, the World Conference Against Racism, Racial Discrimination, Xenophobia and Related Intolerance (WCAR) in Durban, South Africa. This is a continuing campaign, one much longer, more complex, and intense than current engagements with the WSF. It is a dynamic campaign that is being waged on a variety of levels, from the *panchayati raj* (village councils) to the Indian states, to the central government in New Delhi, and beyond India, transnationally (where Canada plays a part), internationally at the UN and finally, globally at the WCAR.

The Dalit campaign highlights the janus-faced nature of globalisation. That is, while globalisation can disempower people, and thus can be seen as a threat, it simultaneously can empower the most marginalised groups who increasingly are acquiring the capacity to project themselves and their causes beyond their borders. All this in an attempt to transform the politics of place, in this case, India.

The first part of the study concerns itself with a number of related theoretical concerns. It initially discusses the relationship between the global and the local with a focus on the centrality of networks as a link between the global and the local. It then discusses how political opportunity structures at the domestic and international level influence the strategies of social movements. Given the centrality of the "local", "place", and the "domestic" it is also important to understand some of the dynamics of social movements within an Indian context.

Once this stage has been set the paper then considers the nature of the Dalit movement itself and the decision to internationalise their human rights struggle at the United Nations and subsequently in terms of the UN sponsored WCAR. Taking the Dalit cause beyond the Indian state illustrates the desire and need of Dalits to create public spaces in which to highlight their causes and to give voice to the voiceless. The chapter concludes addressing the question of what difference has internationalising the Dalit cause made, among the Dalits, within India and at the UN.

Globalisation, Networking and the Local

Initially globalisation was portrayed one-dimensionally as the triumph of space over place. For example, Caroline Thomas argued that the concept of globalisation "refers broadly to the process where power is located in global social formations and expressed through global networks rather than through territorially-based states."

While most other analysts do not go so far as to foresee the end of the relevance of states, nonetheless, territory and place are often marginalised in their analyses. According to social theorists such as Manuel Castells, the "space of places" (territory, place, locality) are being subordinated to a "space of flows" of commodities, capital, technology, ideas and culture across national boundaries. Both power and function are becoming organised in a space of flows. Thus, according to Castells, "the dominant tendency is towards a horizon of networked, ahistorical space of flows, aiming at imposing its logic over scattered, segmented places, increasingly unrelated to each other, less and less able to share cultural codes."

This has considerable consequence for agency. According to Harvey groups opposed to globalisation are better able "to command place better than space." In Harvey's words oppositional groups "are relatively empowered to organise in place but dis-empowered when it comes to organising over space."

Viewed from this perspective, a lapsided optics of globalisation emerges with the global becoming the dominant unit of analysis to the relative exclusion of place and territory. In recent years, however, there has been a growing awareness of how messy, complex and contradictory globalisation is. (Kellner) Other analysts reject the notion of place as static and bounded. Doreen Massey, for example, sees place as "open and porous networks of social relations." According to Massey places are produced through social contestation and are inseparable from globalisation in its various manifestations—trade, finance, production, migration, and social movements. Place thus has a dynamic, interactive relationship with the global. Building upon Massey Laura Chernaik insists that:

Harvey's expression, 'place-bound' is quite misleading; local practices are not bound to place but are potentially possible to articulate through space, globally. The form that this global articulation takes, though, is more often a network than a system; a coalition of specific, different groups rather than a universalisation of any one political identity.

In this perspective, networks provide the bridge by which the global and place are linked thus facilitating a complex relationship between the two. James Rosenau comes to much the same conclusion arguing, for example, that a focus solely on the global occludes as much as it reveals. Rather, he argues:

> Globalisation is but one component of the transformative dynamics that underlie the emergence of a new epoch in the human condition. It is, to be sure, a major component, but all too many analyses suffer from treating it as the primary component and thus risk underplaying the complexity of the emergent epoch.

There is a need, for example, to recognize that localisation (place) is also a powerful force at work throughout the world.

Moreover, argues Rosenau, the two are inseparable, "there can be no global without the local." Rosenau refers to two expressions "distant proximities" and "fragmegration" to capture the complex interplay between globalisation and localisation, and the integrative and disintegrative forces at play in world affairs. Moreover, claims Rosenau:

> Locating distant proximities at the centre of our perspectives on politics enables us to avoid the disciplinary trap of maintaining an analytic separation between foreign and domestic politics, as is the case when international politics and comparative politics are treated as different fields of inquiry with each holding constant the dynamics at work in the other.

Like Chernaik, Rosenau agrees on the centrality of networks as a link between the global and the local. Importantly, the spread of horizontal networks can be viewed as "serving to restructure the underpinnings of world affairs."

According to Rosenau, networks symbolise the world explosion in connectivity between organisations. Although networks are known for "voluntary, reciprocal, and horizontal patterns of communication and exchange" as organisations they do have structure. Commonly networks are "defined as a set of organisational arrangements midway between horizontal coordination (markets) and vertical coordination (hierarchies)." In addition, as Hardtmann notes, networks are highly elastic, "they may be stretched out over vast geographical distances, or rapidly reduced for narrower situations."

Thus networks can traverse a broad range of organisational relationships from face-to-face relations to the local, regional, national and beyond. The Dalits, as we shall see, have proven adept at moving across this entire spectrum of local to global politics. As such networks can serve as catalysts of empowerment and agency from below for marginalised groups and social movements.

While networks can take a variety of forms the focus here is on "advocacy networks" that work beyond national borders. For Keck and Sikkink advocacy networks "plead the causes of others or defend a cause or proposition. They are organised to promote causes, principled ideas and norms." Of critical importance "networks are communicative structures" and "political spaces in which differently situated actors negotiate - formally or informally—the social, cultural, and political means of their joint enterprise."

In a network world, with its dynamic interaction between the domestic and the international environment, advocacy networks also have a greater range of political opportunity structures in which they can operate. These structures may include domestic institutions, international institutions or institutions in civil society. Keck and Sikkink offer one example whereby international opportunity structures provide an outlet for nonstate domestic actors faced with repression and blockage at home can "bypass their state and directly search out international allies to try to bring persuasion on their states from outside." This is a tactic commonly used by human rights advocacy networks to place their issues on the international agenda. In a latter work Sikkink, in collaboration with Khagram and Riker, acknowledges that while "repression is the most obvious form of blockage ... a lack of responsiveness may also compel groups to work internationally" among them feminist groups and indigenous peoples. This is important inso far as it acknowledges that even in democratic regimes groups may feel frustrated by unresponsive state and societal structures.

Sikkink also refined the analysis of interaction between domestic and international opportunity structures by formulating the concept of a "spiral model." Whereas the boomerang model suggested that advocacy networks engage in a single move, the spiral model involved a series of political moves over time designed to help create a more open domestic opportunity structure. This is clearly applicable to the Dalits.

Just as domestic political opportunity structures may vary and have greater or lesser degrees of openness, so too may international opportunity structures. The United Nations and its related institutions, for example, provide for relatively open opportunity structures permitting non-governmental organisations (NGOs) to have consultative status, to speak and make presentations at meetings, and place written materials on the record. This is particularly true in the area of human rights. This helps to explain, as we shall see, why the UN became such an attractive venue for the Dalit movement.

Globalisation and Social Movements

For most Indian social movements globalisation has been perceived negatively, as an imposition, as primarily an external economic force. Neo-liberal globalisation, or as it is commonly referred to in India, "Liberalisation, Privatisation, and Globalisation", arrived in 1991 in the form of the New Economic Policy of Prime Minister Narishma Rao when India opened the market for foreign products and companies. Until then, the state had been a decisive actor in the Indian economy since 1947.

For most social movements in India, particularly new social movements, globalisation represented a threat, the latest chapter in Western imperialism and capitalist expansion, and had to be resisted. For the Dalits it represented both a threat and an opportunity to globalise their plight by actively networking from India or through overseas supporters. (Ahmed) For the Dalits globalisation threatened the limited gains they had secured through the state, including anti-discriminatory measures such as reserved employment in the state as well as the state's welfare role which was being eroded by privatisation.

The Dalit and non-Dalit social movements drew upon distinct intellectual traditions. According to Gail Omvedt "most of the social movements today draw upon the ideologies that originated in nineteenth century India ..... Gandhism ..... and the Dalit ideology of the anti-caste movement." Today, outside of India, perhaps the best know exemplar of these Neo-Gandhian ideas is the eco-feminist Vandana Shiva. Shiva's website makes explicit her indebtedness to Gandhi. For example, her lecture before the Gandhi Peace Foundation in January 2004, "The Spinning Wheel and the Seed: Gandhi's legacy, Humanity's Hope," pays tribute to Gandhi in her struggle against globalisation:

> Gandhi Lives—as a perennial source of inspiration and political motivation to defend our freedoms. Globalisation as a project is a plan to extinguish all freedoms of people through total control of trade, technology and property rights.... Globalisation is often presented as a process of new interconnections between societies. However, if it is geographical, it is about the global reach of giant corporations—not about a global joining of the hearts of people worldwide.

Shiva concludes by underscoring the continuing relevance of Gandhi's ideas:

> Gandhi's creative vision of swadeshi [self-reliance, protectionism], swaraj [self-rule], satyagraha [non-violent resistance], and sarvodaya [welfare of all] inspires us to build living economies and living democracies.

Shiva's vision, like Gandhi's, is clearly grounded in a vision of local empowerment. Gandhi emphasised de-centralisation, the traditional village as a self-contained republic, social harmony, and anti-secularism, sentiments that many new social movements in India share.

Dalit Movement

While Gandhi's ideas underwrite the activities of most social movements in India the Dalit Movement today rejects Gandhism in favour of another towering figure in Indian history, the Dalit, Dr. Bhimrao Ramji Ambedkar (1891-1956). For Dalits, Ambedkar is a source of immense pride and respect, not for only his remarkable educational achievements —two doctorates, one from the London School of Economics, the other from Columbia University—but also for his leadership against untouchability, Hinduism, and his role as a founder of the modern Indian state. Today, Ambedkar serves not only as an inspiration for the Dalit movement but also as a source of legitimacy for actions including fighting casteism not only internally but externally.

In comparison with Gandhi, Ambedkar is a study in contrast. Whereas Gandhi dressed in the simple garb of Indian peasant, Ambedkar's portrait -projected everywhere in India where Dalits reside—is of a modern man, an important man, with glasses, suit and tie and, in some portraits, with a copy of a book in his hand which represents the Constitution of India and Ambedkar as a contributor to the nation. It is an image according to Zelliot, "that says 'education to the literate and the illiterate alike." In philosophical terms whereas Gandhi saw the world in terms of harmony, Ambedkar saw it in terms of contradictions, the most pre-eminent being the caste system although those of capitalism and class were also critical.

In this sense, Ambedkar is a precursor to the post-modern criticism of Marxist claims that class is the principle source of oppression. Ambedkar felt that culture and ideology must be seen as sources of oppression and that caste trumped class as a source of oppression. Ambedkar was a committed socioeconomic egalitarian and an internationalist whereas Gandhi was oriented to the traditional village.

Ambedkar's hostility to caste is exemplified in a historic quarrel with Gandhi in the 1930s in this regard. In terms of caste, Gandhi was an opponent of untouchability but he did not want to abolish the *varna* system, only reform it. According to Gandhi, the untouchables could be added to the four fold *varna* system of Hinduism. These four *varnas* were the Brahmins (priests), Kshatriyas (warriors), Vaishyas (merchants), and Shudras (servants). Outside of the *varna* system, and, therefore, polluted, were the untouchables. Gandhi felt the untouchables, who he called "Harijans"—men of God could be incorporated within the *varna* system (Hardtmann). In effect, Gandhi saw untouchability as an aberration within Hinduism and through a change of heart and mind by the "higher" (dominant) castes it could be rooted out.

Ambedkar, on the other hand, felt untouchability was not an aberration of Hinduism but was inextricably bound up with it and could not be rooted out as simply as Gandhi implied, a judgement that has proven historically accurate. Whereas Gandhi was willing to accept the hierarchical varna system for Ambedkar caste was a "monster." Caste was everywhere, blocking the path of Dalit advancement at every turn, and, according to Ambedkar "you cannot have political reform, you cannot have economic reform, unless you kill the monster [of caste]" (As quoted in Nanda, 192) At the fag end of his life she demonstrated his contempt for Hinduism by embracing Buddhism interpreting Buddhism as a rational, "modernistic, 'liberation theology.'"

While most Dalits have not followed Ambedkar's conversion to Buddhism, it is true that Dalits "have been extraordinarily hostile to Gandhi" and today, "anti-Gandhism is one theme that permeates the Dalit discourse in various contexts." Elliot asks the question of why Gandhi should be so disliked when for most non-Dalits Gandhi is the one leader most responsible for bringing the plight of the untouchables to the consciousness of India. Her response is as follows:

> I think the answer to this is quite simple. Gandhi's 'Harijan' is an object of pity. Compassion also, but also pity. Ambedkar's 'Dalit' is a man or woman filled with pride and self-respect. Social movements thrive on pride. The multifaceted Dr. Ambedkar stands for both qualities, pride and self-respect.

It is this pride and respect and desire for socioeconomic equality and recognition, that drive the disparate elements of the Dalit movement and their self-identification with the term Dalits (oppressed.) Whatever their differences "all Dalits, irrespective of creed, caste, and political affiliation consider Ambedkar their leader."

Ambedkar's Influence on Dalit Movement

Ambedkar casts a huge shadow not only over the Dalit movement but India itself. He is, with Nehru, considered a "co-inventor of India" although it is Ambedkar who has been described "as the principal author of the Constitution." Ambedkar's imprint on the Indian constitution is clear in its many clauses intended to protect the human rights of the Dalits and improve their social welfare and education. Article 17 abolishes "Untouchability" and forbids its practice in any form. Article 335 provides for "reservations", i.e. affirmative action for "scheduled castes" (Dalits) in terms of government employment.

Ambedkar was fully cognizant that formal constitutional and political rights could not be realised without social and economic equality. On the occasion of the adoption of the Indian constitution he warned:

> On the 26th of January 1950, we are going to enter into a life of contradictions. In politics we will have equality and in social and economic life we will have inequality. In politics we will be recognising the principle of one man one vote and one vote one value. In our social and economic life, we shall, by reason of our social and economic structure, continue to deny the principle of one man one value.... How long shall we continue to deny equality in our social and economic life? If we continue to deny it for long, we will do so only by putting our political democracy in peril.

Ambedkar's observation is *apropos* to contemporary India. According to Oommen a prime source of discontent in India today is the "inculcation of values of equality and social justice into an extremely hierarchical society through the agency of Indian constitution."

Internationalisation of Dalit Movement

Today, more than ever Dalit activists are demanding socio-economic equality and the destruction of the caste system. Increasingly frustrated in the arena of representative politics by limited progress the Dalit movement in the 1990s reorganised on a network basis. They widened the basis of their struggle against caste beyond the nation-state, a struggle very much based on the ideas of Ambedkar. In so doing, they chose as their primary venues the United Nations and the WCAR.

The move to international advocacy in recent years has been most forcefully spearheaded by the National Campaign on Dalit Human Rights (NCDHR) founded in 1998. However, this was not the first foray of the Dalits in the international arena not would be it accurate to portray the NCDHR as the first, or only, flag-bearer in the international arena fighting casteism. Dalit literature outlines four phases of the emergence of caste discrimination as an international issue. The first phase, not surprisingly, are Ambedkar's interventions before the British Round Table Conferences in London, 1930-31. In the lead up to independence India leaders met in London in an attempt to find agreement on the key elements of a constitution for an independent India. Ambedkar was adamant that the future constitution had to abolish the practice of untouchability and guarantee the "Depressed Classes" (untouchables) equal citizenship and fundamental rights. For his stance Ambedkar was attacked by many dominant caste leaders for dividing the Independence movement. Not unlike today he was told this was an internal matter, one to be settled after Independence. Today, Ambedkar's intervention is credited for ensuring the formal rights and freedoms to the untouchables in the Indian Constitution. For contemporary Dalit activists Ambedkar's external advocacy of an internal problem set an important precedent, one that provided legitimacy to the internationali-sation of the Dalit human right's struggle. According to two leading activists in the NCDHR:

> Ambedkar showed that boundaries for solutions to the problem of caste discrimination are not to be drawn around the village, district, state or nation. What is an internal solution or an external solution should not be determined by geographic borders or national borders.

The second phase of the internationalising of the Dalit issue was one of invisibility and transition. In terms of invisibility, one of the leading statements on human rights in the twentieth century, the Universal Declaration of Human Rights of 1948, to which the Indian government is a signatory, is silent on the issue of caste despite Ambedkar's representation of the case of the untouchables to the UN. The UDHR makes no reference to caste as a basis for discrimination focussing as it did on questions of race and colour. This is largely a result of North American and European dominance at the UN. The emphasis on questions of race and colour as norms became heavily institutionalised at UN institutions becoming significant limitations and constraints within which Dalit activists have had to work.

During the second phase, internationalising of the Dalit issue was not done so much by Dalits in India but by a transnationally linked Dalit diaspora. During the 1950s and 1960s Dalits began to emigrate, to the United Kingdom, United States, Canada, and a number of other countries. Their numbers are fewer than the much larger numbers of the dominant castes who were able to emigrate and they were often scattered. They kept in touch where they could and during the 1990s the series of networks among themselves and the Dalit movement in India became more extensive "not least due to their communication *via* the Internet."

Gail Omvedt traces the start of transnational Dalit activism back to the declaration of Emergency in 1975 when Dalits in solidarity with Black Americans mobilised and protested against a visit to the United States by Indira Gandhi. For the first time Americans were hearing stories of Dalit atrocities from what they knew only as the "land of Gandhi." In the U.K., an extensive transnational Dalit movement also began to form. (Hardtmann) About the same time, in Toronto a Dalit small businessman, Yogesh Warshade, founded the Ambedkar Mission which since has developed into a global NGO, the Ambedkar Centre for Justice and Peace. As the ACJP website notes the centre "has been globalising the issues for Dalits .... of India for last 15 years." Since 1991 the ACJP has been appearing in various venues including the Canadian Parliament and at various human rights forums at the United Nations. Prominent among these forums is the UN Committee on Elimination of Racial Discrimination (CERD).

CERD operates under the International Convention on the Elimination of All Forms of Racial Discrimination (ICERD) to which the Indian government is a signatory. ICERD in 1965 defined the term 'racial discrimination' as:

> any distinction, exclusion, restriction or preference based on race, colour, descent, national or ethnic which has the purpose or effect of nullifying or impairing the recognition, enjoyment or exercise on an equal footing of human rights and fundamental freedoms in the political, economic, social, cultural or any other field of human life.

As is evident, the provision does not refer to discrimination to other identities than those listed above.

In August of 1996, Yogesh Verhade was invited by CERD as an observer and to present evidence of Indian atrocities on untouchables and tribal peoples. Verhade was already an accredited participant to the UN Working Group on Indigenous Populations in Geneva and where he had been campaigning for the UN to recognise untouchability as a crime against humanity. In 1996 CERD was deliberating on the question of caste discrimination. That CERD had taken this step is due, in part, to pressure from NGOs such as that expressed when a thousand NGOs wor'dwide attended the UN Vienna Human Rights Summit in Jur e 1993 and pressured the Summit to pass a resolution urging the UN to act. (Press Release, ACJP, October 4, 1996) By 1996, the attitude of the UN on the issue of caste discrimination was in clearly in flux.

In the fall of 1996, CERD harshly criticised the India government of former Prime Minister Deve Gowda for the widespread discrimination and abuse of the Scheduled Castes and tribes. For the first time, a UN body made reference to caste discrimination under the heading 'descent':

> The Committee states that the term 'descent' mentioned in Article 1 of the Convention does not solely refer to race. The Committee affirms that the situation of the Scheduled Castes and Scheduled Castes and Scheduled Tribes fall within the scope of the Convention.

Globally, for all Dalits this was a significant development, the first of several to come. The AC JP "hailed the move as perhaps the most significant development and an important first step for CERD" (Press Release, October 4, 1996). In India there was rejoicing in the Dalit movement.

No doubt the UN had proven itself to be an important venue to advance the Dalit cause. Over the next two years the spotlight of the UN and its related institutions began to shine ever more strongly on the Indian government and its poor human rights performance in terms of caste discrimination. For example, in 1997 the UN Special Rapporteur on Racism and Racial Discrimination chastised the Indian government for its unwillingness to be forthcoming to the request for more information concerning the situation of caste discrimination stating:

> The Special Rapporteur noted the discrepancy between the facts alleged and the government's reply and stated that a visit to India would permit him to evaluate the situation in cooperation with the government and the communities concerned.

In 2002, another UN body, the Committee for Elimination of Discrimination Against Women (CEDAW) criticised the Indian government on the situation of continuing violence and discrimination against Dalit women.

While the networks of the Dalit diaspora transnationalised the Dalit issue and internationalised it at the UN, it was only in 2001 that the Dalit issue was globalised, at the WCAR, held in Durban, South Africa in September 2001. While the UN discussion and reports are of great significance it was the WCAR that brought the issue of caste and untouchability-based discrimination to wide public audiences internationally but particularly in India. The WCAR became, in effect, an important means of creating public space in India for the Dalits present by reflecting the controversy over caste-based discrimination back to India igniting a huge internal public debate.

Formation of the National Campaign on Dalit Human Rights

By 2001, a global Dalit movement had taken shape, one composed of a variety of networks within India and abroad. While there is no central hub to the Dalit movement in 1998 a key node emerged, the National Campaign on Dalit Human Rights (NCDHR). Its name belies the fact that this is an international and global campaign as well. Formation of the NCDHR reflects a growing capacity and confidence within the Dalit movement. Unlike the diasporic networks it is India-based and operates on all levels from the local, to the regional, to the national, transnational, international, and global levels. It is the NCDHR that today has brought the Dalit movement to a new level organisationally taking a leading role in the series of meetings up to the WCAR and after to another significant victory at the UN in 2005.

The events leading up to, and at, WCAR were intense and fiercely contested. However, before I discuss these events it is necessary to discuss the NCDHR as a network organisation in terms of its purposes, objectives, organisation, and activities.

The NCDHR originated in 1998 when, in a response to a call from the United Nations to celebrate the fiftieth anniversary of the Universal Declaration of Human Rights, Dalit activists met in Bangalore. These activists included people working in a variety of NGOs, including, prominently, the National Federation of Dalit Women, and other associated Dalit networks consisting of intellectuals, academics, trade unionists, writers, journalists and social workers. Many came from southern India but the campaign extends across the country. (Hardtmann) Underlying the formation of the NCDHR is one primary concern, to publicise the plight of the Dalits at both the national and international levels, the latter with the intent of internationalising the Dalit issue at the United Nations. In this regard the NCDHR has proven particularly adept with a keen sense of its audiences and symbolism. For example, it launched its first national campaign on December 10, 1998 (World Human Rights Day) and concluded it on April 14, 1999, April 14 being the birthday of Ambedkar, thus symbolically linking the global and the local.

According to the NCDHR documents the NCDHR has two overarching aims closely linked to its primary concerns of publicity:

- That India and the International Community recognise that Dalit Rights are

Human Rights and decide to effectively abolish untouchability.

- To cast out caste so as to build a new, just social order.

In addition to these aims the NCDHR has laid out a number of objectives that reveal the types and levels of activities it is engaged in. These objectives include :

- Creating awareness and support for Dalit Human Rights in civil society
- Strengthening the unity and solidarity of Dalits and Dalit movements worldwide

- Preparing research and status reports in such areas as education, land and labour, gender equality for Dalit women and employment
- "Pressurising" central (federal) and state governments and other National agencies to give top priority to Dalit Rights
- Pressurising United Nations bodies and other international organisations to give top priority to Dalit issues
- Highlighting the culture and contribution of Dalit communities to society.

While the NCDHR is organised as a campaign in the international language of human rights it interprets this language in two ways that need underscoring. First, as is evident from its lists of demands the NCDHR's concerns about human rights go beyond caste-related discrimination and violence, to include cultural, socioeconomic, and political rights and protections. Second, while it subscribes to the universal language of human rights, it does not view them in Western terms, as individual rights, but rather, as group rights. The campaign's Charter of Dalit Human Rights makes this pointedly clear :

> We are shocked by the fact serious discussions on human rights have been clouded by an excessive focus on individual liberty because of the predominant focus on the individual contemporary Western thinking. An individualism of the type and intensity that is being promoted by the West... is in sharp contrast to the indigenous people in general and Dalits and tribal peoples in particular.

Organisationally, the NCDHR is a loose network structure with a National Secretariat in New Delhi. Its aims, objectives and changing circumstances within Indian and internationally require that it operate on a variety of levels and within a variety of networks. For example, given that caste discrimination is worst at grassroots levels (Interview, November 8, 2004) it is imperative that the campaign have a presence there, particularly at the panchayati raj (village councils) whose powers were expanded in the 73rd amendment to the Indian Constitution in 1992. The amendment also reserved one-third of panchayati seats for women in addition to quotas for Dalits and *Adivasis*. Dalit women and men (as well as *Adivasis*) are frequently intimidated from participating in panchayats but panchayats are emerging as important sites of Dalit resistance nonetheless.

To all this, the NCDHR has added an extensive system of monitoring local atrocities. Todate, nearly 500 youth in 15 states have been trained by the NCDHR to monitor human rights abuses to international human rights standards. Any atrocities occurring in the name of caste are investigated and reported with the media alerted and complaints made. In addition to monitoring the NCDHR also works with local NGOs in a variety of advocacy interventions, demonstra-tions, rallies, mobilisations in an interconnected manner described as "Push from above and pull from below."

Elsewhere, economic globalisation has accelerated the decentralisation of power to the state level in India (Sáez) meaning that increasingly the NCDHR must engage with elected state representatives, ministers, policy-makers, bureaucrats and law enforcement agencies. In addition, the NCDHR must engage the central government and its related agencies. Given that Dalits perceive these levels of government to be controlled by the dominant castes their expectations of a sympathetic ear and compliance are not high, a point made in a report on its website:

> For more than 50 years since Independence, Dalits have utilised the laws and mechanisms existing within the country to try to promote and protect their rights, only to find that dominant caste values, prejudice and vested interests prevalent across all levels of government and society so seriously debilitate the political will to implement and enforce these laws that they have been emasculated and reduced to the status of mere paper tigers.

The consequence the same report says is that "Dalits have the right to look for solutions at the international level when they have exhausted the national mechanisms to little or no positive effect."

As a part of its process of seeking international solutions when domestic opportunity structures are blocked the NCDHR has associated itself with a wide range of international networks. In 2000, for example, the NCDHR played a formative role in establishing the International Dalit Solidarity Network (IDSN) based in Copenhagen, Denmark. The IDSN exists to:

- promote the global recognition of Dalit human rights
- act as an advocate with governments and international bodies and institutions
- monitor enforcement of anti-caste discrimination
- facilitate interventions at international and multilateral bodies including the European Union, the European Parliament, the UN, the International Labour Organisation, the World Trade Organisation, World Bank, and Asian Development Bank.

The IDSN is composed of three distinct types of networks: (1) international human rights organisations; (2) national Dalit Solidarity Networks; and (3) national advocacy groups. International associates of IDSN include an extensive number of organisations including Human Rights Watch, the Lutheran World Federation, the World Council of Churches, and the Asian Human Rights Commission. National Dalit Solidarity Networks have been established in the U.K., France, Denmark, Sweden, the Netherlands, and the United States by development and human rights NGOs and individuals. These networks conduct local campaigns, alert media, and lobby governments to promote action to eliminate caste discrimination. The national solidarity networks work closely with Dalit organisations in South Asia. Finally, there are four national advocacy platforms in the caste affected countries of India, Nepal, Sri Lanka, and Japan. The first three are specifically Dalit platforms but a similar caste phenomenon exits in Japan where the Buraku Liberation League campaigns for the eradication of Buraku discrimination. Beyond this the NCDHR is linked to other networks and NGOs including the Ambedkar Centre for Peace and Justice discussed previously.

Most of these organisations have extensive websites, which provide a national and international presence to the Dalit cause. Many provide extensive well-documented reports, news bulletins, articles, lists of books, activities, rallies, and conferences. The website of the NCDHR, itself, is used to promote a positive image of itself internationally. Its material is extensive, well-researched and well-documented. In promoting its activities the NCDHR is careful to avoid criticising Gandhi on its website despite contrary sentiments internally. This is, no doubt, implicit recognition that Gandhi is a global icon and little good would come from it.

Since 1998, but particularly after 2000, the NCDHR, assisted by its complex of networks, has moved vigorously onto the international and global stage. As it has done so it has been vigorously contested by the Indian government. For its part the NCDHR has attempted to portray itself and its cause in the broadest manner possible in order to legitimise itself both nationally and internationally. On the other hand, the Indian government until very recently has attempted to define the issue of casteism as narrowly as possible, as solely an internal manner. A clear attempt to contain the caste issue as an "India" only problem. Similarly, the government has refused to acknowledge the existence of no more than 170 million Dalits that are recognised as the categories of 'scheduled castes' by the Indian constitution. To the official base of 170 million 'scheduled castes' the NCDHR has added 20 million Dalit Christians, 50 million Dalit Muslims, and 20 million Dalits residing 'abroad" for a total of 260 million Dalits worldwide. (Hardtmann, 202) Above and beyond these numbers the NCDHR has created links and promoted the issue of caste-based discrimination and violence in Nepal, Sri Lanka, and Pakistan as well as in countries with similar forms of discrimination, the Buraku in Japan, the Roma (gypsies) and certain communities in Senegal and Mauritania. The point is obvious. Caste is an international issue.

The WCAR and Beyond

At the international and global level, the most significant opportunity to highlight the issue of caste discrimination came with the UN sponsored WCAR in Durban, South Africa, in September 2001. This was both an international and global event, international in so far as it was an intergovernmental conference, global in the breadth of its issues and the thousands of people from civil society organisations that attended, both before, at an NGO forum, and during the WCAR itself. Upon hearing that the WCAR would take place Dalits realised that this was a golden opportunity to publicise the issue of caste-based discrimination, both internationally and nationally.

Getting to Durban was no easy matter. Prior to Durban the NCDHR and other Dalit and pro-Dalit organisations had to make a series of interventions to UN human rights bodies and at international meetings held to prepare for the WCAR. The purpose of the interventions was to place the inclusion of caste discrimination on the main agenda of the WCAR.

In the meetings from January 2000 to May 2001 the NCDHR appeared to be enjoying a fair degree of success in placing caste discrimination on the WCAR agenda. The first meeting in which the NCDHR took part was the Bellagio Consultation to the WCAR organised by the International Human Rights Law Group and held in Italy in January 2000. This was a meeting of discriminated communities, human rights NGOs, and various UN human rights bodies. At Bellagio, a resolution was passed recommending that caste discrimination against Dalits be put on the agenda of the WCAR and future Prep (Preparatory) Com (Committee) meetings.

Subsequently in May 2000 at the First WCAR PrepCom Meeting held in Switzerland the NCDHR delegation received support from Human Rights Watch and other NGOs to ensure that caste discrimination was put on the WCAR agenda. The Indian government of former Prime Minister Atal Bihari Vajpayee adamantly opposed the submissions but since this was more of a general organising meeting nothing was concluded in this regard.

In between the first and second PrepCom meeting the NCDHR activists lead by Prakash Ambedkar, the grandson of Dr. Ambedkar, and supported by several human rights NGOs, attended a meeting of the UN Sub-Commission on the Promotion and Protection of Human Rights in Geneva held in August 2000. There they managed to convince the Sub-Commission to pass two resolutions, the first authorised a working paper on "discrimination based on occupation and descent" to be prepared by Rajendra Kalidasa Goonesekere, Expert Member of the Sub-Commission from Sri Lanka.

The second resolution recommended that descent-based discrimination should be placed on the agenda of the WCAR. To Dalit activists 'discrimination based on work and descent' provided sufficient scope to highlight the issue of 'untouchability'.

The resolutions were passed despite the strong objections of the Indian government. In Geneva, the Indian government made the same case as it had at the first Prepccom meeting in May, that race was not caste and therefore beyond the scope of CERD. This, however, was a shop worn argument, one that had been made before CERD in 1996 and that had been rejected. CERD had stated that 'descent' does not refer only to race and could apply to scheduled castes and scheduled tribes.

To the Indian government's claims a document posted on the NCDHR website responded claiming:

> The reality is that caste is a basis for discrimination on par with racism and apartheid and severely reducing the quality of life for at least 160 million of India's own citizens. To attempt to smoke screen this reality behind semantic gymnastics on the

> definitions of race and descent obviously never intended by CERD is nothing but sophistry.

Furthermore, they argued, it was fallacious for the Indian government to claim that caste was solely an internal issue, the boundaries between the external and internal had disappeared on the issue:

The United Nations World Conference Against Racism is an internal mechanism with respect to India, because India freely chose to ratify CERD in 1969. Therefore, to raise the problem of caste discrimination for attention and action by CERD and the WCAR is not to seek an external solution.

Subsequent related area meetings in Bangkok (September 2000) and Tehran (February 2001) were supportive of the Dalits. However, between the Second WCAR PrepCom meeting in Geneva in May 2001 and the Third WCAR PrepCom meeting in July-August 2001 disaster struck. The Second PrepCom draft of the WCAR agenda included a paragraph by Switzerland prohibiting discrimination on the basis of work and descent. Mysteriously, the inclusion disappeared in documents in the next few days. So did other paragraphs on Palestine. No explanation has been given so far, although many assume that they were a victim of power politics of the Indian and United States governments. Despite frantic efforts by the NCDHR it was unable to have the paragraph reinstated on the official WCAR agenda.

Despite the setback NCDHR decided to send a large contingent of 200 representatives to Durban. They were buoyed by the release of the Goonesekere Report by the UN Sub-Commission on August 9, 2001. The Report reconfirmed CERD's decision that interpreted 'descent' to mean "not solely race but tribal or caste distinctions as well." (As quoted in Hardtmann, 218) India was also cited as the main example of a country where discrimination based on work and descent exists. What the Dalits were losing in terms of the official intergovernmental agenda they were now starting to gain back in terms of publicity. In addition, just prior to Durban the

National Human Rights Commission of India, an independent state body, acknowledged that the Dalit situation was intolerable and gave its support to the Dalits. The NGO Forum held prior to and overlapping with the intergovernmental conference in Durban also lent its support to the Dalit cause. The media savvy Dalit delegation attracted mass media attention from India and internationally. According to Thekaekara:

> This conference grabbed the headlines of every Indian newspaper and TV station and brought caste back into the news with a vengeance. Dalits have seized the opportunity, and used the Durban WCAR to rally people around the issue which for too long has been ignored.

At the conference, itself, the Dalits received the support of UN Human Rights Commissioner, Mary Robinson, UN Secretary-General, Kofi Annan, and South African President, Thabo Mbeki.

The balance sheet for the Dalits at the WCAR is thus mixed. Clearly, the Dalits did not get everything they wanted. However, this was not to be the end of the international debate on caste discrimination as the issue was subsequently taken up again at UN institutions by the NCDHR, the IDSN and several supporting NGOs. Once again, the Dalits found the UN to be a supportive environment. In August 2002 CERD openly condemned caste discrimination. In Geneva, on April 19 2005, the UN Commission on Human Rights adopted by consensus a decision to appoint two Special Rapporteurs to prepare a three year study and analysis of the problem of caste-discrimination and find solutions for its eradication (W. Chandrakanth, *The Hindu,* April 21, 2005). India, while the prime example of caste discrimination, was not the only country cited, so were twenty other countries in South Asia, Asia (Japan), and Africa (Thekaekara, *The Hindu,* May 2, 2005). Each year the Special Rapporteurs will present their findings to the UN. The decision means that the UN considers caste discrimination to be on a par with other forms of human rights discrimination. A leader of the NCDHR welcomed the decision this way.

This is a belated victory in the internationalisation of the plight of the Dalits. We also welcome the stance of the new Indian Government, which did not come in the way of passing this resolution.

Conclusion

There can now be little doubt that the Dalits have succeeded in internationalising the issue of caste discrimination. What this means in India and other countries where the practice exists is not clear. The UN has few powers to impose its human rights decisions on other countries by any coercive means. Moreover, caste discrimination is still well entrenched and has existed for thousands of years in India although it is eroding.

There can be little doubt that the Dalits have enjoyed a measure of success by:

- Creating strong viable platforms such as the NCDHR
- Creating a global network of supporters
- For the first time getting an Indian government not to stand in their way at the UN
- Publicising their issues and creating alternative public space in India and abroad.

Where they have not succeeded, as indicated, is in eradicating the caste system.

However, the India government has lost control of public debate and the public agenda and thus the ability to contain the issue as an India only problem. The Dalits have been able to name and shame the practice of caste discrimination internally and externally as the *The Telegraph* Calcutta edition freely admits:

> It is a sorry state of things when one of the greatest shames of the Indian social arrangement has to be dragged into international daylight because the stubborn Indian mind has not changed in attitude in spite of pious announcements against casteism.

As India becomes a significant player on the global stage it will lead to greater external scrutiny of Indian society by media which may lead to greater scrutiny of its human rights record. Its global competitors may also express concerns that the caste system by depressing overall wages gives India an economic advantage. Whether or not this occurs a robust global Dalit network exists which will continue to put the global spotlight on the flaws in India's human rights record.

Yet, in criticising the human rights record of the Indian government the Dalits are not rejecting the state Ambedkar helped found. There is a recognition that the state is janus faced, that while it has failed in a number of respects that there have been some gains in employment, health, and education that need to be augmented and preserved. A small Dalit middle class has emerged in part with the assistance of the state. Moreover, the Indian state is not monolithic and can be contested. Parts of it such as the National Human Rights Commission have indicated an ability to speak for the Dalits. What the Dalits want is a state shorn of casteism and corruption, an equitable and fair state with capacity, one responsive to their needs. As Corbridge and Harris state, "the history of independent India continues to be written around the state and the state idea."

In sum, we are back from where we started. The state, territory and place still matter. But so do the international and the global and the dynamic networked interaction between the local and the global. Politics in India, like elsewhere, it seems, will continue to played out between contending forces of the vertical and horizontal at levels of society and governance.

REFERENCES

Castells, Manuel, *The Rise of the Network Society.* Malden, MA.: Blackwell Publishers, 1996.

Chandrakanth, W., "Rapporteurs to probe discrimination." *The Hindu,* April 21, New Delhi, 2005.

Corbridge, Stuart and Harriss, John, *Reinventing India: Liberalisation, Hindu Nationalism and Popular Democracy.* 2nd edn. Oxford: Oxford University Press, 2003.

Courchene, Thomas , "Celebrating Flexibility: An Interpretive Essay on the Evolution of Canada Federalism" (Montreal: C.D. Howe Institute) October 16 as quoted in Rosenau, James N. (2004) *Distant Proximities: Dynamics Beyond Globalisation.* Princeton: Princeton University Press, 1995.

Divakar, N. Paul and Ajai, M., "UN Bodies and the Dalits: A Historical Review of Interventions." Reprinted in *Caste, Race and Discrimination: Discourses in International Context.* (2004) Eds. Sukhadeo Thorat and Umakant. New Delhi: Rawat Publications, 2001.

Held, David; McGrew, Anthony; Goldblatt, David; Perraton, Jonathan, *Global Transformations.* Stanford, CA.: Stanford University Press, 1999.

Keck, Margaret E. and Sikkink, Kathryn, *Activists Beyond Borders: Advocacy Networks in International Politics.* Ithaca, NY.: Cornell University Press, 1998.

Kellner, Douglas, "Theorising Globalisation." *Sociological Theory,* 2002.

Khagram, Sanjeev; Riker, James; Sikkink, Kathryn, "From Santiago to Seattle: Transnational Advocacy Groups Restructuring World Politics." In *Restructuring World Politics.* Eds. Khagram, Sanjeev; Riker, James; Sikkink, Kathryn. Minneapolis, MN.: University of Minnesota Press, 2002.

Omvedt, Gail, "The UN, Racism and Caste," in *The Hindu,* April 9, 10, 2001. Reprinted in *Caste, Race and Discrimination: Discourses in International Context.* (2004) Eds. Sukhadeo Thorat and Umakant. New Delhi: Rawat Publications, 2001a.

—, "Ambedkar and After: The Dalit Movement in India." In Ghanshyam Shah, ed., *Dalit Identity and Politics.* New Delhi: Sage Publications, 2001, 143-159.

—, "Social Movements in Western India: Visions for the Future." In *Globalisation and Social Movements.* Eds. P.G. Jogland and S.M. Michael. Rawat Publications: New Delhi, 2003, 78-108.

Oommen, T.K., *Nation, Civil Society and Social Movements.* New Delhi: Sage Publications, 2004.

Rosenau, James N., *Distant Proximities: Dynamics Beyond Globalisation.* Princeton: Princeton University Press, 2004.

Sáez, Lawrence, *Federalism Without a Centre.* New Delhi: Sage Publications, 2002.

Shah, Ghanshyam, "Introduction: Dalit Politics." In Ghanshyam Shah, ed., *Dalit Identity and Politics.* New Delhi: Sage Publications, 2001, 17-44.

Sikkink, Kathryn, "Patterns of Dynamic Multilateral Governance and the Insider-Outsider Coalition." In *Transnational Protest and Global Activism.* Eds. Donatella della Porta and Sidney Tarrow. New York: Rowman and Littlefield Publishers, Inc. 2004, 151-174.

Thekaekara, Mari Marcel, "What Next for India's Dalits?" *The Hindu,* New Delhi, September 13, 2001. Reprinted in *Caste, Race and Discrimination: Discourses in International Context.* (2004) Eds. Sukhadeo Thorat and Umakant. New Delhi: Rawat Publications. 313-316.

Thekaekara, Mari Marcel, "Discrimination against Dalits." In *The Hindu,* May 2, 2005, New Delhi.

Thomas, Caroline, "Globalisation and the South," in *Globalisation and the South,* ed. by Caroline Thomas and Peter Wilkin. New York: St. Martin's Press, 1997.

Thorat, Sukhadeo and Umakant, "Introduction" in *Caste, Race and Discrimination: Discourses in International Context,* Eds. Sukhadeo Thorat and Umakant. New Delhi: Rawat Publications, 2004.

Zelliot, Eleanor, "The Meaning of Ambedkar." In Ghanshyam Shah, ed., *Dalit Identity and Politics.* New Delhi: Sage Publications, 2001, 129-142.

9

HUMAN RIGHT VIOLATIONS AGAINST INDIAN DALITS

The main purpose of this study is not only to publicise the gross human rights violations against India's 250-300 million untouchables (now known as Dalits), but also to create international awareness and to seek international support for the plight of the Dalits in India. It is evident that the Afro-Americans suffered slavery for some centuries. The Jews suffered holocaust and martyrdom for some time, but Dalits have been suffering humiliation, loss of respect, dignity, culture and above all, unspeakable horror of the caste system for the last three thousand years of human history (Thind, *Our Indian* n.pag; Thind, *Tentacles* n.pag). The world communities must assume responsibility in bringing total justice to the Dalits who have been systematically deprived of their respect, dignity, culture and rights by the upper caste people of India. What is amazing that even after 55 years of India's Independence, and as India is signatory to many international agreements such as the Universal Declaration of Human Rights and the International Convention on the "Elimination of All Forms of Racial Discrimination," and even though untouchablity was abolished by India's constitution in 1950, there is no difference in the lives of India's Dalits as their fundamental human rights are violated on a daily basis. India has been called the "world's largest democracy." It is merely "A democracy of the few for the few, and by the few" and is probably the largest violators of human right acts in human history. What is worse to notice is that untouchables can not fetch a bucket of water from the village well or socialise in village tea stalls or cafes, as their touch pollutes every thing (Thind, *Our Indian;* Thind, *Tentacles).*

In fact, Dalits have been considered the most degraded, downtrodden, exploited and the least educated in Indian society. They are considered to be *"untouchable"* because their touch to high caste people is considered polluted and uncleaned. The caste hierarchy has excluded these people from the caste system and therefore, they are *"outcaste."* For decades and until today, they have been barred from sharing water, food and shelter and are forced to live in ghettos, and hence are referred as *"segregated."* They have been socially, culturally, and politically subjugated and marginalised through three thousand years of India's history. What is still surprising is that the Dalits experience the agony of untouchability very deeply in all walks of life: social, economical and political.

Until today, India's caste system has compelled them to perform the most inhuman jobs, from the manual scavenging, skinning animals, disposal of the dead animals, cleaning streets, landless labour, bonded labour, child labour and performing the most inhuman tasks, such as cleaning the toilet and disposal of human waste (Thind, *Our Indian;* Thind, *Tentacles;* Narula).

Caste System in India

India is a country with a lot of traditions, culture and beauty. The most pathetic part of these traditions is an unwanted, ugly, and inhuman structure called the *Caste System.* One cannot but feel ashamed of the caste system as this system continue to discriminate the human persons and stratifies them into different groups (Ambedkar, *Annihilation*). In Hindu society, caste is still the most powerful factor in determining a person's dignity. Socially, Dalits are placed outside the fourfold graded caste system of Indian Society. Hindu Scriptures divide the people on the basis of birth (descent-based discrimination). The social structure of India is stratified, with inbuilt inequalities and injustices, based on the caste system sanctified by *Brahmins (Hindus)* (Ambedkar, *Castes* n.pag; Viyogi n.pag). Although social stratification exists in almost all societies, the caste system is quite unique to Indian society. Sanctioned by the religio-philosophical system, the Dalits are socially placed outside the fourfold caste system and they are referred to as the fifth caste.

India's caste system has existed for more than 3000 years and appears to be deliberately and intentionally developed by the Brahmins (priests) in order to maintain their superiority over the other castes. Typically, the caste system is divided into four distinct classes. This is referred as "Varnas". At the top the caste hierarchy are the Brahmins, the priestly class. According to the Hindu religious book called *Manusmruti,* the Brahmins came from the head of God. They are eligible for learning, teaching and perform religious ceremonies. The others cannot teach and perform sacrifice, hence they have 100 per cent control on religion, education and Vedas. Next come the *Kshatriyas.* The people in this class are warrior, and according to *Manusmruti,* they originated from the shoulder of God. They are eligible for learning. Their work is to protect the people by waging war against the enemies. The *Vaisyas* are the trading class and came from the thigh of God. Their work is to trade and feed the above two classes. Finally stand the *Sudras.* This is the servants class and came from the feet of God. Their work is to do all menial work for the above three classes. They are not entitled to learn anything. In addition to the above four classes, there is a fifth class called "untouchables" or outcaste. They literally have no caste and means oppressed, downtrodden, broken and exploited social group.

Such a rigid caste system is not found anywhere in the world outside India. Once born in the caste, a person's status is predetermined and immutable. Birth decides any talent the person may develop, and one cannot alter one's status or wealth the person may accumulate. Similarly, the caste in which a person is born predetermines what profession or activities he or she will pursue. What is surprising is that even today most Hindus who are living abroad still practice the caste system in their country of residence.

Human Rights Violations against Dalits in India

According to the Hindu religious belief, "*All human beings are not born equal.*" This creates caste-based discrimination against Dalits, which is then open to various forms of violence against them, which include public humiliation, torture, rape, beating, and killing, etcetera.

The untouchability is the basis for atrocities and violence, denial of basic needs, land rights, legal discrimination, infringement of civil liberties, inferior or no people status, de-humanising living and working conditions, impoverish-ment, malnourishment, bad health conditions, high levels of illiteracy and continuing social ostracism is continue to the reason for human rights violations against dalits.

Even today in rural India, Dalits are prevented from most common social activities such as sharing water, food and drinks. They are barred from wearing shoes when meeting high caste Hindus. They are not allowed to cycle through village streets in which higher caste people live. They can be publicly dehumanised by small crimes such as shooing away a chicken, dogs, and other pets that belong to higher caste people. They are discriminated against, denied access to land, forced to work in the most degrading conditions, and are routinely "abused by the hands of the police and higher caste Hindus who enjoy government protection. Most Dalits continue to live in precarious conditions and are not allowed to use the same well, visit the temples, drink from the same cups in tea stalls or even cannot claim the land that legally belongs to them. Most Dalits continue to live in extreme poverty, without land, and they lack opportunities for better employment and education.

According to the National Commission of Human rights of India, more than 62,000 human rights violations are recorded annually. On average, two Dalits are assaulted every hour, three Dalit women and children are raped, two Dalits are murdered, and at least two Dalits are tortured or burned every day (Narula; *National Commision* n.pag). Due to scarcity of space, it is not possible to describe an individual human rights abuse. Following are some of the most inhuman "Human Right Violations" that took place in recent time in India. For instance, recently, five Dalits in the Northern district of India, Haryana, were lynched by a mob of 4,000 Hindus on the allegation that they skinned the cow as these victims denied a bribe to police. In another incident, a four-month pregnant Dalit women from Tamil Nadu district (Southern part of India), was beaten by upper caste Hindus from the same village. She was stripped naked and paraded in front of the village as well as her family members. Later, police beat her in jail, which resulted in her miscarriage.

Less than 3.5 per cent culprits are prosecuted for such crimes, and out of 10 cases of atrocities against Dalits, only one is prosecuted. The problem is not the law; implementation is a total failure because the less than 15 per cent high caste Hindus who control 85 per cent of the wealth, power, justice system, police and 100 per cent of the media. Hence, the culprits go unpunished. Most importantly, these violations are not only performed against Dalits, but also on other minority communities in India. For the last few years, Hindu masses have been directly associated with the human rights violations against Muslims, Christians and Sikhs throughout India. For instance, Hindus killed more than 3,000 Muslims in a Mosque demolition in 1992. In 1984, more than 4,000 Sikhs in the Delhi area were killed in Communal riots. In recent years, more than 2,000 Muslims in Gujrat and hundreds of Christians have been killed in Orissa.

Human Right Violations against Dalit Children

According to the National Commission for Scheduled Caste (SC) and Scheduled Tribes (ST), there are an estimated 115 millions children working in slavery, and amongst those, approximately 80-90 per cent are Dalits who work as bonded labour in order to pay off debt *(National Commission;* Varhade). In slavery, children, often from poor families, are picked by a high caste restaurant or shop-owner and are forced to work 16-18 hours a day at wages of not more than 2-3 dollars per year (Ambedkar *Annihilation;* Varhade). Their denial to the order of their owner or trying to escape can result in severe beating and no food and water for several days.

According to Government statistics, an estimated 800,000 Dalits are manual scavengers who are involve in clearing human feces from pubic and private latrines and disposing of dead animals (Ambedkar, *Annihilation).* A recent survey conducted by two teams of *National Geographic* stated that "in one toilet there can be more than 400 seats which all have to be manually cleaned. This is the lowest occupation in the wold, which is performed by the community occupying the lowest status in the caste system" (O'Neill 8-31). In addition to the above, there are approximately 50,000 Dalits girls who are forced to practice a Hindu religious practice of child prostitution, called *Devdasi.* Devadasis, literally meaning "female servant of god," and they usually belong to the Dalit community. Amazingly, this practice still exists in Indian states like Andhra Pradesh, Karnatka, Orissa and Maharashtra. Once dedicated, the girl is unable to marry, is forced to become a prostitute for upper-caste community members, and is eventually auctioned off to an urban brothel, where she may die due of many sexual diseases, including HIV/AIDS.

Human Rights Violations Against Dalit Women

According to Arpita Anant, researcher on the behalf of South Asia Partnership of Canada, Dalit women in India face the triple burden: caste, class and gender. As stated by another woman activists in India, "No one practices untouchability when it comes to sex." Rape is a common phenomenon in rural areas. Women are raped as part of caste custom or village tradition. According to Dalit activists, Dalit girls have been forced to have sex with the village landlord. In rural areas, "women are induced into prostitution *(Devadasi system)*, which [is] forced on them in the name of religion." The prevalence of rape in villages contributes to the greater incidence of child marriage in those areas. Early marriage between the ages of ten years and sixteen years persists in large part because of Dalit girls' vulnerability to sexual assault by upper-caste men; once a girl is raped, she becomes unmarriageable. An early marriage also gives parents greater control over the caste into which their children are married. Moreover, Dalit women are also raped as a form of retaliation. Landlords and the police use sexual abuse and other forms of violence against women to inflict political "lessons" and crush dissent within the community.

One of the reasons that Dalit woman continue to be target of atrocities is that in rural areas, due to extreme poverty, lack of education, and as high caste Hindus own 80 per cent land, Dalit women are forced to work on minimal wage. A slight denial to their orders or daring to ask for a raise in wages can result in humiliations, beating, torture, rape, killing and jail. More often, Dalit womens and children are held by as ransom to catch their spouses on minor charges (Ambedkar, *Annihilation)*.

Opportunities for Dalits in Education

The Government has made reservations for Dalits, so that they can enter into jobs in the public sector, parliamentary State Assemblies and Universities. This reservation, however, makes them even more vulnerable in the society. Most Dalits continue to live in extreme poverty, without land or opportunities for better employment or education, with the exception of a minority who have benefitted from India's policy of quotas in education and government jobs. According to Constitution of India, reservation for Dalits in Government jobs is secured, but in reality, only a few are filled out as they have full control of recruitment. According to the National Commission for SC and ST and as per India's constitution, total job reservation for Dalits is 22.5 per cent but only 2.1 per cent in case of class-I (Dalits serving in pubic commission, civil services, chief executives in major companies) and 9.0 per cent in the case of class-II (this includes Dalits serving as college lecturers, bank manager, in government, etcetera). To date, most Dalit students are prevented from entering in government as well as the public sectors as a part of the caste-based discrimination, hence there is a stiff increment in unemployment.

Many bright Dalit students are prevented from sitting in the front classroom row, sharing water or food, and mixing with high caste students. Teachers are often violent against them for showing greater aptitudes in classrooms. Often humiliated in front of class by the teacher and high caste students, most of those students return back to their family profession. For instance, most recently a Dalit girl student who accidentally joined a street dance performed by high caste performers was humiliated and was threatened with rape if she complained to the police. Turning to the police for a complaint only exaggerated the situation. Later, she committed suicide (Narula).

Role of International Non-Government Organisations in the Highlighting Dalit Issues

Now the United Nations and the Human Right groups have exposed the sufferings of these voiceless peoples to the rest of the world. Many Non-Government Organisations (NGO) both in India and as well as abroad have been involved in raising the plight of India's 250 million untouchables.

Amongst many, one of the NGOs in North America is called "The Ambedkar Centre for Peace and Justice" (ACJP), named in honour of Dr. B. R. Ambedkar (1891-1956), who was India's foremost human right activist and an untouchable. He has been recognised as the Chief architect of India's Constitution. Dr. Ambedkar was an emancipator, scholar, extraordinaire, social reformer and a true champion of human rights. He was the first Dalits who received a Ph.D. and L.L.D. from Columbia University, USA, D.Sc. and Bar-at-Law from the London School of Economics, and D.Litt. from Osmania University, India. Moreover, he was the first law minister of Independent India.

The most immediate task of the ACJP is to bring the plight of the Dalits to the attention of the International community and to document and publicise human rights abuses. The mission of this organisation is to foster recognition of the human rights of, and to develop support for, the indigenous peoples of India. The long-term objectives are to enfranchise Dalits as full citizens of their society. This will require broad-based financial and political support for the Dalits, as well as legal and educational changes in India, so that they may re-establish their dignity, culture and civilisation.

As warned by the Vice President, Yogesh Varhade, since fundamentalist Hindu forces are pushing this caste system to the limits, this will result in civil war, instability in South Asia and Global Peace will be in danger. Millions of refugees could infiltrate North America and Europe, further resulting in a complete collapse of the economy, and could cost million of dollars.

The Indian Government is only interested in developing trade with Canada, but does not reveals its "dirty secret" of human rights violations and caste-based atrocities on millions of Dalits. The Canadian government should show compassion towards dissolving untouchability. For this, Canada should put pressure on the Indian government to recognise untouchabilty as "racial discrimination" and put policies in place to protect human rights and the dignity of million Dalits. Moreover, the Canadian as well as the world media should take an active role in publicising the plight of Untouchables.

I wish to thank R. Kamble and Yogesh Varhade for their valuable comments on this chapter, and the following websites (www.ambedkar.org and www.ambedkar.net) for providing useful information on human rights violations against Dalits in India.

REFERENCES

Anant, A., *Human Rights of Marginal Communities: The Low Caste Dalits In India.* South Asia Partnership of Canada.

Chakrabarty, Renu, *Communists in Indian Women's Movement, 1940-50* , People's Publishing House, New Delhi, 1980.

Chakravarti, Uma, *Rewriting History. The Life and Times of Pandita Ramabai,* Kali for Women, New Delhi, 1998.

Custers, Peter, *Women in the Tebhaga Uprising,* Naya Prakash, Calcutta. Dasgupta, Kaberi, 1998.

De Haan, Arjan, "Towards a Single Male Earner: the Decline of Child and Female Employment in an Indian Industry" in *Economic and Social History of the Netherlands,* 6, 1994.

Keer, D., *Dr. BabasahebAmbedkar.* Bombay, India: Popular Publication, n.d.

Moon, V., *Dr. B.R. Ambedkar, Writings and Speeches.* Vol 7. n.p. 1990.

Narula, S., *"Broken People" Caste violence against India's Untouchables.* Human Rights Watch, 1998.

National Commission for Scheduled Caste and Scheduled Tribes, India, 2000.

O'Neill, T., "Untouchables." *National Geographic.* June 2003, 8-31.

Talukdar, S.R., *Merit: The Aryan Bluff.* Bluemoon Books, n.d.

Thind, G.S. *Our Indian Sub-Continent Heritage.* Vancouver, BC: Crosstown Press Ltd., n.d.

10

VIOLENCE AGAINST DALIT WOMEN

Vulnerably positioned at the bottom of India's caste, class and gender hierarchies, Dalit women experience endemic gender-and-caste discrimination, and violence as the outcome of severely unbalanced social, economic and political power equations. Their socioeconomic vulnerability and lack of political voice, when combined with the dominant risk factors of being Dalit and female, increase their exposure to potentially violent situations while simultaneously reducing their ability to escape. Violence against Dalit women presents clear evidence of widespread exploitation and discrimination against these women subordinated in terms of power relations to men in a patriarchal society, as also against their communities based on caste.

As the National Commission for Women has commented, "in the commission of offences against... scheduled caste women the offenders try to establish their authority and humiliate the community by subjecting their women to indecent and inhuman treatment, including sexual assault, parading naked, using filthy language, etc." Hence, violence, which serves as a crucial social mechanism to maintain Dalit women's subordinate position in society, is the core outcome of gender-based inequalities shaped and intensified by the caste system.

This situation exists in India, today, despite constitutional guarantees of non-discrimination on the basis of caste and gender *(Article 15(1))*, the right to life and security of life *(Article 21)* and the constitutional directive to specifically protect Dalits from social injustice and all forms of exploitation *(Article 46)*. Moreover, the Indian State has enacted a series of laws protecting the rights of Dalits and women, acknowledging the prevalence of discrimination and violence against these sections of society. A key law in this regard is the *Scheduled Castes/ Scheduled Tribes (Prevention of Atrocities) Act 1989*. The presence of laws, however, without concomitant implementation to ensure personal security to Dalit women, and without concerted efforts to emancipate the Dalit community and eradiate entrenched gender-and-caste biased notions of (in)equality and (injustice, is not enough. The Indian government has itself acknowledged that the institutional forces—caste, class, community and family— arraigned against women's equal rights are powerful and shape people's mindsets to accept pervasive gender inequality. If human rights are the legitimation of human needs, then the needs of Dalit women for personal security, socioeconomic development and social justice are priority areas for intervention.

In order to understand, therefore, the reality of Indian society in general, and the Dalit community and Dalit women in particular, an analysis of caste-class-gender dynamics is imperative. It is only by adopting this threefold lens focusing on the cultural and material dimensions of the intersection of gender and caste discrimination that a true comprehension of key social relations and social inequalities in India emerges. This analytical lens, grounded in Dalit women's subjective experiences, highlights how these women become instruments through which the social system replicates itself and systemic inequality is maintained: violence against Dalit women is systematically utilised to deny them opportunities, choices and freedoms at multiple levels, undermining not only Dalit women's dignity and self-respect, but also their right to development. An intersectional caste-class-gender analysis also fulfils the need to make Dalit women visible to the public eye through exposing their reality of violence and dis-empowerment intrinsically related to their social position, in recognition of their selfhood and human dignity.

Moreover, analysing these social relations which convert "difference" into systemic oppression and violence enables not only policy-makers, but also women's movements and Dalit movements, to better strategise and implement policies and programmes towards the protection of Dalit women's rights: that is, programmes that facilitate wider processes of change, that ensure the comprehensive eradication of caste and gender discrimination and violence, and enable Dalit women to be mainstreamed into the planned development process in India. At the international level, examining patterns of violence against Dalit women can contribute towards an enhanced human rights understanding of racial and gender discrimination, as interacting factors perpetuating violence against racialised and often marginalised women.

And yet, very little information or government data exists today as regards the specific situation of Dalit women in the country. A study was initiated in 2004, therefore, to examine the forms and manifestations, frequency, caste and social status of perpetrators, causes, effects and responses to violence against Dalit women over the period 1999 to 2004. A total of 500 Dalit women were selected, based on information supplied by knowledgeable persons or organisations working with the Dalit community, from a sample of 32 panchayat unions/mandals/blocks falling within 17 districts of the states of Andhra Pradesh, Bihar, Tamil Nadu/Pondicherry and Uttar Pradesh. These were women who were willing to speak out about their experiences of violence in either or both the general community and in the family, without serious repercussions for their personal security such as threats and further violence from the perpetrators, or renewed caste tensions in the village.

The wide-ranging experiences shared by the Dalit women in this study, when analysed, reveal the multiple layers of violence that pervade their lives. Dalit women endure violence in both the general community and in the family, from state and non-state actors of different genders, castes and socioeconomic groupings. An overview of the forms, frequency and locations of violence, perpetrators and causal factors for violence highlights the incongruence between Dalit women's reality and the universal right of women to freedom from any gender-based violence that results in physical, sexual or psychological harm. This data, therefore, serves as an indictment of both the Indian state and Indian society for failing to respect, protect and fulfil Dalit women's rights.

As an initial comment, it must be noted that the overwhelming majority of the 500 Dalit women's case narratives were never reported in the media. Given that these cases were selected, in collaboration with those working with the Dalit community, from a small sample, it is likely that many more unrecorded instances of violence exist. The reasons for this "silence" when it comes to violence against Dalit women are that cases that are not spoken out in public by the women themselves, or not reported in the media, or not registered by law enforcement authorities, or hidden by the Dalit women's families, relatives and community, or suppressed by the *diktat* of the perpetrators and/or the perpetrators' caste community. The effect is the creation and maintenance of a *culture of violence, silence and impunity* when it comes to violence against Dalit women. This further exacerbates the denial of their rights to security of life and basic human dignity.

Forms and Frequency of Violence

Twelve major forms of violence constitute the basis of this study, nine being violence in the general community—physical assault, verbal abuse, sexual harassment and assault, rape, sexual exploitation, forced prostitution, kidnapping and abduction, forced incarceration and medical negligence—and three being violence in the family—female foeticide and infanticide, child sexual abuse and domestic violence from natal and marital family members. The majority of the 500 Dalit women have faced several forms of violence over the past five years, either in one incident, or in a series of incidents of violence, in either or both the general community and the family.

The more frequent forms of violence that are perpetrated against the majority of Dalit women are verbal abuse (62.4 per cent of total women), physical assault (54.8 per cent), sexual harassment and assault (46.8 per cent), domestic violence (43.0 per cent) and rape (23.2 per cent), in descending order. Although the remaining forms of violence are faced by relatively fewer Dalit women (less than 10 per cent of total women per form of violence), this does not discount their gravity, precisely because of the qualitative factor of force present in these forms of violence.

Violence in the General Community

Verbal abuse from members of the general community, experienced by 312 women in this study, includes derogatory usage of caste names and caste epithets arguably amounting to "hate speech", as well as sexually explicit insults, gendered epithets and threats. One-third of these women have faced violence regularly, indicating the habitual nature of this form of violence. This verbal abuse also highlights the perpetrators' worldview wherein Dalit women are seen as without any rights in the "natural" caste hierarchy, as devoid of any entitlement to resources or respect, and as always sexually available without any requirement for the women's consent.

Saiamma, a 32-year-old Dalit woman who was elected as president of the local Mandal Praja Parishad in Chittoor district, And Andhra Pradesh in 1999, was abused and intimidated by the dominant caste men who initially encouraged her to contest elections. They said, "You are a Mala woman; you are not eligible to be in this post... you cannot sit in the MP seat in front of us. If you sit in that chair, it degrades us; you are eligible to sit only in a normal chair. Just sign wherever we say and apply for three months' leave and go away! ...If you don't listen to us, you cannot survive in this village." She considered her options, and eventually resigned from the position, allowing the dominant caste Vice-President to take over the work.

Verbal abuse often accompanied *physical assault,* perpetrated against 274 women in the study. Over 500 incidents of physical assault on these women were recorded, with 30 women facing regular physical assaults. This combination of violence further links in many cases to a spectrum of sexual violence, from *sexual harassment and/or sexual assault* (234 women), to *rape or gang rape* (116 women). While many women had been raped in one or more incidents, when it came to sexual harassment and/or sexual assault, often the violence occurred several times or was regular, as was the case for 72 women. Where the male perpetrator has some social or economic hold over the woman, such as her employer, or simply belongs to a dominant caste, then this violence sometimes developed into regular, coerced or induced sexual encounters or *sexual exploitation.* In the case of the 44 women, who had been sexually exploited, this violence was most commonly perpetrated through false promises of marriage or lifelong economic maintenance, made to Dalit women in order to sexually exploit them for a period of time.

Kidnapping or abduction of Dalit women, as experienced by 24 women, often led to their forced incarceration and even rape or sexual exploitation. The targets are Dalit women from the time they attain puberty. Hence, parents' fear of their daughters being sexually assaulted and thereby becoming "unmarriageable" explains why, especially in northern states such as Bihar and Uttar Pradesh, Dalit women are getting married at ages as young as five years. At the extreme end of the sexual violence spectrum also lies *forced prostitution,* experienced by 24 women across the four study states. Half of these women are *Joginis,* dedicated to temple goddesses from early ages in Andhra Pradesh and thereafter considered as religiously-sanctioned village prostitutes. Other women had been forced into prostitution after being sexually exploited by their dominant caste landlord-employers, or by their husbands, or in one case by the police.

Incidents *of forced incarceration* have been endured by 23 Dalit women, involving for some women false cases leading to their detention, or arrest and imprisonment. The failure of the police to fulfil their duty to uphold law and order in these cases stemmed from police negligence or bias in initiating these cases against the women. Otherwise, half of these women had experienced being incarcerated in the perpetrator's home, or workplace, or in some isolated or rented building, bringing in the element of kidnapping and sexual violence from various non-state actors. When it comes to *medical negligence,* doctors and nurses have also demonstrated failure in their professional duty of care towards 17 Dalit women, through careless or pressurised operations especially as regards family planning, or discrimination in turning away Dalit women in need of serious medical attention.

Violence in the Family

Within the family, domestic violence is prevalent. A total of 215 Dalit women have recorded regular incidents of domestic violence that span several years of married life. This violence often manifests itself in verbal abuse of the woman, accompanied by physical assault, but also entails sexual abuse including marital rape. Several cases of inter-caste marriages ending in domestic violence reveal caste and gender discrimination against the Dalit wife leading to violence. In most cases, where a Dalit husband is concerned, the violence takes on a strong patriarchal dimension: women are tortured within the home for not bringing enough dowry, for not bearing male children, for being supposedly ugly, or too beautiful, or allegedly unfaithful, for talking back to her husband, etc. Alcoholism among Dalit husbands is also a strong contributing factor to this domestic violence. Domestic violence resulted in some women being deserted by their husbands, or being forced to leave their marital home. For the majority of women, however, the social norms and pressures of married life and "duties" of wives to their husbands ensure that they continue to endure this violence. Moreover, as this violence often commences when they are but children given in marriage, their ability to question and stand up to this violence is often severely diminished.

Female foeticide and infanticide were not recorded as widespread among the Dalit women in this study, with only two women revealing the occurrence of this violence. By comparison, *child sexual abuse* in terms of particularly early child marriages and sexual relations with minor Dalit girls below the age of 16 years is more common. Otherwise, four cases of sexual violence from a brother, father-in-law, brother-in-law and fathers also emerged. While only 23 girls had experienced child sexual abuse within the past five years, this must be viewed in the light of the fact that 282 women, or 72.2 per cent of the total women in this study, were married below the legal age of marriage of 18 years, of which 39.7 per cent were married below the age of 15 years. These early marriages indicate that the majority of women participating in the study would probably have been legally minors at the age of their first sexual encounter with their husband.

Location of Violence

The sites where violence occurs reveal another aspect of Dalit women's vulnerability, in that Dalit women are seen to be accessible in both public and private spaces for any acts of violence. The result is that they are denied spaces in which they can enjoy their rights to privacy and security of life. The majority of Dalit women have faced violence in *public spaces* —streets, women's toilet areas, bus stands, fields, etc.—in and around their villages and towns. The open or public nature of violence committed against them indicates both their specific vulnerability outside of the home, as well as the element of combined individual and collective community punishment meted out through particularly public physical assaults and verbal abuse. Many Dalit women in the study pointed out the perceived additional humiliation of public violence they face from dominant castes, as compared to the generally more private nature of violence committed against dominant caste women.

The next most common place for violence is *within the home.* Aside from domestic violence, a number of women have faced physical assaults, verbal abuse, sexual harassment and sexual assaults in their very home from non-family members. This reveals a common pattern of infringements of their right to privacy where perpetrators of violence invade the women's homes in order to attack and abuse them.

Violence at the *workplace* ranks third in terms of common locations for violence. This relates to Dalit women's greater work participation rates as compared with other women. Their mostly informal sector, daily wage labour occupations, bereft of employment security and many other rights, provide fertile ground for violence. Moreover, given their economic dependence, Dalit women often do not report violence from employers at the workplace, instead keeping silent in order to retain their means of livelihood. In addition, as many Dalit women either work in the perpetrators' home, or have to go there to receive their wages or ask for loans, etc., the *perpetrator's home* also becomes another site for violence perpetrated by general community members.

Finally, *government spaces* become grounds for violence particularly where medical negligence occurs in government hospitals, or where women are forcibly incarcerated, verbally abused, sexually harassed or raped in police stations. Otherwise, verbal abuse is the most common form of violence meted out in government spaces from a range of government actors including the police, district administration officials and doctors.

The multiple sites for violence against Dalit women indicate that while in the brahminical patriarchal system they have greater "space" in which to function as compared with dominant caste women, this space does not translate into greater "freedom"; in other words, while Dalit women are said to enjoy greater freedom of movement, interactions and work opportunities in the "public sphere" than dominant caste women, they do not necessarily enjoy freedom that is safe, secure, productive and progressive, and that ensures their right to choose and decide for themselves. This is due to limits imposed, restrictions mandated and obstructions placed on Dalit women's movement in the gendered space of the "public sphere" which is mediated by caste; that is, public spaces where men, and particularly dominant caste men, predominantly operate. These public spaces are seized upon as opportune places for exercising power and authority over Dalit women as individuals and as a collective through violence.

Social Status of Perpetrators of Violence

Within the wide range of identified perpetrators of violence against Dalit women in the general community, *dominant caste landlords* emerged as the most prominent group. Landlords are the feudal landed class owning over 10 acres of land, and it is their continuing socioeconomic and political power and authority in rural agricultural regions, as well as their connection as employers of many Dalit women agricultural labourers, that provide them disproportionate scope for perpetrating caste violence against these women with impunity. The violence they mete out is physical, verbal and sexual, often in response to Dalit women asserting their economic rights, that is, challenging caste-class relations by demanding their right to wages or land, or their right to sexual integrity, that is, the right to choice in sexual relations.

Police and forest officials, as well as *business people,* also emerge as key perpetrators of violence against Dalit women. Where police are not active perpetrators, they also act in a significant number of cases in collusion with the perpetrators by failing to enforce the law when violence against Dalit women takes place. *Goondas and thugs* also play a role in supporting other perpetrator categories in their acts of terrorising Dalit women with actual or threats of violence.

Two other groups of perpetrators whose numbers are significant belong to the *professional category,* namely hospital nurses and doctors and teachers, and the *political category,* namely local political party leaders and elected panchayat members, and all these cases, except for *goondas* and thugs, these perpetrators hold positions of authority or positions entailing a duty of care and responsibility towards other people. Hence, their presence as perpetrators indicates their gross misuse of the power and authority conferred on them by virtue of their professions.

In addition, there are a large number of *"other dominant caste persons"* as perpetrators, for whom only their caste, and not other social status, has been identified by the woman victim-survivors, and other words, these are dominant caste men and women in the village whom the Dalit women have been unable to identify as having any specific social, occupational or political status in the village such as a landlord or teacher. Their significance lies in the fact that they are often ordinary community members who, by virtue of their "higher" caste status *vis-a-vis* the Dalit women, engage in violence against these women. Moreover, often this violence is committed by these perpetrators not only as individuals, but also as group violence involving people of the same status (for example, where landlords get together to attack a Dalit woman), or different status (for example, where dominant caste villagers join with panchayat or political party leaders to commit violence against a Dalit woman). The group nature of violence (particularly physical assaults, verbal abuse, sexual harassment and gang rapes) often against an individual Dalit woman highlights the particular vulnerability of these women where they are outnumbered by the perpetrators.

Finally, a number of *"other Dalit persons"* have been identified as either active perpetrators of violence against Dalit women, or colluders in the violence. While family members become perpetrators when it comes to dedication of their daughters as Joginis, Dalits often collude in violence when it comes to specific allegations against women of being "witches", or "loose women", or where Dalit women protest against the production and sale of liquor in the villages. Otherwise, their presence indicates both the inter- (sub) caste as well as intra-caste violence that exists within the Dalit community, albeit on a smaller scale to violence against Dalits by the dominant caste groups.

Caste Background of Perpetrators of Violence

Castewise, both forward castes (FCs) and backward castes (BCs) are seen to engage in violence against Dalit women, either as individuals or as a group. Roughly equal numbers of women across the different forms of violence have faced violence at the hands of these two major caste categories.

Dalit perpetrators are also present in significant numbers, as mentioned earlier. Their concentration lies in four forms of violence, namely physical assaults, verbal abuse, sexual harassment and sexual assaults, and rapes. Together, however, they account for around 10 per cent of all perpetrators of violence against Dalit women in the study.

While in some instances, the perpetrators of violence belong to one homogenous dominant caste, there are instances where they cut across all dominant caste lines, that is, backward caste and forward caste. This is particularly so where the Dalit woman is seen to transgress established caste norms, for example, by asserting her rights in defiance of "untouchability" practices. The punishment meted out, therefore, takes on the form of collective punishment that is both expressive of caste outrage as well as instrumental in terms of teaching the woman and her community a lesson of "obedience" to caste norms. Otherwise, sexual violence against Dalit women often takes a collective caste aspect, in terms of gang rapes or forced prostitution.

There are also instances of violence wherein the dominant castes—whether forward caste or backward caste—draw in the Scheduled Castes (Dalits) to engage in violence. To be noted is that this tactic is increasingly utilised by dominant castes to thwart the applicability of the *SC/ST (Prevention of Atrocities) Act 1989*, which only applies to atrocities committed by persons not belonging to the Scheduled Caste or Scheduled Tribe community. Dominant caste and Dalit collaboration in violence is also often present in witchcraft cases, with the accusation of witchcraft targeted at the Dalit woman by her family, her community or the dominant caste community. Other traditions such as the Jogini system also yield multiple caste perpetrators of sexual exploitation against Jogini women, as do some gang rapes and some physical assaults where Dalits and dominant castes are engaged together in illegal activities such as logging or illicit liquor production and sales.

Perpetrators of Violence in the Family

As far as violence in the family is concerned—husbands, the Dalit women's in-laws, her relatives and husbands' relatives are perpetrators of violence, in descending order. Pressures exerted from both natal and marital families lead to female foeticide and infanticide, while child sexual abuse takes the predominant form of child marriages (as per the law rape of a minor refers to girls below 16 years of age, though a legal anomaly reduces this age to below 15 years in the case of a husband raping his wife). Less commonly recorded forms of child abuse are incest (where fathers and brothers are perpetrators) and sexual abuse by other male relatives (by brother-in-laws and father-in-laws). Husbands are also the key perpetrators of domestic violence, followed by mothers-in-law, the women's other relatives, fathers-in-law and their husband's other relatives. Given that most of the Dalit women's natal and marital families are very poor, the day-to-day struggles for survival, caste oppression and gender oppression often translate into frequent violence against Dalit women within the home. In other words, the subjugation, and lack of power and authority in the general community for the women's husbands, marital and natal families, is often replicated in violence in the family, a phenomenon noted in many socially marginalised communities. This domestic violence is further bolstered by the internalised dominant caste ideology of wife fidelity *(pativrata)* and duty of chastity, placing premium on notions of women's "honour", "purity" and "obedience".

CAUSAL FACTORS FOR VIOLENCE

Violence in the General Community

In most cases of violence in the general community, where the perpetrator belongs to a dominant caste, the Dalit women clearly identified their gender-caste-class status as the overall or key cause for the violence. Clear examples were given not only in terms of *ihejogini* system or violence related to untouchability norms, but also more generally in terms of the petty reasons that often triggered violence against the Dalit women by dominant caste men, women and children (for example, trying to cross a dominant caste's fields, asserting equal rights to access water from common taps, or asserting the right to own economic resources). These reasons fall broadly into two categories: reasons related to coercive violence utilised to maintain caste norms or caste-based gender norms, and reasons related to Dalit women's assertions of their rights by defying untouchability norms or asserting their rights to cultural, economic and political resources.

The verbal abuse that is integral to many women's experiences of violence also indicates the dominant caste perpetrators' worldview as regards Dalit women's 'inferior' caste, class and gender status, and consequent powerlessness and vulnerability. Buil' ;nto the patriarchal caste system is the assumption that Dalit women are available for any form of exploitation and violence, as a consequence of their "low" and "impure" character, and hence the low character of their caste that does not deserve honour and respect. The impunity with which much of this violence is carried out reinforces the normality of this culture of violence. The gender-caste-class axis, therefore, provides the systemic base for violence against Dalit women; that is, this violence is an in-built component of the caste system.

As far as Dalit perpetrators are concerned, the majority being male, many assimilate and reproduce the gender inequality structured into the caste system by using patriarchal norms to commit violence against women of their own community. This is particularly manifested in terms of physical and sexual violence, where patriarchal norms of female subordinate status and submissiveness influence Dalit women's abilities to enjoy their sexual integrity, equality and dignity, freedom, life and physical security in particular.

Flowing from and interlinked with this systemic causal factor for violence (that is, being a Dalit and a woman), Dalit women identified four main discrete and overlapping categories of causal factors for violence against them in their recorded narratives. The primary identified factor for violence in the general community related to the issue of Dalit women's *sexual or bodily integrity.* Accompanying Dalit women's low caste status and the socioeconomic and political power of the dominant castes is the latter's view of their superior caste and gender status and accordingly a perceived right over Dalit women's bodies. Dalit women are seen as sexually available as they move in gendered public spaces and engage in productive labour. Sexual violence is understood in caste ideology as ennobling 'lower' caste women; that is, dominant caste perpetrators of sexual violence against Dalit women expect their "victims" to be grateful for the sexual attention they are receiving from 'higher' caste men. Sexual violence is also a tool utilised by dominant caste men to reinforce the caste 'impurity' of both the Dalit woman and her community, given the hegemonic discourse of women symbolising the group identity and bearing the honour of their community. Hence, socially legitimised reasons for sexual violence and its accompanying physical and verbal assaults against Dalit women include:

- the women's perceived sexual availability;
- retaliation against women who rejected men's sexual advances;

- reaction against women who expressed a desire to leave prostitution work.

A second frequent causal factor for violence in the general community directly links to *gender inequality and the 'natural' caste hierarchy* as often manifested in untouchability practices, and Dalit women's counter discourse of equality, rights, dignity and self-respect. As the caste system hinges on the power of the dominant castes to enforce caste-based rules, including those rules governing what Dalit women should and should not do as impure, low caste women, violence also serves a functional aspect. Thus another set of causes for violence—mostly physical assaults, verbal abuse and sexual harassment or assault—includes:

- when women broke "customary" laws by trying to access places of worship, hotels or other public places on equal par with the dominant castes;
- when women allegedly disrespected the caste status of a dominant caste or the gender status of a Dalit male by speaking up, questioning, or raising their voices in protest or to assert their rights;
- when women tried to participate in religious or cultural life;
- when women tried to access water rights or the public distribution system (PDS) ration shop on equal par with dominant castes.

Almost as frequently identified a causal factor for violence in the general community lies in the area of Dalit women's *civil rights.* The violence is either a response to the Dalit women's alleged breach of caste norms by exercising their freedom of expression in speaking out on an issue, or seeking to protect her family or community, or as a means used to reinforce their submissiveness and voicelessness as demanded under the caste system. These issues include:

- revenge or retaliation to settle scores with either the woman, her family or her community;

- response to the women when they questioned the perpetrator/s for violent acts done to them, their children, their family members or other Dalit community members;
- response to the women when they questioned illicit arrack sales or corruption in government schemes meant for Dalit welfare;
- where a male member of the woman's household was wanted for questioning by the police;
- where a woman scolded dominant caste children for destroying the *anganwadi* garden;
- where women were involved in a road blockade protest;
- resort to supernatural beliefs to explain sudden illnesses, or family pressures, that led to girl's dedication as a Jogini;
- doctors' carelessness or negligence in treating or operating on women;
- insecurity faced as a widow, or a Jogini.

A fourth causal factor for violence in the general community, given the aspect of economic exploitation built into the caste system, related to *economic resources*—land, or other economic resources/capital such as wages, payment for services, etc.—and particularly Dalits asserting their rights to own or utilise resources. Violence also related to Dalit women's poverty levels or economic status, in terms of their landlessness combined with their dependence on dominant castes for their livelihood; that is, with regard to work, wages and loans. Causes for violence related specifically to land and common property resources, being key economic resources in the villages, include:

- women and their families asserted their rights to own land;
- women tried to access forests or other common property resources;
- women questioned dominant castes for destroying, or for their cattle destroying crops;

- in order to appropriate the land belonging to the Dalit women or their families;
- reaction against Dalit women and their families owning or leasing land;
- retaliation for women allowing water to flow onto the dominant caste perpetrator's land, or allegedly wrecking the dividing line between their two fields.

Economic development factors triggering violence against the Dalit women include:

- where women failed to repay debts;
- women asked for loans;
- women asserted their economic rights by asking for monetary payment for services performed or goods sold, or loans given out, or their pensions;
- women asserted their rights to access government relief schemes or housing schemes;
- woman asked for the return of her ration card given as surety for a loan she had repaid;
- women attained or tried to attain a higher economic status than allegedly befitted a Dalit, such as by trying to become quarry owners;
- women won a contract to cook school midday meals;
- poverty that led the women's family to dedicate their daughters as Joginis, or that led doctors to discriminate against the women in providing medical care or be negligent in their provision of medical care.

Similarly, causal factors related to Dalit women's labour and work include:

- women protested against forced or bonded labour;
- women challenged working conditions;
- women questioned the delay or part-payment or under-payment or non-payment of wages;

- women asked for workers' compensation following their husbands' deaths;
- women allegedly arrived late for work, or allegedly did not work properly, or slept during work, or did not come to work due to illness;
- woman refused to clean her dominant caste employer's muddy shoes;
- woman did 'polluted' work of burying unwanted corpses;
- where a Dalit man wanted to wrest a woman's job away from her;
- where a dominant caste man did not want a Dalit woman working with him.

Seen together, these four afore-mentioned broad categories of causal factors indicate the crucial areas of sustaining Dalit women's lives, their integrity and their identity. Hence, Dalit women are often attacked in these vulnerable areas in order to deprive them of an economic base and economic independence from the dominant castes, to deny them civil freedoms to express their rights, to damage their bodily and sexual integrity as means of attacking their dignity and identity, all of which are necessary to maintaining their gender-caste-class subordination.

Otherwise, other causal factors that provoked violence include those related to Dalit women's *basic livelihood* outside of economic issues:

- women asserted their rights to access or enjoy housing, or water, or the public distribution system (PDS), or education, or open spaces for defecation;
- women questioned the perpetrator for polluting their housing premises with rubbish or sewage water;
- women asked for immediate medical treatment due to being in intense pain;
- women did not come to hospital early enough, or were not able to pay for medical treatment due to poverty.

In the realm *of political rights,* several Dalit women spoke of their assertions of basic political rights as provoking violent dominant caste backlashes. The issues that led to violence included:

- woman canvassed for votes in the dominant caste section of the village;
- women exercised or attempted to exercise their right to an independent vote in elections;
- women contested panchayat elections;
- women exercised or attempted to exercise political authority as elected panchayat representatives.

Another category of causes for violence relates to *relationship issues,* including:

- women asserted their rights to equality and dignity in relationships, by protesting against violence, or demanding fidelity from man in the relationship, or questioning man for deserting her;
- women allegedly had illicit relationships with other men, or allegedly were prostitutes, or allegedly encouraged others to have illicit relationships;
- women asked the perpetrators of rape or sexual exploitation to marry them;
- women accused perpetrator's son of having raped them;
- reaction against Dalit woman whose son married a dominant caste woman;
- women questioned perpetrators for abandoning them after having sexual relationships with them.

This category is very much related to that of sexual integrity, in that the causes for violence expose the underlying ideology of Dalit women's availability for illicit relationships, though not marriage, and the stringent punishments proscribed for inter-caste marriages. Moreover, the Dalit men's and Dalit community's control over Dalit women's sexuality is seen in their violent responses to Dalit women asserting their rights in relationships, or in punishing women whose so-called immoral behaviour allegedly influences other women to have illicit relationships.

Two categories of causal factors are related, in dealing with the dominant caste discourse of *criminality* that claims Dalit women as inherently criminal, a consequence of, as well as reinforcement of, their alleged impurity and low caste status. This discourse pervades conflicts and consequent violence arising out of accusations of trespass, or criminal activity. Examples of accusations of criminal activity against Dalit women includes :

- alleged to be witches or accomplices to witches;
- allegedly helped bomb a police station;
- allegedly gave false evidence to the police;
- allegedly took firewood, or mud, or grass from the perpetrators' fields
- alleged theft from perpetrator's house or fields;
- alleged misappropriation of money from Old Age Assistance Fund.

Similarly, examples of accusations of *trespass* includes :

- women's animals strayed into the dominant castes' fields and sometimes ate or destroyed some of the crops;
- woman bathed in the perpetrator's pond;
- women simply passed by or crossed the dominant castes' fields;
- women's animals or children went to the toilet in the perpetrators' fields.

The issue of trespass in particular is worth considering in the context of the systemic denial of economic resources to Dalits under the caste system. Where Dalit women are so often excluded from ownership or enjoyment of land or common property resources, and lack basic livelihood amenities such as toilets in their homes, then it would seem unrealistic to draw a line between public and private resources in villages. Unless issues of land reforms and basic public amenity provisioning, for example, are implemented by the state on a priority basis, can one speak of trespass by persons who are kept systematically excluded from such resources or amenities?

Finally, violence also took place when Dalit women *sought justice and the protection of the law* for violence done to them, or to forestall such action, by any of the following acts:

- women filed or tried to file a police complaint;
- women brought or tried to bring incidents of violence to the traditional village panchayat for arbitration;
- women refused to accept compromises following acts of violence;
- to prevent women from telling anyone of the violence or filing a police complaint;
- to prevent women from being witnesses against the perpetrators in a court case.

This revisiting of violence upon Dalit women in order to forestall any efforts by them to seek justice, or to punish them further for daring to seek justice, functions to build, maintain and reproduce a culture of impunity for perpetrators and their colluders in violence.

Violence in the Family

Similarly, Dalit women faced violence in the family over a range of issues, suggesting the assimilation of the larger patriarchal caste system's norms by particularly Dalit men, with negative implications for Dalit women's personal lives and interactions in their community.. As previously mentioned, the internalised ideology of brahmanical patriarchy, with its notions of women's "honour", "purity" and "obedience", produces and influences the causal factors for violence in the family. Female foeticide and infanticide stemmed from gender discrimination, combined with poverty or a response to the child being born of an illicit relationship. By comparison, child sexual abuse was primarily seen as the result of husbands asserting their perceived right to sexual relations with their child brides.

When it comes to domestic violence, however, the causes for this violence are much more nuanced and varied. *Gender inequality and norms of female subordination* formed a major category of causal factors for violence meted out by natal and marital family members to Dalit women. Examples of causal factors falling within this category includes :

- women allegedly failed to be dutiful wives;
- women asserted their rights;
- women were unable to bear children, or unable to bear sons;
- caste discrimination from dominant caste husbands and in-laws in inter-caste marriages, or reaction from dominant caste husbands on being ostracised from their dominant caste communities as a result of marrying Dalit women;
- dominant caste husbands did not want children from their Dalit wives, or did not want their children to visit their Dalit grandparents' house, or not wanting their children to marry a Dalit.

A second major category was *economic* causal factors for domestic violence, including:

- poverty;
- insufficient dowry;
- women earned more income than their husbands, or their natal families had a higher economic status than their marital families;
- women asked their husbands to account for money given from their earnings to the husbands, or refused to give their earnings to fund their husbands' drinking habits, or refused to mortgage jewellery to satisfy their husbands' spendthrift habits;

- to deny women their share of their deceased husbands' property, or to appropriate their dead father's pension.

A third prominent category of causal factors related to Dalit women's *civil rights,* which include:

- women's insecurity due to their husband's unemployment or alcoholism;
- women's insecurity as widows, or orphans, or differently abled, or stepchildren.

Finally, two related categories of causal factors related to rights in *family relationships* and to *sexual integrity.* Internalised brahmanical patriarchal norms entail strict control over Dalit women's sexuality. Hence, reasons for violence surrounding marital relations include:

- women allegedly having illicit relationships;
- women's alleged breaches of family honour, particularly in response to women surviving sexual or physical violence in the general community;
- women caught up in internal family power dynamics.

Evidence of the lack of similar norms applicable to male household members was seen in violence against Dalit wives arising from their husbands having illicit relationships with other women, or marrying again, or wanting to marry again.

In a similar manner Dalit women faced violence arising out of *disregard for their sexual integrity,* including:

- when women did not want to have sexual relations with their husbands, or in one case with her husband's friends;
- either in furtherance of sexual relations, or retaliation for women having refused to have sexual relations with male relatives;
- negative or blaming responses from women's natal or marital family members after women were sexually assaulted or exploited.

Overall, much of the domestic violence arose out of a combination of factors such as internalised gender discrimination, poverty, dominant discourses of dowry, wifely fidelity and duties, and distrust of women to guard their own sexuality all leading to husbands' perceived rights over their wives, or their husbands' alcoholism. The message effectively sent home to Dalit women is that they must keep "in their place"; that is, they must remain submissive daughters or wives, and should not assert their rights against Dalit men and other dominant family members.

Remedial Action for Justice

The Indian Government has an obligation under international human rights law to act with due diligence to prevent, investigate and punish acts of violence against Dalit women in both the general community and in the family, at the hands of state or non-state actors/Any case of violence against a Dalit woman has to pass through the hands of the local police and the judiciary in order for the woman to receive justice under the law. Safeguarding the impartiality of this process, the Indian Constitution stipulates in *Article* 14 that all Indian citizens have the right to equality before the law. However, deeply ingrained normative values of appropriate gender and caste roles and behaviour patterns influence government officials, police and even judges who have the power to interpret and actualise rights. These socio-culturally-religiously rooted biases enforce the discriminatory *status quo* to the detriment of Dalit women's right to justice where violence takes place. As the United Nations Special Rapporteur on Violence against Women has noted with regard to the situation in India, "constitutional and legislative provisions that have been enacted to protect women from discrimination have not proved to be an effective deterrent.

Moreover, the Indian government's consistent inaction in protecting, promoting and fulfilling rights for its Dalit women citizens—evidenced in official data indicating the increasing rates of crimes against women and Scheduled Castes, its failure to resister many cases of violence against Dalit women, and low disposal rates of Scheduled Caste atrocity cases combined with low conviction rates—all points to structural injustice being perpetuated and the Indian state's failure to comply with its international human rights obligations. These conclusions are substantiated by the justice-seeking efforts of the Dalit women in this study.

Considering all 500 Dalit women in the study, in 40.2 per cent of instances of violence the *women have been unable to obtain legal or community remedies for the violence.* A culture of silence exists when it comes to especially sexual violence, due to the dominant discourse emphasising women's "honour" and the stigma attaching to sex outside of marriage, whether forced or by consent. Other reasons for not attempting to obtain justice includes :

- fear of the perpetrators, arising from the perpetrator's threats of further violence to the women or their family members should they file police complaints, or to deny them work;
- fear of dishonour or further shame by publicising the violence;
- ignorance that the violence was an illegal act for which there are legal remedies;
- lack of money to approach the police, or pay the often requisite bribe in order for the police to take action, or to follow a police case through to the courts;
- lack of family or community support for the justice-seeking attempt.
- The overall effect is to reinforce a culture of impunity for violence by the perpetrators and their colluders, further exacerbating the denial of Dalit women's rights to security of life and basic human dignity.

In 26.5 per cent of instances of violence, the women attempt to obtain legal or community redress for the violence, but are *prevented from obtaining justice by the perpetrators and their supporters, and the community at large.* The existence of traditional village panchayats of caste elders/leaders that exists parallel to the formal panchayat system in most Indian villages, in particular, often systematically suppresses women's and Dalits' voices using patriarchal and dominant caste notions of social and moral justice. Reasons for these thwarted justice-seeking attempts include:

- perpetrators, or their families, or their caste community threatening or intimidating the victim- survivor into silence;
- perpetrators foisting false police cases against the victim-survivors to pressurise them to drop their legitimate cases;
- traditional village or caste panchayats, and in some cases formal elected panchayats, refusing to take up Dalit women's cases, or refusing to accuse dominant caste perpetrators, or portraying the affected woman as the wrongdoer instead of the perpetrator, or pressurising the affected woman to accept an informal "compromise";
- victim-survivor's family pressurising her to drop the case out of fear of family dishonour of dominant caste reprisals;
- dominant caste community pressurising the victim-survivor to accept informal "compromises" that involve no proper and adequate remedial or justice action.

In cases of panchayat rulings, justice may appear to be done to the Dalit women. Often, however, the perpetrators and supporting dominant caste members/groups contrive "compromises" by taking advantage of their socio-political power and status, instead of dispensing true justice.

Of all the instances of violence, only in 1.6 per cent are the Dalit women able to *obtain informal justice rulings in her favour.* In most of these 33 instances, traditional village panchayats or elected panchayats or local NGOs manage to broker informal justice rulings rewarding the victim-survivor with financial compensation and a public apology, while extracting from the perpetrator a fine and/or apology and promise for improved behaviour in the future.

A further 17.4 per cent of all instances of violence reach the notice of the police, but *the justice attempts are blocked by the police* themselves. These include cases in which:

- police pressurise the woman victim-survivor to drop the case or to accept a "compromise";
- police frame false cases against the victim-survivor or her supporters in order to force them to drop their legitimate case;
- police file victim-survivor's complaints but neglect to take action;
- police accept bribes from the perpetrators to drop or scuttle the case;
- police simply refuse to file FIRs.

By rendering futile the women's attempt to seek justice through the criminal justice system, the police collude to reinforce the culture of impunity for violence against Dalit women.

Finally, in only 13.8 per cent of instances of violence in this study is *appropriate police or judicial action underway.* The majority of these cases are all pending: investigations are being carried out, chargesheets are yet to be prepared, cases are currently before the courts, etc. Hence, leeway still exists for the cases to be scuttled by the police and/or perpetrators and their community. Notably, only 3.6 per cent of all instances of violence have actually reached the court, and of those, only three cases (that is, less than 1 per cent of total instances of violence) have ended in convictions. Eight other cases have been dismissed by the courts or ended in acquittals of the accused, due to either a forced "compromise" dictated by the accused while the case was under trial, or the perpetrator pressurising the woman victim-survivor or witnesses into turning hostile, or the victim-survivor being unable to obtain the requisite evidence for her case, or the perpetrator dying before the end of the trial.

Hence, the long process to obtain justice for Dalit women victim-survivors of violence is too often effectively stymied by different actors—the perpetrators, their caste community, police, the traditional village panchayats or formal elected panchayats. The brahminical patriarchal discourse of "honour" and fear of further dominant caste reprisals, moreover, influences Dalit women, their families and their communities, not to seek justice where violence takes place. Impunity for violence, therefore, is an intrinsic factor in the maintenance of the caste system and caste- and-gender based norms circumscribing Dalit women's fundamental rights and freedoms.

The overall performance of the Indian State, therefore, comes into serious question when measured against the standard of due diligence to prevent violence against Dalit women. This is true for violence at the hands of both non-state actors, as well as state actors themselves. Giving effect to Dalit women's rights requires not only building structures of protection—including investigation, prosecution, fair punishment and compensation for violence—but also rigorously implementing laws and policies designed to facilitate the enjoyment of equal citizenship rights for the 80 million Dalit women in the country today.

Taking into account the situation of rising rates of crimes against Dalits, combined with failure of the state machinery to check this rise with stringent action, the Parliamentary Committee on the Welfare of Scheduled Castes and Scheduled Tribes has stated that atrocities on Scheduled Castes and Scheduled Tribes constitute an internal disturbance under *Article 355* of the *Indian Constitution,* and has called for Central Government intervention under various provisions to take strict action against offending states. The Committee has also castigated the Home Ministry for using "police and public order" being "state subjects" as an excuse for absolving themselves of the responsibility implied under *Article 355.* Finally, the Committee recommended taking "extreme steps," wherever warranted to protect the Dalit community and punish perpetrators of violence against them.

Effects of Violence

Violence against Dalit women causes social, physical and mental trauma to women, much of which is long-term suffering. Where violence is committed with impunity, aided by the failure of the police to effect arrests and prosecutions, the fact of the perpetrators and their colluders in the violence freely moving about the village and often intimidating the woman and her family has a deep *psychological impact.* Significant are feelings of the futility of legal justice and fatalism about positive changes to address such violence, hi total, 71.2 per cent of Dalit women in the study expressed their feelings of helplessness to stop the violence, while 60.4 per cent indicated the atmosphere of constant fear in which they carry on their daily lives. Feelings of depression or low-self esteem and shame also marked out the lives of around 60 per cent of women, while 24 women had tried to commit suicide because of the violence they endured.

At the level of *physical effects,* among other effects of violence, 92 Dalit women experienced long-term physical health complications arising out of the violence, and a further nine women now live with a permanent physical disfigurement or disability. Twenty-three women endured long-term sexual health complications, while seven women miscarried as a result of violence meted out to them. Sexual violence resulted in 40 women becoming pregnant, though 18 women either opted for or were forced to undertake abortions, and one woman's family killed her child at birth.

Social effects of violence include economic punishment in terms of the destruction of Dalit women's livelihood or loss of employment (11 women), or social boycotts (four women). Around 8 per cent of Dalit women (39 women) expressed their inability to get married or to get their child married where especially sexual violence had occurred. Violence also restricted many Dalit women's freedom of movement, while eight girls quit their education due to violence. Otherwise, Dalit women were ostracised from their families (57 women), or their community (16 women), or deserted by their husbands (17 women), or forced to leave their homes (80 women) because of violence in either or both the general community and the family. Finally, 9.6 per cent of women (48 women) experienced contempt or ridicule in the villages following the violence perpetrated against them, often reinforcing the idea that somehow the women were to be blamed for the violence meted out to them.

Thus, the harm caused to Dalit women by violence does not stop at the act itself; it has long-term and multiplying social, psychological and physical effects that are not being addressed. Outside of the social movements and organisations working with the community, little supportive or counselling mechanisms exist in India today to deal with caste-and-gender based violence meted out to Dalit women. The result is that the lives of many Dalit women are underwritten by layers of trauma, hindering their rights to live with dignity and reach their full potential.

Courage, Strength and Resilience of Dalit Women

Despite all these experiences of violence that leave grave marks on Dalit women's lives and dominant caste perpetrators constantly reiterating gender-based caste norms and Dalit gender subordination, the narratives of the Dalit women also evidence their courage, strength and resilience to assert their right to live a life with dignity. Apart from the courage that Dalit women have shown during violence, their resilience in the post-violence phase is manifested in two respects: first, their determination to pursue a course of action, whatever may be the expected or unexpected outcome, to set right the harm done by the violence; secondly, the tenacity they have shown in their various attempts to sustain their lives against all odds, refusing to let their lives disintegrate further as a result of the violence they have experienced. Whether this was done with success or otherwise in terms of achieving a legal remedy for the injustice, they had faced or improving their living conditions, what is significant are their efforts to survive and sustain their lives in some form or another.

It is ironic that instead of the Indian State being the custodian of constitutional rights, it is Dalit women themselves who often dare to uphold the rule of law in the face of the "rule of caste". This is evident from cases where Dalit women assert their rights to equality and fundamental freedoms of life, and also where they approach established legal justice mechanisms instead of taking the law into their own hands as the perpetrators have done. And yet, in only a few cases does the state rise up to meet Dalit women's expectations of justice. Therefore, what Dalit women look to is not a paternal way of providing them remedial justice, but support mechanisms that clearly establish and uphold their rights, and bring them into mainstream society with dignity.

Failure by the Indian state and civil society to respond to Dalit women's legitimate expectations results in these women experiencing greater marginalisation, to the detriment of a healthy and vibrant democratic polity. There also lies a possibility of increased questioning of the rule of law as the appropriate means to securing justice. What Dr B.R. Ambedkar said in 1949 on the occasion of the Third Reading of the Indian Constitution is well worth noting in this regard:

> "On [enacting the Constitution], we are going to enter into a life of contradictions. In politics, we will have equality and in social and economic life we will have inequality. In politics we, will be recognising the principle of one [wo]man one vote and one vote one value. In our social and economic life, we shall, by reason of our social and economic structure, continue to deny the principle of one man one value. How long shall we continue to live this life of contradictions? How long shall we continue to deny equality in our social and economic life? If we continue to deny it for long, we will do so only by putting our political

democracy in peril. We must remove this contradiction at the earliest possible moment or else those who suffer from inequality will blow up the structure of political democracy which this Assembly has so laboriously built up."

Concluding Reflections

In contravention of both national laws and international human rights standards that prohibit any physical, sexual or psychological violence against women, varying forms of violent acts specifically targeting Dalit women are occurring on a large scale across India today. That physical (affecting bodily integrity), verbal (affecting the psyche), and sexual (affecting bodily/sexual integrity) violence are the most common, and often combined, forms of violence suggests that at every level Dalit women's dignity is being attacked. Moreover, given that most of this violence is occurring in public spaces, the additional humiliation of being violated in public drives home a message not only to each Dalit woman, but also to her family and community, that she is not considered worthy of being treated with honour, respect or human dignity. As Dalit women also experience violence within the family, they are effectively left with no safe spaces in which to freely express themselves and reach their full potential.

Dalit women would appear to be extremely vulnerable to aggression primarily by dominant caste persons in their villages and towns. Dominant caste status, often combined with patriarchal status and reinforced by a dominant class position (for example, being a landlord), effectively legitimises many dominant caste men's exercise of power, authority and force over Dalit women. Moreover, reading through the 500 Dalit women's narratives reveals the pan-religious element in that perpetrators of violence come from all major Indian religions—Hindus, Muslims, Christians and Sikhs, indicating that even in non-Hindu traditions the caste hierarchy trumps religious ideals of equality and respect for all human beings.

The range of causal factors for violence in the general community is directly attributable to systemic caste-class-gender factors that ascribe Dalit women's low status in society and consequent disempowerment and exploitation. At the core is patriarchy, which is gender-based and gender-biased against women. Male exercise of patriarchal power to subjugate women is overtly manifested in their attacks on Dalit women's sexual and bodily integrity, as well as their rights in inter-personal relationships with men. At the same time, patriarchy in India is influenced by the caste system and its inherent inequalities arising from hierarchal structuring of the system. Dalit women become specifically targeted for violence as an outcome of their positioning at the bottom of both gender and caste hierarchies, which condone violence against those Dalit women who contravene caste and untouchability norms by asserting their right to equality, or criminalises Dalit women's actions, or deems it socio-culturally acceptable to perpetrate sexual violence on Dalit women.

Moreover, reinforcement of Dalit women's lack of or denial of access to land and other economic resources through violence points to their effective class subordination in order to retain them as an exploitable labour force for their mainly dominant caste employers. There are also interconnections between denial of Dalit women's socioeconomic rights or right to livelihood, and the denial of their civil rights; that is, their ability to protest and protect themselves depends to a great extent on their having a sound economic base. Finally, the lack of civil and political freedoms, including the right to justice and protection of the law in the event of violence taking place, reinforce the disempowerment of Dalit women at all levels. Such violence is crucial to the maintenance of caste structures and unequal power relations in society, which serves to highlight key areas requiring urgent intervention to safeguard Dalit women's fundamental rights. Similarly, the multiplicity of causal factors for violence in the family suggests the reproduction of the larger patriarchal caste system's norms in Dalit women's personal lives and interactions in their community.

Finally, the culture of impunity built into the caste system has wide-ranging implications as far as violence against Dalit women is concerned. Impunity for violence reinforces that caste-based notions of (injustice prevail over democratic rights and the rule of law in the country. Justice itself becomes defined in terms of caste-and-gender privileges, with violence serving to reinforce caste law and order at the heavy expense of Dalit women's rights. Violence against Dalit women thus presents one of the greatest challenges to the social justice system in the country, calling for immediate and holistic remedial action at all levels of the government, law and order agents, the judiciary and civil society.

Future Prospects

The Indian Government has identified in its 10th Five-Year Plan 2002-2007, the empowerment of socially disadvantaged groups such as Dalits and women as priority strategies for development of the nation. Complementing this development priority is the elimination of discrimination and all forms of violence against women and the girl child, which is a central objective of the National Policy for the Empowerment of Women 2001 in attempting to bridge the gap between *de jure* equal status and *de facto* pervasive gender inequality. As the National Policy states,

> All form of violence against women, physical and mental, whether at domestic or societal levels, including those arising from customs, traditions or accepted practices, shall be dealt with effectively with a view to eliminate its incidence. Institutions and mechanisms/schemes for assistance will be created and strengthened for prevention of such violence, including sexual harassment at workplace and customs like dowry; for the rehabilitation of the victims of violence and for taking effective action against the perpetrators of such violence. A special emphasis will also be laid on programmes and measures to deal with trafficking in women and girls.

Similarly, the National Human Rights Commission has summed up recommendations from the National Commission for Scheduled Castes and Scheduled Tribes, national conferences and various non-state organisations such as the National Campaign on Dalit Human Rights *vis-a-vis* protection of Dalits' rights to life and security of life: sincere and effective implementation of the law to protect Dalits against "untouchability" practices and atrocities; capacity building within government to protect and promote Dalit human rights; capacity building of statutory watchdog bodies; strict enforcement of Supreme Court guidelines on treatment of persons in custody; convergence of regulatory and development programmes; information for social change in civil society; code of conduct for state agencies; overcoming procedural handicaps to Special Courts taking cognisance of atrocity cases without prior committal by Magistrates; right of separate settlement for Dalits; enhanced central share in schemes for Dalits; and the setting up of independent, non-official monitoring agencies to review cases of atrocities against Dalits.

Attacking systemic violence against women demands that patriarchal structures and attitudes in India be contextualised by caste, the eradication of caste inequality being intrinsic to the solution of gender equality. It is the institutionalised inequality of the caste system that underpins and reinforces gender inequality in India, rendering marginalised Dalit women particularly vulnerable to violence with impunity. Therefore, an understanding of the intersection of gender and caste discrimination incorporated into government policies is vital to ensuring that Dalit women's rights to life and security of life are respected and protected. This also open up the challenge to Dalit and women's movements, as for other social movements across the country, to incorporate a gender-and-caste perspective in their work, in recognition of the specific identity and corresponding unique intensity of Dalit women's subordination by gender and caste.

By fulfilling its national and international obligations to protect Dalit women from violence, complemented by adequate focus on improving the socioeconomic conditions of Dalit women, the Indian State could contribute to enlarging the choices and agency of Dalit women. Increased Dalit women's agency, in turn, would contribute to social change not only for their families and their communities, but also for the wider Indian society. As the National Federation of Dalit Women has stated in its *Declaration of Dalit Women's Rights 2002,* Dalit women have the right to life and to freedom from oppression and violence, the right to expression, conscience and autonomy. It is only when support is extended to Dalit women across the country that these women will become empowered and enjoy these fundamental rights on par with the rest of the Indian citizenry.

Finally, it is the voices of women such as Rohini Devi from West Champaran district in Bihar that must be heard and respected: when asked if she would standup publicly for her community and fight for justice through the legal system, Rohini Devi said, *"Yes. I may lose my life in the process, but I want to live with dignity... Tell me, is there any Dalit family left in our village in which someone has not been raped [by the dominant castes]? We will no longer tolerate it!"*

REFERENCES

Ambedkar, Dr B.R., "Annihilation of Caste", in Moon, V. (ed), *Dr. Ambedkar Writings and Speeches,* Volume 1.

Chakravarti, U., *Gendering Caste: Through a Feminist Lens,* Stree, Calcutta, 2003 on the use of the term "brahminical patriarchy" to refer to the interlinking of patriarchy and caste structures in India.

Government of India report to the Committee on the Elimination of All Forms of Discrimination against Women, UN Doc. CEDAW/C/IN/1, 1 March 1999, para 83.

Government of India, *National Policy for the Empowerment ofWomen 2001,* Policy Prescriptions: para.7.1. See, for example, Aloysius

Irudayam., *Black Paper: Broken Promises and Dalits Betrayed*, National Campaign on Dalit Human Rights, Bangalore, 1999.

National Commission for Women, *Women of Weaker Sections: Socio-Economic Development of Scheduled Caste Women*, New Delhi, 1996, p.33.

National Human Rights Commission, *Report on Prevention of Atrocities against Scheduled Castes: Policy and Performance, Suggested Interventions and Initiatives for NHRC*, New Delhi, 2004, pp.193-4.

Parliamentary Committee on the Welfare of Scheduled Castes and Scheduled Tribes, Fourth Report on Ministry of Home Affairs, Ministry of Social Justice and Empowerment and Ministry of Tribal Affairs (14th Lok Sabha): *Atrocities on Scheduled Castes and Scheduled Tribes and Pattern of Social Crimes towards Them*, Government of India, 2004-2005; news report in *The Pioneer*, 28 April 2005.

Rege, S., 'Dalit Women talk Differently: A Critique of 'Difference' and towards a Dalit Feminist Standpoint Position', 6(2) Vikalp Alternatives, Vikas Adhyayan Kendra, Mumbai, 1998.

11

AMBEDKAR'S VISION FOR DALIT UPLIFTMENT

Born as an untouchable with no rights to be an equal in Indian Society, Dr. B.R. Ambedkar educated himself as the most qualified person of his time, inspired untouchable castes to reject Brahamanical Social Order (BSO) that kept them socially degraded, economically poor, culturally despised, politically powerless, and denied them the " basic human rights". He challenged the leadership of his time by exposing follies of their proposition of freeing India without freeing millions of untouchables, tribals and socially and educationally backward classes living in sub-human conditions under the Socio-economic Raj of the Hindus. As the Chief Architect of free India's New Constitution, he abolished all forms of discriminations and inequalities based on caste, gender, race, or status. But, what was his vision to uplift the Dalits?

Leadership has always been associated with many attributes. These attributes range from individual persona of the leader to a number of skills such as self-confidence, strong convictions, poise, ability to speak and present his concerns, and influence others' thought and actions. But it is the articulation of vision in the leadership that taps the conscious or unconscious needs, values, aspirations and feelings of followers such that the leadership enthuse them with shared ideological goal. This chapter attempts to define the terms vision, and leadership, and then establishes the linkages between the two. Before exploring actions, programmes of Dr. B. R. Ambedkar and vision behind them, attempt has been made to explore the source of his vision.

The Vision

Oxford dictionary gives many meanings of the word *'Vision'*. However, when one uses this word in association with the word leadership, it is the act of faculty of seeing or power of discerning future conditions, or the foresightedness. Therefore, it is the capacity of the leadership to look forward. It suggests the future orientation and perceiving the possibilities or images of the things to come. Vision gives the sense of direction. It can also be referred to as a conceptual road, mapping form the existing position of the organisation to its destination in the imagined future. Vision propels one to change for a better future against the maintenance of a *status quo*. It connotes a standard of excellence, an ideal and implies a choice of values. It has quality of uniqueness. Vision is not for the complacent. Vision articulates a view of a realistic, credible, attractive future for the organisation, a condition that is better in some ways than what now exists. Renowned authority on Leadership, Kouzes and Posner reports that not every leader they interviewed used the term vision. They used purpose, focus, mission, legacy, dream goal, calling or personal agenda.

The Leadership

Based on leader's personal traits, behaviour, functioning style, decision-making process, leader-follower relationship in relation to different situations, a number of models and approaches of leadership have been developed. However, there exists low notions of leadership, which are (1) the traditional and (2) the new notions.

The traditional notions of leadership are based on power and control. Leaders are supposed to detach themselves from mundane routine work, and limit themselves to the inventing a grand plan. Magnetise a band of followers with courageous acts. Separate emotions form work and remain lonely at the top. Being on the top makes them automatically leader, and the leadership is reserved for few. Traditional notions are based on the assumptions that leadership can't be learnt.

Notions of leadership, however, have changed. The changed notions, we refer to them as new notions of leadership, contradict the assumptions of born-leaders. They characterise leadership with challenging the process, changing things, and shaking up the organisation. It could be a mother, a small model of leadership in her family, a teacher, a principal, and environmentalist, a Chief Executive Officer, CEO or a leader of a community, party or nation.

The new leadership attracts constituents not because it is in a position to command (*e.g.* Minister) and control them, but because of its unquestionable faith in the human capacity to adapt, grow, and learn. The new leadership believes in long-term strategy. Supernatural powers are not their source of dynamism. Their powers come from strong belief in a purpose, and willingness to express that conviction. Instead of commanding and controlling, this leadership serves and supports. It is involved and in touch with those whom it leads. The credibility of action is the single most determinant of whether the leader being followed or not. Therefore, the new leadership is not about a place or a position. It is an art of mobilising others to strive for shared aspirations. Leadership communicates these shared aspirations—the vision. The new notion of leadership, therefore, emphasises the role *of vision in the leadership*.

Importance of vision in leadership has been adequately acknowledged. Burns referred to this kind of leadership as 'Transformational Leadership'. Kotter expressed it in terms of three elements, establishing direction i.e. vision, strategies for achieving it and aligning people with the chosen direction and producing change.

Vision in Leadership

Vision provides strength and reflects depth in thinking process of the leader. Vision gives a clear idea of the objectives of the leader. Warren Bennis in his book *On Becoming A Leader* says that leaders come in every size, shape and disposition, but they seem to share the basic ingredients of a guiding vision. Robert Swiggett, as quoted in 'The Leadership Challenge' says "the leaders job is to create a vision. Without vision the leadership has no meaning because the people won't know where the leader wants to go and what he/she wants to do and how he/ she wants to do it." It is the vision that unites the leader and the followers for achieving common goals, and precisely that is what leadership is about.

Vision brings effectiveness to leadership. It is a bridge between the present and the future constructed by a leader. Vision is the manifestation of a leader's judgement and character and a fresh approach or new option to longstanding problems. Leadership must provide a framework of thought to the people he is leading, as they would not follow without being convinced.

Dr. B.R. Ambedkar and the Source of his Vision

Dr. B. R. Ambedkar returned to India in 1917 after spending three years at Columbia University in United States of America and one year in London School of Economics. He has earned a degree of Master of Arts in June 1915 and a Ph.D degree in June 1916. He came to London in October 1916, and enrolled for the degrees of M.Sc. (Economics) and D.Sc. (Economics) in London School of Economics and Political Science. He also joined Gray's Inn for Law for the degree of Bar at Law. He returned back to India in August 1917, as the duration of his scholarship granted to him by the Maharaja of Baroda was over. He was appointed as the Military Secretary to the Maharaja Sayajirao Gaikwad. The Maharaja's intention was to appoint Ambedkar his finance Secretary after some experience. But soon Ambedkar had to leave Baroda in sheer disgust at the harassment and treatment he received as an untouchable.

In 1918, he became a professor at Syndenham College, Bombay. He resigned in 1920, and went again to London to complete his studies. He returned to India for permanent settlement in April 1923.

Highly educated and articulate, from the very moment of his return in 1917 he was looked to as a leader of the community. In 1919, during a brief period in India between segments of his overseas education, he testified to the Southborough Committee, which was gathering information to determine the franchise for the Montagu-Chemsford reforms. He also appeared at two major conferences of untouchables during 1920, and launched a Marathi fortnightly *MOOKNAYAK* (Voice of the Mute or Dumb) in January 1920. Dr. Ambedkar's testimony reveals the difference between the Ambedkar and the other Mahar leaders as well as the leaders of Untouchables in other parts of India. In this testimony before the Southborough Committee he spoke for no group, only as the college graduate among the Untouchables of Bombay province.

Eleanor Zelliot in her essay on the Leadership of Baba Saheb Ambedkar says, "His testimony was lengthy, sophisticated, passionate, but never beyond the bound of a lawyer's plea. He fit his proposal into a total plan for the election procedures in the province for all the groups, asking only that "the hardships and disabilities entailed by the social system should not be reproduced and perpetuated in political institutions. He claimed that the Depressed Classes were entitled to representation because there was no "like-mind ness" and no "endosmosis" between Untouchables and Touchables and hence Touchables could not represent Untouchables. The Depressed Classes were "slaves" "dehumanised", and so "socialised as never to complain" and they must have communal representation "in such numbers as will enable them to claim redress", and under franchise "so low as to educate into political life as many as Untouchables as possible". Terminology used by Dr. Ambedkar in this testimony, indicate formation of his vision.

Vision in the leadership may spring from its original thinking or may be derived from an outside source. Vision, however, is generally expressed as the inner voice, the insight or the intuition in a leader, which helps him in visualising. Kouzes and Posner have defined intuition as the bringing together of knowledge and experience to produce new insights. Vision may not necessarily be a pure conception of the leader, but the leader is the one who chooses the image and articulates it into a vision and focuses attention of the people on it. Where from Dr. Ambedkar's vision sprang? What were the sources of his vision?

Lord Buddha: Dr. Ambedkar choose his three gurus from three era of Indian History—Ancient, Medieval, and Modern - all historical figures, who chose to stand up and challenge the decaying societies of their times. His first Guru was Lord Buddha, who had profound influence on him. Dr. Ambedkar appreciated these beliefs. He learnt from the life of Lord that a man could achieve greatness not merely by his royal birth, but because he was motivated by the dynamics of a social purpose and acted as 'the scourge and scavenger of the society. Lord Budha led him to question the infallibility of the Vedas; the faith in the elevation of the soul; the efficacy of rites, ceremonies, and sacrifices as means of obtaining salvation; the theory that God created man or that he came out of the body of Brahma; and the doctrine of Karma, which is the determination of man's position in present life by deeds done by him in his past life. The impact of Lord Buddha's teaching can be seen his writings.

Saint Kabir: He was the second guru of Dr. Ambedkar. Again a historical figure St. Kabir was a weaver-cum-poet of medieval period. In fact he was the leader of the band of Untouchable poets. Saint Kabir opposed Varnasharam system vehemently and challenged the superiority of Brahmans. He opposed fundamentalism of Hindus and Muslim both, and unified himself with the suffering of the downtrodden, lower castes, and untouchables. Kabir's liberalism and opposition to fundamentalism of Hindus and Muslim can be seen in

Dr. Ambedkar's book on Pakistan, where he has criticise both the communities in unequivocal terms.

Jotiba Phule: His third guru died in November 1890, merely five months before Dr. Ambedkar was born. Jotiba Phule was the Mahatama of the poor and Untouchables. Jotiba Phule Shudras and ati-Shudras and women educated and worked for their upliftment. He was the first modern Indian who questioned the hegemony of Brahmins and exposed the priest-craft through his speeches, ballads, writings and programmes. Phule's stress on education and knowledge showed a striking contrast with the upper-caste efforts to acquire technology while maintaining 'traditional' values of many cultures; he made it clear that education was a weapon to change 'eastern morals' and to bring about a kind of Cultural Revolution as well as technological one. He and his wife, Savitri Bai Phule founded Satya Shodhak Samaj, which launched a strong movement for the rights of the downtrodden. Dr. Ambedkar considered him the greatest *Shudra* of Modern India who made the lower classes of Hindus conscious of their slavery to the higher classes and who preached the gospel of that for India, social democracy was vital than Independence from foreign slavery. He dedicated his book, *who were the Shudras?* to this greatest Shudra of Modern times. Following his third Guru Jotiba Phule, Dr. Ambedkar's also considered struggle against social bondage more important than the foreign bondage.

Apart form these three personalities, John Dewey, famous American intellectual and his mentor at Colombia University in New York, Karl Marx, and Booker T. Washington, Justice Ranade also had profound influence on Dr. Ambedkar. History of Roman Empire, Irish Struggle, and Slavery in United States also shaped his actions and vision.

Dr. B.R. Ambedkar and his vision of Upliftment of Dalits

As mentioned above that the leaders job is to create a vision. Without vision the leadership has no meaning because the people won't know where the leader wants to go and what he/she wants to do and how he/she wants to do it. In fact it was the vision that differentiate Dr. Ambedkar from his contemporary leaders. His contemporary Dalit Leaders were though educating the Dalits, but have hardly analysed the socio-economic causes of their degrading and inferior position in the society. Dr. Ambedkar was fully equipped to go into the depth of the socioeconomic problems and fix the problem. In contrast to other leaders, who were petitioning to the British Government for the upliftment of the Dalits, Dr. Ambedkar emphasised on the concept of self-help or *Atta Deepo Bhava.* He realised the lack of ideological hollo wness of the Dalit Movement and provided necessary ideology to it.

Not improvement in caste status, but Annihilation of Caste: In contrast to earlier efforts of Dalit leadership claiming higher social status of *Khastriyas,* Dr. Ambedkar never claimed high caste status for Untouchables, since such claim implied an acceptance of upper caste superiority. He did not claim that the Untouchables were pre-Aryan, the original settlers of the land. Dr. Ambedkar argued that the Untouchables' position in the Indian Society was of social, not racial, origin and therefore subject to change. By 1935, Dr. Ambedkar had concluded that unless caste is totally annihilated, degrading position of Dalits in Indian society wouldn't improve. For him, caste embodied Brahamanical superiority.

Alternative to Brahamanical Social Order (BSO): For Dr. Ambedkar eradication of Caste required a repudiation of 'Hinduism' as a religion and adoption of an alternative to this religion. He considered Buddha Dhamma and alternative to Brahamanical Social Order or alternative to Hinduism. His choice of Buddhism was essentially linked to his strong dedication to the reality of India, its rich historical heritage, which he sought to wrest from the imposition of a 'Hindu' identity.

Rationalism: He stood for rationalism. His commandments are reflecting his rationalism.

State Socialism: He stood for a responsible state, taking due care of the despised, downtrodden and socially and economically weaker sections.

Autonomous Dalit Movement: Dr. Ambedkar firmly believed in an Autonomous Dalit Movement with a constantly attempted alliance of the socially and economically exploited.

If we analyse these cornerstones, we find that he stood for an alternative form of society, economy, polity, religion and culture. His programmes were intended to integrate the Untouchables into Indian Society in modern, not traditional ways, and on as high a level as possible. This was in contrast with Gandhi's 'Ideal Bhangi' who would continue to do sanitation work even though his status would equal that of a Brahman. Dr. Ambedkar wanted depressed classes "to raise their educational standard so that they may know their own conditions, have aspirations to rise to the level of highest Hindu and be in a position to use political power as a means to an end."

Ambedkar vociferously advocated equality. He meant not equal status of *Varna,* but equality in social, economic and political opportunity for all. He said "Equality may be a fiction but nonetheless one must accept it as the governing principle."

Educate, Agitate and Organise

Realising the divisive and water-tights compartmentalisation, Dr. Ambedkar stressed on self-help. He adopted quadrilateral strategy of empowering the Dalits. The first step of this strategy was to educate the Dalits, so that they know the ills, evils that prevent them from progressing. He realised that a community that has been totally deprived from acquiring any kind of resources, education would be the easiest and within reach of the Dalits. He visualised that no Government can afford to keep such a big mass of people illiterate and ignorant. However, he stressed that Dalit themselves have to take lead in educating their lot. He founded People's Education Society for this purpose, which established first educational institute run in Bombay by an Indian Agency. By this, Dr. Ambedkar showed that Dalits were not solely dependent on the Government.

Considering education as the basic and necessary investment, Dr. Ambedkar expected that by acquiring education and knowledge, many more people like him would take up the cause of the Dalits. Educated Dalit mind would agitate over the injustice inflicted and would fight against it. Though Dr. Ambedkar recognised the indifferentism perpetuated by the Brahamanical Social Order, but left this to be addressed by the Brahamanical curriculum designers, which continue to hold this indifferentism. Therefore, agitation of mind is yet to be seen in proportion to the education.

Agitated mind, as Dr. Ambedkar presumed, would force educated people to form organisations and they would act to fix the problems. Many people, quite often, who profess Dr. Ambedkar, limit his slogan to these three points. But to this author, the actual message of Dr. Ambedkar lies in "have faith in your strength." Right from the beginning, Dr. Ambedkar emphasises self-help. He says, "Self-help is the best help". He also made it loud and clear to Dalits that "it is out of hard struggle and ceaseless struggle alone that one derives strength, confidence and recognition." He directed Dalits on many occasion that you must stand on your feet and fight as best as best you can for your rights. Power and prestige will come to you through struggle. Many political leaders, who eye on our numbers, profess that politics is the key that can unlock all the locks, forgetting that 'it is not enough that a people are numerically in majority. They must be always watchful, strong, well-educated and self-respecting to attain and maintain success. Therefore, Dalits have to organise themselves to improve their lot themselves. No more begging pots.

EDUCATION OF DALITS : BEYOND LITERACY

Education of Dalits has sprouted from the seeds of socio-political awareness nurtured by the great visionary Dr. Baba

Saheb Ambedkar and various Social reformers like Narayan Guru, Mahatma Phule, Raja Ram Mohan Roy and so on so forth. Education of Dalits is still in its infancy. History is a mute witness to the nagging truth that a particular group of people has been marginalised merely because of their identity as a caste in the Hindu society. The caste formed the basis for a high degree of polarisation in access to knowledge and means of production. The perpetuation of social and economic inequalities further heightened the division of society along the caste lines wherein the occupation and the status used to be determined at the time of birth and not by the calibre of the individual. The instrument used for perpetuation of the socioeconomic differentials was the separation of work from knowledge and power. The working class was denied the access to education as it was considered a privilege of few upper castes. The denial of education was essential to prevent them from acquiring rights in productive assets, mainly lands, which were in the hands of upper castes who seldom worked on it. On the other hand , the lower castes being without land had no option except to seek employment from the land owning class at their mercy.

The Indian political system underwent transformation. The bases economy also underwent change posing a new set of economic challenges and the solution did not come from the landholdings alone, thus the Sun of a new politico-economy era arose sprinkling a new light of hope to the depriveds. New avenues of employment appeared and the monopoly of Oriental studies was challenged; Macaulay's education replaced the traditional system of education and thus Dalits got an opportunity of having access to education.

Education is a broad term, which encompasses the whole gamut of knowledge. However, today, Education of Dalit, in terms of Govt. is confined to Literacy only. Not to speak of educated Dalits, even the literate are very few among the Dalits. A statistical profile of literacy of the Dalits in the chapter ahead, will prove undoubtedly, that a lot is to be done to make the Dalits even literate. Literacy of the masses is an obligation on the Govt. in welfare democratic system of the Country. Literacy is the first step towards education. No Govt. would deny the fact that education is the real investment. The economic value of a good education has been known to the economists for a long time; e.g. Marshall! (1890) And Smith (1776). People with higher level of education earn more on the average. They contribute more in the process of economic development. Presently with the introduction of the human capital theory the relationship between schooling and future earnings has been stressed. The human capital theory has become very popular these days and U.N.O has started publishing Human Development Report wherein education/ literacy is an indicator of the human development.

At present, 35 per cent of the total Indian population is illiterate. It is coincident that among the illiterates the SCs and STs form the major chunk. The reasons can be seen in the mirror of the past history of India. Govt. of India would, therefore, be interested more in raising the literacy level than providing relevant education to the commoners, and among the commoners incidentally majority happen to be the Dalits (SCs and STs). The reasons for not taking an appropriate action by the Govt. are best known to the people at the helm of affairs.

Education in India : A Comparision

It would be injustice to the topic if any weightage is not attached to the overall scenario of education in India in comparison to other countries. Please bear with to have a statistical and comparative analysis of the education in India. There are 165 countries in the world, which are seriously concerned about education and spend certain amount of their budget on education. Fortunately India is one of them. India has a full-fledged Department of Education under Ministry of Human Resource Development. I am sure, you must be very curious to know the ranking of India among 165 countries. Please hold your breath. India is one of the few countries where higher education is highly subsidised. Besides all, India holds 115th position among 165 countries.

Though there are various reasons responsible for the above situation, however a few of them can be enumerated here. India spends just 3.8 per cent of its G.D.P. towards education whereas developed countries spend more than 9 to 10 per cent of their G.D.P on education. Forty per cent of schools function in without-roofed structure. Numbers of dropouts are many. Attendance of teachers in rural areas is dismal and last but not the least the failure of Government in enthusing the importance of education in common masses.

Difference between Literacy and Education

The word 'Literacy' has been derived from the word 'Literary' where the connotation of literary may have a reference to 'Literature' in general, and books, language and authors of books and articles in particular. Literacy may therefore, by implication, relate to the lowest and crudest form of education, as it refers to the familiarity with the written alphabetical forms, which should automatically involve the ability to read and write in a given script. Literacy provides merely a wheel of learning. It enables an individual to read and write and also to understand the thing upto a certain limit based upon the inherited ability of an individual to comprehend the things. The process further continues and the literate is exposed to the whole gamut of learning, which if perused, can make the person educated.

Education refers to the provision of learning opportunities in a purposeful and organised manner through various means including, but not limited to schools and other education. Basically, education shapes an individual in a desired manner. It depends upon the type of education, being imparted to the people as to what is supposed to be taught. Education is considered the next destination after literacy. However, education devoid of literacy becomes difficult but not impossible. Education has further been divided into various types, such as Formal and Informal education, Basic education etc. The then Prime Minister of India Indira Gandhi had once rightly stated "Education is a liberating force, and in our age it is also a democratising force, cutting across the barriers of caste and class, smoothing out inequalities imposed by birth and other circumstances."

Literacy Situation among the Dalits

Economic disparity and prejudice have always been associated with the Dalits. They restrain and restrict them from coming out of the vicious circle of socially and economically distorted lifestyles and also prevent the fuller development of their academic and intellect aspirations. Frankly speaking, the socio-economic factors obstruct and prevent the fuller growth of a Dalit child, putting him at a relative disadvantage against the child belonging to Non-Dalits in the competition for advancement in life whether it is in the form of acquiring education or for competing in the labour market for employment.

As such the Dalits socially occupying the lowest rung of the hierarchical ladder, have been living under the weight of socio-psychological alienation of powerlessness, meaninglessness and complete social estrangement. in spite of the fact the govt.'s efforts towards amelioration of their condition is much below the expectation. *What is more frightening that the govt. is yet to realise the intensity of the fact, not the problem. Every problem has a solution and if any problem has no solution it is no longer a problem but a fact to be accepted. Once this fact is accepted, the ways can be searched.*

Since India's independence almost five precious decades are over and India has been able to achieve only 65 per cent of literacy. India where women are considered to be an epitome of love and the essence of origin are more illiterates than men. The importance of an educated mother is known to all. It is irony to note that women among Dalits folk are educationally the most backward. A table covering all the states and Union territories of India in respect of literacy rates by sex of general, Scheduled Castes and Scheduled Tribes population on the basis of 1991 Census can throw light upon the educational condition of the Dalits men and women.

The author prefers to call both SCs And STs Dalits on the ground of the commonness of the nature and intensity of atrocities committed upon both of them. It may be taken in a different connotation by few of us because of some sociological reasons.

Literacy among Different Caste Groups of Dalits

There is no denying the fact that among the Dalits there are castewise variations in attainment of literacy. In every state of India there are some castes which have much higher literacy rate than the other castes among Dalits. Although the over all literacy is very low but certain caste groups either because of their rank in the caste hierarchy or due to their small numerical strength or otherwise have attained a unique position as far as the educational attainment is concerned. For example, Bhartar in Kerala have attained an overall literacy rate of 79.8 per cent; Adi-Dharmi has 80 per cent literacy rate in Delhi.

However, when it comes to deprivation and illiteracy, the position in respect of many castes is very depressing. The gap in literacy rate of different caste groups even within the Dalits is extremely high—ranging from almost total illiteracy to that of almost universal literacy. For example, the Mushars in Bihar with a population of about 1.7 million have been reeling under total illiteracy. The literacy in their case is less than 5 per cent.

The fact that the over all literacy among the Dalits is low as a group, vividly indicates that excepting a few castes, the educational attainment among the Dalits is significantly low. Warranting immediate attention of the govt. in general and the few fortunates among the Dalits who have seen the Sun of education in particular to rise and do the needful immediately.

Education and Employment Position of Dalits

The prospects of employment have always been a matter of consideration in so far as education is concerned. Irrespective of the castes almost every one, who pursues education, has an aspiration to get employment matching one's educational qualification. Education has always been attached economic value. Role of education in economic growth at micro level and its impact on private incomes have got worldwide acceptance of the economists.

The pivotal role of education in the development process has been recognised right from the inception of planning in India. Third five year plan (1962-67), for example, had emphasised the role of education in the process of economic development. Thus, education is the single most important factor in achieving rapid economic development and technological progress and in creating a social order founded on the values of freedom, social justice and equal opportunity.

Employment, which is the only and solitary means of the economic and social elevation of the Dalits have acquired direct relation with the education. It would be blunder to talk, at this stage, of literacy only when the knowledge explosion has shrunk the world in a global village. Education for all has become *sine qua non* for the over all development of the country in general and the Dalits in particular. Educational development will determine the share of a group of persons in the economy, which will act as a deciding factor for social advancement too.

Role of Government in Dalit Education

We must acknowledge that whatever growth and development have been made in the furtherance of literacy and education of the Dalits, the role of the Govt. has, undoubtedly been significant. One may, of course, say that the pace has been slow and much below the envisioned level. The orientation and thrust of the education is undergoing tremendous change. The relative change is lacking in the case of the Dalits. The Govt. is expected to play pro-active-role but the Govt. is moving with the speed of tortoise which is bound to take the Dalits to the same position of socio-economic estrangement from where they had started. The growing apathy of the Govt. is mainly attributed to the following factors:

(*a*) Non-association of the Dalit-intellectuals either in formulation or implementation of the education policies.

(*b*) Inherent biased approach of the policy makers towards the downtrodden because of the threats of social upheavals.

(*c*) Lack of educational infrastructure in rural areas where the major chunk of the Dalits population lives.

(*d*) Widespread existence of attitudinal discrimination (mental untouchability) in the name of caste in place of physical untouchability.

(*e*) Lack of awareness among the Dalits about the importance of education with regard to their social standing.

Concept of Merit in Education

The concept of higher marks has always been made a yardstick of merit. Knowingly or unknowingly the concept of merit has been wrongly propagated to keep the Dalit talents away from the mainstream. Without giving any consideration to the limitation under which a child of the Dalit acquires the education and without having the right kind of mechanism to assess the merit, one is dubbed to be less meritorious than the convent educated, who is of no worth except being versed colloquially and dexterously.

Nobody will deny the importance of merit in any sphere of life. Merit must be given due place in education. There should be a proper mechanism to assess the merit, it so happens that, if somebody scores good marks just by cramming, is bestowed with medals. Merit is a subjective term, it should not be quantified. Talent constitutes an eminent part of the merit. Talent is of two type—first is man made and second is god-gifted. Thus, anybody can be talented. The Hyppocratic stand on merit is also a criterion of discrimination. Dalits are generally the victim of this h pocrisy.

Vision for the Education of the Dalits

Education is not an education if it does not imbibe the value of education. Howsoever educated one may be but lack of values will put him or her at worse position than that of an illiterate. The values of education as perceived today are Equity with Justice, Uprightness, Scientific temper, Mutual regard and appreciation, Socialism, Secularism and democratic principles. Educated are divided in two categories today. One, having acquired the above values act as soothers trouble shooters while the others, who do not acquire the above values are trouble makers. Both have one similarity that both are educated but one has been able to shape the knowledge acquired through education in right perspective while the other has mixed education with the mythical and the Hyppocratic values. The outcome of the first type of education is development and growth of the ability to accept one's mistake boldly, pardon the others easily and siding with the justice invariably. The outcome of the others is to behave in pseudo fashion, (To say something and to do something) Create the atmosphere to hate others and allow others to hate in turn, and finally to suppress the scientific temper with mythical science.

Thus, the vision for the education of the Dalit should be *"Spread of right type of education among the Dalits beyond literacy.*

In order to achieve the said mission the following objectives/goals should be drawn:

(*a*) All the educationally and economically capable Dalits should be appealed to contribute their mite for the cause of the education of the Dalits

(*b*) The Govt. should be impressed upon to play pro-active roles in spread of the education for the Dalits

(c) Education should be linked with employment so that the relevance of education is not lost.

(d) Awareness campaign towards education must be launched forthwith.

Plans to give a practical shape of the above objectives can be further chalked out by the Dalit Organisations participating in the National Conference.

REFERENCES

Ahir, D.C., *The Legacy of Dr. Ambedkar*, B.R. Publishing Corporation, Delhi, 1990, p. 9.

Burns, J.M., *Leadership*, Harper and Row, New York, 1978.

Gujrati, Anita, Vision in Leadership, assignment paper of Master of Educational Management, 1999, Flinders University of South Australia, Australia, p. 1.

James, Kouzes M. and Posner Barry Z.: The leadership Challenge: How to get Extraordinary things done in the Organisations, Jossey-Bass Publishers, USA, 1995.

Kotter, J. P., *The Leadership Factor*, Free Press, New York, 1988

Omvedt, Gail, *Dalits and the Democratic Revolution- Dr. Ambedkar and the Dalit Movement in Colonial India*, Sage Publications, New Delhi, 1994, p. 144.

Warren, Bennis & Nanus Burt: Leaders, Harper and Row, 1995. *Quoted in Anita Gujrati:* Vision in Leadership, assignment paper of Master of Educational Management, 1999, Flinders University of South Australia, Australia, p. 1.

Zelliot, Eleanor, *Leadership of Baba Saheb Ambedkar in her Book From Untouchable to Dalit Essays on the Ambedkar Movement*, Manohar Publishers and Distributors, New Delhi, 1998 p. 65.

Zelliot, Eleanor, *Gandhi and Ambedkar: A Study in Leadership in her Book From Untouchable to Dalit Essays on the Ambedkar Movement*, Manohar Publishers and Distributors, New Delhi, 1998 p. 158.

12

DEVELOPMENT OF SCHEDULED CASTES AND SCHEDULED TRIBES

In the ancient India, the backward castes had been denied all kinds of social and economic endowments. Hence, they had been lagging behind in the process of development. The social and economic deprivation among Scheduled Castes had been most common during pre-and post-Independence. Therefore, there was a need of number of special safeguard policies. One of that is, 'Reservation Policy' in the Government Recruitment. The objective of the reservation policy is to eradicate the socioeconomic disparities which existed in the society.

Article 15 (4) and 16 (4) of the Indian constitution has made provision of reservation for backward classes in educational institutions and public employment. The reservation policy has to be followed by both, Central and State government. "When the first Backward Classes Commission was constituted on 29th January, 1953 under the chairmanship of Kakasaheb Kalelkar, he wanted economic backwardness to be the criterion and not caste in deciding backwardness. But he had to field to the majority of the members who wanted caste to be the criterion, to decide the backwardness".

Finally, the government accepted the reservation policy. The social and economic up-liftment of SCs/STs could be made through the reservation policy. Social inequality is a product of Hindu-Caste System. Hence, protective discrimination policy like 'reservation policy' must be adopted. The Government of India has been following this policy in the recruitment. The reservation policy is being followed in recruitment and also in education. The author has analysed here, the position of reservation in the Central recruitment and has tried to find out the rate of disparity in the implementation of reservation policy for Scheduled Castes. The disparity has been calculated in accordance with the reservation rate prescribed by the Government of India compared with the reservation position in the Central Government.

An Overview of Indian Scheduled Castes

The 'Sudras' were classified as inferior and the last varna to other three varnas, in ancient social system in India. Along with this several social, economic and political restrictions were imposed on them. This classified 'Sudras' includes various caste groups, which have suffered social and economic inequity since ages. They had to stay outside the village. The concept of pollution was attached to them and they were treated as untouchable castes. These untouchables or castes were officially defined as depressed castes in 1932 and they were systematically listed in the 1931-Census of India. Gandhi called the untouchables as *'Harijans'*. *'Hari'* means 'God' and 'Jan' means 'People', *i.e.* 'People of God'. The meaning of this word in *Hindi, Marathi* and other languages is, ' a child, whose father's identity is unknown'. Therefore, the name *'Harijan'* was opposed and hated by the untouchables.

The Simon Commission in 1935 first coined the term 'Scheduled Castes'. All the untouchable castes, which were listed in 1931-Census of India, came to be known as the 'Scheduled Castes' (SCs) through the Government of India Act of 1935. In the mean time, the Government published a list of Scheduled Castes under the Government of India (Scheduled Castes) Order, 1936. The Government of India in post-Independence period carried the same idea. According to the Constitution of India, under article 341(1), the President of India, after consultation with the Governor, may specify, "the castes, races, tribes or parts of groups within castes or races, which shall be deemed to be Scheduled Castes". Accordingly, the President has notified the Scheduled Castes in the order called 'Constitution (Scheduled Castes) Order-1950' and the 'Scheduled Castes and Scheduled Tribes List (Modification) Order-1956'.

However, under article 341(2), the Parliament of India by law can include or exclude the above-mentioned groups from the list of the Scheduled Castes. In a simple way, in contemporary period, the Scheduled Castes are defined under article 366 (244) of the Constitution of India as, "the Scheduled Castes means such Castes, Races, Tribes or parts of or groups within such Castes, races or tribes, deemed under article 341 to be Scheduled Castes for the purpose of this Constitution." Thus the Scheduled Castes are those castes which are listed as Scheduled Castes in the Constitution of India.

The Scheduled Castes constitute a significant demographic strength in India. In the year 1935, the Scheduled Castes were estimated as about 5 crores., in the year 1981, estimated as 10.475 crores and in the year 1991, population was estimated as 13.822 croes, which constitutes 16.48 per cent of the total population. The decadal growth of Scheduled Castes in India over 1991 was 30 per cent, which is more than decadal growth of general population 81 per cent of Scheduled Castes are living in rural area. Nearly 84 per cent of the SCs. population live in ten states. In the states of 'Himachal Pradesh', 'West-Bengal' and 'Uttar Pradesh', 25.34 per cent of its total, 23.62 per cent of its total and 21.04 per cent of its total population, respectively, belongs to Scheduled Castes. In 'Maharashtra', 11.10 per cent of its population is SCs, interestingly, 28 per cent of the total population of 'Punjab' belong to 'Scheduled Castes'. Other states like 'Bihar' (14.56 per cent of its total), 'Haryana' (19.75 per cent of its total), 'Karnataka' (16.38 per cent of its total), 'Madhya Pradesh' (14.54 per cent of its total),

'Orissa' (16.20 per cent of its total) 'Andhra Pradesh' (15.93 per cent of its total) and 'Tamil Nadu' (19.18 per cent of its total) have significant strength of Scheduled Castes population.

According to the 2001 Census, the Scheduled Caste population in India is 166,635,700 persons, constituting 16.2 per cent of the country's total population. Being rural people, four fifth (79.8 per cent) of them live in rural areas and rest one-fifth (20.2 per cent) live in urban areas. The sex ratio of 936 females per thousand males is slightly higher than national average of 933 sex ratio. The highest percentage of Scheduled Caste population to the total Scheduled Caste population of the country live in Uttar Pradesh (21.1 per cent) followed by West Bengal (11.1 per cent) and Bihar (7.8 per cent), Andhra Pradesh (7.4 per cent) and Tamil Nadu (7.1.per cent). In fact, more than 57 per cent of total Scheduled Castes population inhibit in these five States. Proportionately, the largest proportion of population of the Scheduled Castes to total population of the State is in Punjab (28.9 per cent), followed by Himachal Pradesh (24.7 per cent) and West Bengal (23 per cent). In Andhra Pradesh, Karnataka and Pondicherry proportion of SC population is exactly equal to the National average of 16.2 per cent. The smallest concentration of the Scheduled Caste population is in the North-Eastern tribal States such as Mizoram (with negligible or only 272 persons) followed by Meghalaya (0.5 per cent) and Arunachal Pradesh (0.6 per cent).

Implementation of Reservation Policy in India

The Central Government recruitment has been an important and largest area, where the reservation policy can be implemented effectively. But over the years, the status of reservation in this area has been weak. (See Table No.1) Immediately, after the Independence, since, the educational status of Scheduled Castes (SCs) was poor, this factor must be considered. The class of the post can be classified into four, namely, 'Class I', 'Class II', 'Class III' and 'Class IV'. The Class I posts are very important, which are involved in the decision making process. Whereas, Class II posts are also equally important. But Class III and Class IV posts are classified as inferior posts. It includes, *'peons'*, *'sweeper'* etc. Over the years, the representation of SCs in class I posts, has been increasing at a steady rate. It was just 0.35 per cent to the total number of posts in 1953, which reached to 10.13 per cent in 1995. The prescribed quota of reservation for SCs is 15 per cent of the total posts.

Yet there remains a backlog of about 4.87 per cent of the total. At national level, this figure may include hundreds of posts. It means, the SCs have been kept away from the decision making process. This could be stated as, one important reason, for huge backlog of SCs in the recruitment. Similar trend could be found in Class II posts, where the representation of SCs was 1.29 per cent in 1953, which reached 13.13 per cent in 1995. Here also backlog could be estimated at about 1.87 per cent of its total posts. Altogether, Class I and Class II backlog in the reservation has been in significant size. The growth of reservation in the recruitment has been slow.

The reservation status of SCs in class III posts in 1953 was 4.52, which increased to 15.46 per cent in 1995. The representation in the present era is satisfactory. More interestingly, in Class IV, the representation of SCs has been higher from the beginning, i.e. in the year 1953, it was 20.52 per cent and in the year 1995, it was 20.46 per cent. The reservation status in Class IV has more than the requirement. This is because, except SCs/STs and other backward castes, no one from upper castes, applies for the post like 'sweeper'. It means, in the government recruitment also, there could be found a *'Varna'* System. The caste system has been percolated in the government services. The main part of the reservation policy is that, the Class I and II backlog must be filled as soon as possible. But the problem is that, in the contemporary period, the government is adopting 'Zero Recruitment Policy'. In this situation, the SCs may be losing its posts or the rights of reservation. This could be stated as an injustice to the SCs.

Table 1
Reservation Status of Scheduled Castes in Central Government Recruitment

Year	*Class I*	*Class I*	*Class II*	*Class*
1953	00.35	01.29	04.52	20.52
1965	01.64	02.82	08.88	17.73
1970	02.36	03.84	09.27	18.09
1975	03.43	04.98	10.27	18.64
1979	04.83	08.07	11.54	19.16
1992	09.70	11.60	15.80	20.70
1995	10.13	13.13	15.46	20.46

Source : 1. Department of Personnel, Government of India, Report-1993 2. Social Welfare Committee for SCs/STs Report-99-2000.

Relative Disparity in the Implementation of Reservation Policy in India

The reservation policy for Scheduled Castes is most important, since it is linked with their social and economic identity. Reservation is the right of the Scheduled Castes, however, there have been high rate of disparity in the implementation of reservation policy in India. The rate of disparity can be calculated after 1979-80, since before, the educational level of Scheduled Castes was not satisfactory. But in the present context, the Scheduled Castes have achieved a satisfactory level of education all over India. Therefore, the author has calculated the rate of disparity after 1979-80 in relation to the rate of reservation determined by the Government of India. As per the Government of India, the reservation quota for Scheduled Castes is 15 per cent. The rate of disparity over the years has been declining. In Class I posts, the disparity was higher (67.8 per cent) in 1979, which declined to 35.3 per cent in 1992 and further declined to 31.3 per cent in 1995. However, there still exists a significant level of disparity in the implementation reservation policy. In case of Class II posts, the disparity was 46.2 per cent in 1979, which declined to 22.66 per cent in 1992 and then to 12.6 per cent in 1995. In these two categories of the posts, there exists significant level of disparity in the implementation of reservation. These posts are important, which are part of decision-making process. Chart No. 1 explains the trend in the rate of disparity over the years in comparison to other categories of posts. In case of Class III and IV posts, the implemented reservation is more than the prescribed. This indicates negative disparity. These posts are inferior level posts, hence, except the SCs, hardly any one is ready to work. This is a result of 'Hindu Caste System'. And once, in the government sector, the caste structure has been strictly established through the occupations.

Table 2
Disparity in the Implementation of Reservation Policy SCs. in India

(All Figures in Per cent)

Year	*Class I*		*Class I*		*Class II*		*Class IV*	
	AIR	*Disp.*	*AIR.*	*Disp.*	*AIR.*	*Disp.*	*AIR.*	*Disp.*
1979	04.83	67.8	08.07	46.2	11.54	23.06	19.76	-31.7
1992	09.70	35.3	11.60	22.66	15.80	5.3-3.0	20.70	38.0-
1995	10.3	31.3	13.13	12.6	15.46	--	20.46	36.4

Source: 1. Department of Personnel, Government of India, Report-1993.
2. Social Welfare Committee for SCs/STs Report-99-2000.

Note: 1. Rate of disparity in the reservation has been calculated on the basis of above data.
2. A.R.=Actual Implemented Reservation, Disp. = The Rate of Disparity.

Economic Consequences

The disparity in the implementation of reservation policy for SCs has resulted into serious economic consequences, which are closely connected to their life. When one person from SCs family gets a job, the whole family remains dependent on him. The dependency ratio in SCs family is higher. Therefore, the disparity has resulted into huge economic losses to the SCs, as a whole. Although the government is trying to reduce the disparity, in the phase of globalisation, large number of posts have been wiped by the government itself. Therefore, the disparity has affected adversely, the social, economic and cultural life of the Scheduled Castes.

According to the report of the Working Group on the Empowering of Scheduled Castes, over 1,13,450 job opportunities were lost by the scheduled castes in the Central Government during the period 1992-97. Eradication of reservation posts on large scale could be seen in all state Government. The reasons for such step are given as 'Excess Recruitment', 'Globalisation', 'Efficiency' etc. During the last few years, several lakhs of reservation posts have been wiped out. Majority of these posts were high-class posts, which can play important role in the determination of the economic position of the society. This is social injustice; above all, this is an violation of Indian constitution. In the light of economics, the Scheduled Castes lost huge number of sources of livelihood. This policy may create once again, the economic slavery, in the economic system.

Over the years, all the branches of Government Sectors have been neglecting the reservation policy. Even after fifty-nine years of Independence, the reservation status of SCs in all Government branches has been unsatisfactory. The reservation policy has been underutilised. The rate of disparity in the implementation has been high. In the phase of globalisation, the government policy is discouraging the reservation policy. This situation has created various social and economic problems in the contemporary period. In a way, the social justice for the SCs has been denied even in the contemporary period. An inspite of Constitutional provision, the reservation policy has been neglected. This must be taken as violation of Constitution. There must be significant representation of SCs in the decision-making posts, which could help further, for the development of SCs, as a whole. Similar kind of trend could be found among Scheduled Tribes (STs).

POLICY FOR THE UPLIFTMENT OF DALITS AND NEGLECTED COMMUNITIES

All-round development is possible only if the multi-ethnic groups, multi-lingual and various groups and communities within the country develop in proportionate manner. Such type of development will help to utilise their inherent skill, ability and knowledge in the nation development process on the one hand, and on the other, assist to uplift the living standard of the *dalits*, neglected, downtrodden and oppressed classes by creating employment opportunities through the mobilisation of local resources. Taking note of this fact, various programmes are being implemented to uplift of this community. Serious efforts are still needed to bring this class of people who have been backwarded from every aspect of socio-politico-economic issues because of the prevalence of aged old poverty and social deprivation. In number of places, this section of the population could not get social respect in practice due to existence of caste system (though termed illegal) and inhuman behaviour because of ineffective enforcement of acts, which categorically has made the caste system punishable.

As a matter of fact, the community could not fully-establish its role in the socio-economic development of the country. The reasons behind such scenario are lack of proper coordination among various agencies in the implementation of targeted programmes; absence of proper linkage between needs and targeted programmes, for they were implemented without adequate study by the centre; their backwardness in educational field and awareness level; and failure to mainstreaming such community in development activities as an important stakeholder. Keeping these limitations and weaknesses in mind, in order to identify this class/community, extensive study and research work will be undertaken to explore development possibilities of this community. Also, special steps will be taken to implement the outcome of research and studies for their betterment during the Tenth Plan period. The programmes will be initiated from the very beginning of the Tenth Plan to involve them, as co-actors and partners, in the mainstreaming of nation building activities.

Review of the Ninth Plan

The Ninth Plan had given major role to the government to create a congenial atmosphere for exploiting inherent potentiality, skill and knowledge with the people of the oppressed and neglected communities for increasing their living standard through their involvement and participation, as co-actors and partners along with other communities of the country. The Ninth Plan had adopted the objectives to end the existing gap between the people of oppressed groups and other communities by abolishing prevailing social discrimination of the country and to eliminate the poverty and unemployment prevalent among oppressed and neglected community within the next 20 years period as envisaged in long term perspective. The policies and implementation strategies formulated to realise the objectives were to empower these groups economically and socially, to conserve and modernise their professional skill and jobs, to increase access to loan through the creation of social capital, to make obligatory to allocate certain per cent of grant-in-aid provided by the government to the local bodies (i.e., DDCs and VDCs) for their economic uplift and development, to expand coverage of scholarship program in the secondary and higher education and to provide this section/class access to technical education. During the period, scholarship was provided to 513 students from oppressed society in higher education and 5,183 in school level under the neglected, dalits and oppressed community upliftment programme.

However, Rs 25 per month as scholarship provided to children of oppressed community by the Ministry of Education and the various kinds of support programs lunched by different NGOs and social organisations as well as their achievement has not been accounted. During the period, seven projects were implemented in the areas of health, sanitation and drinking water for the backward ethnic groups. In addition, it is recorded that financial support was made available to various helpless-oppressed-children orphanage homes. The seminars were conducted and weekly radio broadcasting programme was operated to increase public awareness about problem of backward ethnic community at the national level for their upliftment. Moreover, 65 income and skill oriented projects were implemented in 37 districts of the kingdom. The employment oriented computer training courses were organised for the unemployed individuals of oppressed classes. The National *Dalit* Commission was constituted for the protection of their rights. The acts and regulations in this area were formulated as well as work related to setting up institutional structure has been undertaken.

Long-Term Vision

The long-term vision is to raise the living standard of *dalits* and neglected communities by empowering them on the basis of equality, and mainstream them into the development efforts while enhancing their self-respect.

Objectivesof the Tenth Plan

Dalits, who have been lagged behind in the society due to the old social systems and beliefs, will be empowered on the basis of equality, and their access to the development efforts will be enhanc ed.

Strategy

Traditional social systems and beliefs have made some sections of the society socially and economically backward. It is necessary to undertake programmes of correcting various human development index HDI related to this section of the population through targeted programmes, since they are generally isolated from the mainstreaming of development. The implementation of programes, such as, making these people capable, for greater representation in the political process, providing access to various income generating activities will not only promote social justice but also contribute to social development. In this context, the strategies of the plan are as mentioned below.

1. By identifying oppressed, downtrodden, neglected communities the social oppression and discrimination against them will be abolished through the development of this class.
2. Through social and economic empowerment, their knowledge, skill and intelligence will be mainstreamed in the development process, and their possible contribution in the national level will be identified and encouraged to implement.
3. The traditional occupations of the downtrodden and oppressed community will be modernised and the goods produced by them will be made competitive. The institutional arrangement for marketing of such products will be undertaken.
4. The dalits and oppressed's social dignity promoting programs will be emphasised, while appropriating national productive resources and opportunities.

Policy and Working Policy

- Special measures will be taken to increase access of this group to programmes like education, health, sanitation, etc.
- The programmes to ensure the rights and development of downtrodden community will be formulated and implemented under the sectoral ministries and local le vel bodies (like DDC & VDC).
- Priority will be accorded to *dalit* (oppressed class) representation in all types of users' committees formed for development works, in the school management committees, local bodies, NGOs and social organisations.
- Necessary arrangement will be made for coordination by undertaking monitoring and evaluation of the I/ NGOs' programmes.

- Efforts will be made from the government, NGOs and private sector to put an end to caste discrimination by identifying discriminatory situation against *dalit* community.
- The award of scholarship programme will be extended to increase the access of the *dalit* community to education for wide coverage. Likewise, access of *dalit* and neglected community to technical subjects under higher education will also be increased along with the extension of programmes related to educational scholarship for this community will be effectively implemented
- The idea that the inherent skill, efficiency and specialisation traits possessed by the *dalit* community is the asset of the nation will be propagated.
- The *dalit* and oppressed community will be empowered economically and socially by involving them in the development process by implementing targeted programmes. In such programmes, *dalit* women will be given due priority.
- Emphasis will be given to institutional empowering of the National *Dalit* Commission
- The ancestral occupational skills and jobs of the *dalits* and neglected communities will be conserved and modernised. Their traditional occupations will be developed as an alternative as well as a dignified source of employment. Access to institutional credit will be increased through the programmes like social savings mobilisation and loan.
- By providing credit and refining their skills, people of the *dalit* and oppressed community will be attracted in foreign employment opportunities.
- The subjects on *dalit* and oppressed community related to their problems, untouchability and existing conservatism in the school level curriculum will be

included and topics of discrimination will be taken out to increase public awareness.

- Major role will be given to local bodies (like DDC & VDC) to formulate as well as implement programmes for economic improvement and social upliftment of *dalit* community.

Social Programmes

- Various programmes will be undertaken to discourage the religious and social conservatism prevalent in the *non*-dalit community and to wipe out the century old inferiority complex of *dalit* community.
- Decision making capacity and leadership quality in the *dalit* women will be developed by abolishing domestic violence and other types of harassment against women

Educational Programme

- Free education up to secondary level will be provided to the children of schoolgoing age of all *dalit* communities.
- The access to higher education particularly technical and vocational institutions will be made easy for *dalit* communities.
- The participation of the *dalit* communities in the education centres is poor. It will be increased by appointing *dalit* females if available and in case they are not available other male members from that community will be appointed to school teaching posts.
- The stipend received by the students of *dalit* communities will be increased and manage all types of scholarships. The campaign for bringing public awareness in the society will be initiated by mobilising *dalit* students receiving stipend.
- By preparing curriculum, which develops and promotes skills of *dalit* communities, arrangement will be made to provide technical and vocational education

- NGOs will be encouraged to use more service of *dalit* and oppressed communities by recruiting them in the posts to the possible extent as well as in the local level programmes related to them.
- Special programmes will be launched to educate the people of *dalit* and so called untouchables like Musahar, Batar, Doom, Halkhor and such other who are educationally backward. In such programmes, special attention will be paid to women of *dalit* community
- The *dalit* literacy campaign will be made as an important part of the National Development Volunteers Service.

Health Programme

- Awareness will be increased through mobilisation of social organisations, government institutions and NGOs to improve the life style, balanced diet including dietary habit and sanitary condition of the *dalit* and neglected community.
- Increase access of *dalit* and oppressed community to primary and basic health services.
- By providing safe and pure drinking water to *dalit* and oppressed community, special health care service will be made available to pregnant women and women of maternity stage.
- Health services will be provided with priority to *dalit* community under the programmes lunched by the health institutions providing basic and primary health care services, such as the mobile health camps. In this manner, if the training and public awareness related seminars are to be conducted, it will be organised in the localities inhabited by *dalit* communities. Special arrangement will be made to provide drinking water and sanitation in their settlement areas. Also, *dalit* people are encouraged to run programmes related to drinking water and sanitation through their users community.

- Infant mortality rate, child mortality rate and maternal mortality rate are quite high in the *dalit* community. In this context, this community will be made as the target group of health and family planning programmes.
- Priority will be given to *dalit* women in the selection of female health workers or female volunteers so long as they are available.
- Awareness programmes relating to health care for *dalit* community in the districts particularly maternity health care of *dalit* women will be launched.
- Health care service will be provided on regular basis by identifying the areas where there is major health problem with the young girls and women in *dalit* community.

Economic Programmes

- Special priority in land distribution will be given to homeless people of *dalit* communities.
- While providing foreign employment to people of *dalit* community under the government initiatives, their traditional skills and resource will be modernised and training will be provided to make their service suitable to foreign jobs.
- Loan in easy installments will be made available to people of *dalit* community to run their traditional businesses. Special training will be provided to modernize their traditional skills.
- There are people of *dalit* community who have skills but have no formal certificate. This is a bottleneck to have jobs. So, measures will be taken to determine the level of skills and provide them certificate by skill testing.
- Priority will be accorded to *dalit* community people in the governmental and non-governmental employment.

- In order to make professional skills of *dalit* community prestigious and to merge them into the mainstreaming, the interest will be created in their occupational skill in the schools.

Study and Research Programme

- Under the government and the non-government sector, people will be encouraged to conduct studies and carry out research works to identify population of different groups of *dalit* communities and different aspects of their life.

Institutional Arrangement

- The District Development Committee will asked to formulate the programmes for the socio-economic development of *dalit* community of the district at the time of district development plan preparation
- Each District Development Committee will be asked to prepare the document on the status and problems of the *dalit* communities of their district.
- In order to coordinate all types of governmental and non-governmental district level *dalit* development programmes and to formulate plan and policy as well as to make responsible of their execution as per local requirement, the responsible person/agency will be pin pointed and focal point will be created in the District Development Committees.
- The process of creating committee at local level to look after the status of *dalit* communities, as watchdog will be initiated. The committee will submit its annual report to its parent organisation.
- The agencies of government, non-governmental organisations NGOs, social and community based organisations working at grass root level will be activated to identify problems and issues as well as for the solution of the area specific *dalit* community.

- By way of coordination, duplication in programmes related to uplift and development of the *dalit* communities of various line ministries, departments and NGOs and INGOs will be avoided. The National *Dalit* Commission and the Committee on uplift of the *Dalit* , oppressed and neglected communities are working separately at present. They will be merged into one single institution for the preparation of appropriate policy and programmes in order to implement all the activities relating to them in an integrated manner.

Monitoring Arrangement

Arrangement will be made to monitor the implementation of the programmes NGO by the users groups and the related local institutions, since these programmes prepared for *dalit* communities will be run under the committee represented by local institution, non-government organisation and consumers' group. Also, considering the nature of the programmes, arrangement will also be made to monitoring and evaluation of such programmes at higher level, such as, the District Development Committee, line ministries, the National *Dalit* Commission and the National Planning Commission. The outlay allocated for the proposed programmes is included in the local development sector.

Total outlay for the sector is Rs 1,600.00 million, of which Rs 500 million at the minimum will be borne by the Poverty Alleviation Fund and Rs 1,100.00 million will be the grant-in-aid provided to the local bodies (like DDCs), but excluding the resources allocated for the targeted programmes of sectoral ministries.

REFERENCES

Bhoite, U. and Boite, A., "The Dalit Sahitya Movement in Maharashtra: A sociological Analysis" in *Sociological Bulletin*, 27(2), 1977, pp. 60-75.

Ramesh, Chandra, Mitra Sangh, *Dalit Identity in the New Millennium*, Commonwealth, New Delhi, 2003.

Roy Burman, B.K., The Problems of Untouchables in Romesh Thaper (ed.) *Tribe, Caste and Religion in India*, Mc Millan, New Delhi, 1977.

Sharma, R.S., *Sudras in Ancient India*, Motilal Banarasidas, Varanasi, 1958.

Verma, J.M.S. (ed.), *Gender Justice in India*, Spellbound, Rohtak, 1999.

13

MODERNITY AND TRADITION IN A GLOBAL ERA : THE RE-INVENTION OF CASTE

India has spent the post-war era attempting to excavate the social inequalities of caste from its social landscape. The various dimensions of caste have been examined and connected with each other and to the past, whilst the consequences of caste have been widely researched. As part of its modernisation programme, the Indian government has repeatedly attempted to legislate caste away. In doing this, the government has dug deep into the Indian cultural psyche to exorcise the tradition of caste. These attempts have run in parallel with the broader social and cultural effects of modern industrial Western capitalism on deeply held traditions, for example, the rapidly changing lifestyles of increasing numbers of Indians employed in the burgeoning information technology, bio-technology, and pharmaceutical sectors.

The tradition of caste in India dates back 3000 years. It is a hierarchical system which divided the population initially into four (that later grew into five) mutually exclusive, exhaustive, hereditary, and occupation-specific *Varnas* dictating all aspects of a person's existence. These are the *Brahmins* (priests and teachers), *Kshatriyas* (warriors and royalty), *Vaisyas* (traders), and the *Sudras* (menial jobs) and the *Ati Sudras* (performing the lowest of menial jobs) (Deshpande, 2000; Thekaekara and van der Gaag, 2005). Whilst the caste system in India originated as a way of dividing labour, Thekarekara & van der Gaag contend that it was and is a method of exercising and maintaining social control.

The economically and socially disadvantaged castes are classified as the Scheduled castes (SC) accounting for approximately 160 million people (Burnad, 2001). People belonging to the SC can aspire to become teachers, government workers, or politicians but rarely a judge, lawyer, senior company executives or journalists. The SC were named 'Harijans' by Gandhi, meaning Children of God, a term now considered pejorative. People of the SC prefer to be known as 'Dalits' or the oppressed, a term first used by Babasaheb Ambedkar. The present day meaning of Dalits denotes people who are struggling for human rights, for a new identity and pride. Representing over one-sixth of India's population Dalits suffer almost complete exclusion by a system of social order and containment.

It is clear that the Indian caste system has deep historical roots. However, contemporary trends such as the development of a 'Dalit' identity and political movement point to a transformation of the caste system and a diverging of perspectives on what the system represents and what its future should be. The next section explores these developments through the theoretical prisms of de-traditionalisation as proposed by Beck, *et al.* and governmentality. The significance of this is that so far, the concepts of de-traditionalisation and governmentality have largely been used in the literature to examine Western societies and have yet to be widely applied to provide insights into the social, economic, political, and cultural effects of modernisation on newly industrialising nations such as India. It is argued here that such concepts are equally useful in both contexts.

In examining the changes to traditional Indian society, the works of Beck, Giddens & Lash and Rose are deployed to provide theoretical insights and analytical structure. Whilst their ideas have so far been applied to explaining the transformation of Western industrial nations, the same processes and forces driving this transformation (*e.g.* globalisation) are being brought to bear on 'developing nations' such as India. According to Giddens, tradition is a way of settling clashes between different values and ways of life. Once a particular set of values is selected by a society, they form a prism through which the world is viewed by that society. Tradition thus incorporates power relations between social groups and tends to naturalise them. The world of traditional society is one in which cultural pluralism takes the form of a diversity of mores and customs, each of which exist in their own space.

The modernisation of India is resulting in a decline of such traditional influences in society. This process is referred to by Beck as 'de-traditionalisation', which he defines as, 'the exhaustion, dissolution, and disenchantment of the collective and group-specific sources of identity and meaning [for example, caste, ethnicity, class consciousness] of industrial society'. Whilst this definition directly refers to the dissolution of Western industrial society, it is equally applicable to the transformations taking place in Indian society. The forces of reflexive modernity are dissolving the traditional social relationships within Indian society as defined by caste causing the system to collapse. For Beck and Beck-Gernsheim this is because the sources of collective and group identity and meanings that characterised traditional social relationships (class, caste, ethnic identity) whose lifestyles and notion underpin the economy, society and culture, lose their mystique and break-up, exhausted. However, Gupta argues that although the caste system has dissolved, caste identity has strengthened, calling into question the idea that group identity and meanings have disintegrated. Beck and Beck-Beck-Gernsheim's argument must therefore, be re-thought in the context of caste in India.

Of particular, relevance to India is the argument mounted by Giddens that de-traditionalisation causes the stripping of successions of generations of the central significance of the past as one of the main means for the transmission of conventional symbols and practices. In this case, one might expect that traditional social practices such as caste would become weaker in their influence. However, as Beck *et al.* point out, as traditions dissolve, the past takes on a new and quite different significance as emotional inertia, a kind of sociocultural baggage. It should come as no surprise then that as India modernises, many traditions are clung to, and caste is one such tradition.

As a result, caste has not and cannot simply be blanked out. It is being re-invented and justified in the present as a necessary and inevitable feature of a modern capitalist society. The notion of de-traditionalisation as detailed by Beck and Beck Gernsheim is correct in that the lifestyles and ideologies that characterise caste in India have brokendown. However, in contrast to Beck and Beck-Gernsheim, the sources of collective and group identity and meanings that characterise caste have strengthened rather than weakened as competition between and within castes for economic and political power has developed. To understand this process, de traditionalisation is connected to Rose's concept of governmentality to provide a useful theoretical framework for analysis.

De-traditionalisation and Governmentality

Employing de-traditionalisation and governmentality as analytical tools means that the formation and transformation of control in all its guises are brought into focus for investigation. This is important because the social, economic and cultural transformations taking place in contemporary India are raising a number of challenges to government, especially in terms of reconciling the forces of modernisation with the immovable tradition of caste. This section is divided into two parts. Firstly, the transformations taking place to caste are discussed through employing concepts associated with de-traditionalisation and governmentality. In terms of de-traditionalisation, three central ideas are used: structural reflexivity, self-reflexivity and institutional reflexivity. Rose's notions of faculty of control (exercise of self-restraint), degree of consciousness (reflection), and force of habit (reflexivity) are then used to focus on the relationships between people, and between people and social structures in post-traditional society in the context of the de-traditionalisation of caste.

The second section examines the issue of caste from a governmentality perspective to analyse that which Rose refers to as endeavours deployed to shape, guide, and direct the conduct of others. According to Rose, governmentality provides a way of taking full consideration of the ways in which people are educated and encouraged to self control through various mechanisms (*e.g.* the market, the law), agencies (*e.g.* health, education, police) and techniques (*e.g.* self-government). This brings into question the means by which consent is manufactured for the continuation of caste as an organising principle in Indian society. In doing so, this research addresses caste as, 'that dimension of ... history composed by the invention, contestation, operationalisation and transformation of more or less rationalised schemes, programmes, techniques and devices which seek to shape conduct so as to achieve certain ends.'

From this perspective, governing caste may be seen as a multi-dimensional phenomenon that includes a variety of thoughts and actions. Rose argues that these dimensions of governing are reflected in the multitude of words used to describe and enact it (*e.g.* education, control, influence, regulation, administration, management, guidance) and the multitude of connected authorities and forces involved in governing caste. Governmentality is thus brought into play to provide insights into how caste has been problematised, the different perspectives, and the ultimate aims of social, political, and cultural strategies utilised to govern its de traditionalisation.

The de-traditionalisation of Caste

Structural Reflexivity—It refers to where people are set free from the limitations of social structures. This means that they are able to critically reflect on the rules and resources of existing social structures and how these affect their social conditions of their existence; they can then begin to create their own rules. The development of structural reflexivity is related to the advance of self-consciousness in that, as Rose argues, people become more aware of their social situation and develop a critical awareness of their place in society. They are now becoming more willing to question the social system that keeps them in the lower strata of society.

Ram examines traces the rise of Dalit identity and consciousness in the Punjab as they asserted their rights to freedom from oppression, political representation, and economic and social equality. Through the development of newspapers devoted to Dalit issues, the founding of Dalit political parties, and the assertion of Dalit culture, Ram demonstrates how the Dalits set themselves free of the social structures of caste that served to limit their life-chances and civil liberties.

Self-reflexivity—It refers to the process by which, in creating their own rules for existence, people reflect on themselves (Giddens, 1994). People must make decisions based on a set of rules that only they can formulate, based on the knowledge they have accumulated about themselves and the world. However, this knowledge is itself in a state of continuous renewal and re-definition in response to the accumulation of knowledge and social interaction. Previous external monitoring, in which many aspects of a person's identity were given or taken-for-granted, dissolves and is replaced by self-monitoring in which people develop the freedom to organise their own biographies. Self-reflexivity provides a way of operationalising Rose's assertion that governmentality draws attention to how control has become a more personalised phenomenon. Rose refers to self-government as the contemporary means of maintaining social order. Gupta outlines the personalisation of caste in terms of a struggle for individual life chances through access to education, the job market, and positions of power. Gupta argues that caste identities have changed to the extent that 'it is now a question of self over others and not self in relation to others' meaning that the caste system is now more a matter of power rather than ideology. Although caste as a formal system has collapsed, contemporary India still embraces caste as a means of social control through competition for status, wealth, and power between castes driven by caste identity and competition for status, wealth, and power between individuals within castes.

Institutional reflexivity—It is different in that rather than focusing on individuals, it refers to a collective form of reflexivity. Just as people have become reflexive, institutions have also become reflexive in that they monitor and control their own performance, adjusting their practices repeatedly in response to changed circumstances or information. As institutions make such continual adjustments, in spite of the efforts of those within institutions to plan and achieve outcomes, what transpires is not necessarily what was intended, nor is there necessarily an awareness of what is actually taking place and its consequences. The uncertainty and insecurity arising from institutional reflexivity undermines the capacity of institutions to exert control as their collective power is dissipated by the fragmenting, ever changing, and increasingly complex environment in which they must operate. Institutional reflexivity provides a way of gaining a deeper understanding of why caste has withstood the rising tide of Western influences brought about by the globalisation of India. It is found that in spite of the best efforts of the major political institutions of India, caste identity has strengthened taking the form of a reflexive habit.

Caste is a strong and enduring feature of Indian society in spite of the constitution outlawing it and supporting legislation. It is enduring because as Lash argues, 'traditions are bound up with collective memory, itself a framework for the reconstruction of past time which in turn organises future time'. On the surface then, caste seems very 'traditional' in that it has a long history and deeply engrained in Indian culture and society. We contend that rather than being a tradition, caste is a social compulsion in that compulsiveness is an inability to escape from the past. Caste looks like a tradition in that it depends on formulaic truths and repetition, but has become shorn of integrity, disconnected from emerging Indian consumption cultures closely aligned to a global attitude, particularly evident amongst young people. As an emerging global consumption culture directly challenges caste, one might expect to see the caste consciousness begin breaking down as previously separate social spheres overlap and merge rather than strengthen. A clue to the persistence of caste in India lies in the way it is been re-invented and justified within the new global consciousness. The new caste consciousness conforms to the logic of the new global social architecture identified by Held and McGrew as one which, 'divides humanity into elites, the bourgeoisie, the marginalised, and the impoverished, re-arranging the world into the winners and losers of globalisation'.

The contemporary challenges to caste come from that which Giddens identifies as the development of the self as the basic characteristic of everyday life in the modern world and as such, there has to be a significant measure of individual autonomy. However, Giddens also argues that this requires the development of purely personal relationships between people in post-traditional society rather than the collective relationships of traditional society. These new personal relationships depend on an intimacy not generally characteristic of traditional society. This goes against and across the grain of caste. In contrast to traditional practices of totally sperate social spheres of caste, the socioeconomic imperatives of capitalist production means that the so-called 'higher castes' cannot escape their connection with the 'lower castes' and one might expect that this inescapable social mixing would result in a destruction of caste as a means of social, economic, political, and cultural separation and control. Rather than being destroyed, caste is transformed. Beck and Beck-Gernshiem argue that de-traditionalisation is not only a destruction of tradition it also involves the reconstruction of traditions either in terms of the invention of new ones or the reinvention of old ones. In the case of India the traditional practices of caste have indeed not disappeared from the Indian social, cultural, political, and economic landscape, instead is has been re-invented, re-structured, and re-justified within the context of global capitalism. The global, propositional truths of modernity, are being appropriated by Indians in everyday life. It is contradictory then that whilst modernity works to effectively disembed traditional meanings of caste, rendering it anachronistic to modern Indian society, it remains an indelible feature of the social, cultural, and political landscape. Insights into how this has come about is provided by governmentality. The next section brings into focus the different perspectives and strategies employed on governing caste as well as how caste has been problematised.

Governmentality of Caste

The main expression of how caste is problematised in India is found in recent reports and research papers. The report by the Human Rights Watch highlights significant economic and educational disparities between lower and higher-caste communities. Further research also defines caste as problematic particularly with regards to the plight of people who are assigned as being Dalit; Deshpande, 2000; Chandra & Mittra, 2003. Dalits are defined as being both socially and economically disadvantaged, with only 15 per cent being literate.

They are treated by wider Indian society as 'untouchable' and thus deprived of equal access to resources such as water and health care facilities. According to Burnad, Dalit people are not allowed to take baths in common wells or to sit on a par with other castes and they have no right to avail themselves of the services such as public transport, parks or hotels. Moreover, children face a higher incidence of malnutrition whilst every Dalit-born woman faces the triple discrimination of class, gender, and caste. Population programmes of the state targets Dalit women for forced sterilisation. As agricultural workers, women are paid half that of a man's salary. Indeed, Dalit women are Dalits among Dalits. Caste has been problematised through being defined in terms of institutionalised discrimination. As such, the different perspectives regarding caste may be seen in terms of those who see the inequalities associated with caste as being unacceptable and those who see caste as a means of maintaining the economic and social status quo of perceived stability and progress.

The different perspectives on caste are a reflection of nearly 60 years of India's post-colonial Independence. Research conducted between 1993 and 1994 reveals that even in more egalitarian states such as Kerala, inter-caste disparity continues to underlie overall social inequality (Deshpande, 2000). Anti-caste radicals such as Dr Ambedkar and Periyar Ramasamy have adopted—at state level—a socialist perspective, demanding that India must redefine its socialist project of multiculturalism and focus on addressing the multiple inequalities within Indian society. Gupta, R.K. contends that the winning of the national elections by the Congress Party in 2004, represents a populist backlash against economic reforms that benefited a privileged minority of the 1.1 billion people of India whilst ignoring a larger community who remain illiterate and impoverished.

In modern India, capital, culture, and the state exist in a cluster of alliances founded on caste hierarchies, and ethnic and religious differences. In recent years, capital growth has created a further divide between and within the hierarchical caste structure. This is creating mounting pressures within India for reform.

The different perspectives discussed here reveal two opposing views on caste. The first is one in which caste is seen as a manifestation and justification of historical social inequalities in India and as such has no place in a modern society. In contrast, the other perspective is one in which caste inequalities are a necessary and inevitable consequence of modern capitalism. The emerging social architecture requires groups of people who are poor and marginalised as well as those who prosper. In India, this social architecture is expressed in the caste system.

The major sources of strategies employed in relation to caste have come from the Indian government. The development of a constitutional and legislative approach to governing the problem of caste had the aim of outlawing discrimination and providing legal protection for people of lower caste. Article 17 of the Constitution of India proclaims Untouchability an offence. Article 35 (a) (ii) confers upon Parliament the exclusive power to make laws prescribing punishment for those acts which are declared to be offensive to SC. In pursuance of Act 35 of the Constitution, the Untouchability (offences) Act, 1955 was passed. The Untouchability Act has since changed to the Protection of Civil Rights Act. Statues such as the Scheduled Castes and Scheduled Tribes (Prevention of Atrocities) Act, 1989 along with policy of reservation in public employment and education for upliftment of people belonging to scheduled castes was enacted. The basic premise of these laws grants the assurance that Dalits would have the same rights as any other person, in using public amenities. These schemes are implemented through State Governments/Union Territories as Centrally Sponsored Schemes. Furthermore, developmental plans, such as the Special Component Plan were evolved as far back as 1979 to bring SC above the poverty line and into the mainstream of national life with equal social and economic status. This was accompanied by action in 1992 to eliminate the manual handling of soil and filth through the National Scheme of Liberation and Rehabilitation of Scavengers and their dependents.

In the area of employment, the problem of caste is recognised and acted on. The government of India initiated affirmative action as a remedial measure with the objective of providing career opportunities for people from lower castes.

All states of India have quotas foı the Scheduled Castes that comprise 16-17 per cent of the population. This means the reserving of 22.5 per cent of: seats in the legislature, places at government-sponsored educational institutions, and public-sector jobs. Prominent private sector employers believe that reform policies such affirmative action will alleviate poverty, however the Dalits debate the misconception of reservation policy. They argue that it should not be seen as uplifting the poor, instead it should focus on reversing centuries of discrimination. Anand Teltumbde, a Dalit managing director of Petronet, states, "It is not the disability of the Dalits but the disability of Indian society that necessitates reservation" (Overdorf, 2004: 43). However, as Rose (1999) points out, government is only one player in the wider process of governing. In the case of caste, other constituencies need to be considered such as employers, public administrators, and law enforcement. These groups have often taken a quite different approach to the issue in that they either passively or actively resist the efforts of legislators.

As a result of the resistance of significant groups in Indian society, the regulation of caste has neither solved nor simplified the problem. The efforts of India to govern caste 'from above' conflict with the practices, logic, and habits of caste 'from below', resulting in a failure of policy. The non-enforcement of protective legislation perpetuates discriminatory employment practices, accentuating hereditary social order. Constitutional and statutory bodies, including the National Human Rights Commission and the National Commission for Scheduled Castes and Scheduled Tribes, have repeatedly confirmed and decried the prevalence of abuses. The practices of law enforcers such as the judiciary on caste discrimination demonstrate failure. In July 1998, in the state of Uttar Pradesh, an Allahabad High Court judge reportedly had his chambers purified with '*Ganga Jal*', water from the River Ganges, because it had previously been occupied by a Dalit Judge. Other government authorities have actually facilitated continued discrimination. The potential of the Prevention of Atrocities

Act, 1989, to bring about social change has been fraught by police corruption and caste bias, with the result that many allegations of caste crimes are not entered in police records. Moreover, ignorance of procedures and a lack of knowledge of the act have also affected its implementation. In a Parliamentary hearing, it was cited that only 2 out of 30 police officials were familiar with the Untouchability Offences Act, 1955. In the area of employment, in spite of policies such as affirmation action being enacted, Dalit leaders allege that high-caste officials responsible for recruitment and promotions leave positions vacant rather than hire or promote those they view as inferior, then justify themselves to superiors by claiming they could not find suitable low-caste candidates.

While the passing of laws hold some influence, caste continues with very little changes in the living standards of Dalits. According to Chandra & Mittra despite protective legislation and positive discrimination improvements in occupational mobility and living standards, the majority continue to be worse off than members of other communities. In literacy rates as compared to the national average figures is below 37 per cent, and yet again women in the SC community are at an even greater disadvantage. Furthermore, it has been asserted, that some state governments dominated by higher castes have attempted to repeal legislation altogether. Dalits have responded to ill-treatment by converting, en masse, to Buddhism, Christianity, and sometimes Islam. Once converted, however, many lose access to their scheduled-caste status and the few government privileges assigned to it. Many also find that they are ultimately unable to escape treatment as 'untouchables.' Indeed it would be difficult to convince Dalits that, over fifty-four years after Independence, the government had done anything to end the violence and discrimination that has ruled their lives.

These practices do not repudiate the achievement which legal reforms aim to accomplish, instead they serve to demonstrate the insufficiency in relation to contemporary challenges. Furthermore, such orientations serve to highlight the lack of integrated programmes, weak implementation and a failure to mainstream disadvantaged communities and repressed people, such as Dalits, into the national development process. This lack of adequate community development demonstrates that whilst the modernisation of India has had the effect of de-traditionalising many areas of the Indian social, cultural, and political milieu, it still remains addicted to caste. This seriously hampers the progress of 160 million of India's citizens ultimately negatively affecting the nation's standing as a global citizen, and its economic, social, and political stability and well-being.

Caste in India, has not been destroyed by modernisation in spite of the efforts of legislators. The perspectives provided by Beck *et al.* and Rose (1999) together help explain the processes at work. The concept of de-traditionalisation illuminates the way in which caste has been transformed from an ancient tradition of social organisation to a modern habit, evacuated of its traditional meanings and functions. Instead it has been re-made as caste consciousness in the mould of the emerging global social architecture. Rose's notion of governmentality has provided insights into the way this re-making has taken place. Using governmentality, caste may be seen as a way of organising the socioeconomic structures of India to mirror Western industrial capitalism in a way that is least disruptive to the current social, political, economic, and cultural power structures. Those who were denied wealth and prosperity in the past will also be those denied it in the future.

The modernisation of India has created the situation where the 'tradition' of caste has been evacuated of its ancient connections with social and economic stability and order and has become a modern state of caste consciousness that is at best a habit and at worst and addiction. The issue that has not yet been addressed in India though is the stark difference between traditional caste structures and their modern equivalent. The work by Beck *et al.* and Rose draw attention to this point of difference. It is now clear is that the so-called 'higher castes' cannot escape their connection with the 'lower castes'. Traditionally, castes were completely apart, moving in separate spheres. Now, they are bound together in a shared community of fate mapped out through engagement with global economic, social, cultural, and political institutions and structures.

This is recognised by prominent Indian authority figures. Nilekani, chief executive of the software-services giant, Infosys Technologies, has a stated recruitment programme that does not discriminate on the basis of age, gender or caste. The Indian Prime Minister, Manmohan Singh, stated recently that, "If a commitment to remain an open society is one of the pillars of India's nationhood, the other is our commitment to remain an open economy—one that guarantees freedom of enterprise, respects individual creativity, and mobilises public investment for social infrastructure". Yet, in its quest towards capital growth, the move towards privatisation of public sector organisations takes precedence, resulting in a dwindling of reserved jobs and a shrinking of the public sector. Calls for private sector organisations to implement reform policies such as affirmative action become more strident. These initiatives are aimed at compelling businesses to implement poverty reduction reforms.

These statements imply that affirmative action is the way to improve the lot of lower caste. Using Rose's conceptualisation, the implication is that the lower castes require assistance. They have the self-control to escape disadvantage; there is no 'culture of poverty' associated with the plight of Dalit people. However, if the Indian government and employers are committed to social reform and economic growth, then the question arises as to the role of consciousness and habit. Overdorf and Deshpande argue that while industrialists think the government should focus on uplifting the poor regardless of caste, Dalit leaders believe such a shift in emphasis would mean only that the lion's share of the benefits. Dalits now enjoy would be transferred to poor members of the higher castes. As land is the prime asset in rural areas that determines an individual's standard of living and social status, lack of access to land makes Dalits economically vulnerable. The relationship of dependency is exploited by upper and middle-caste landlords. Furthermore, social reforms and policies such as affirmative action perpetuate the benefits of a privileged minority belonging to the backward and scheduled castes and tribes. This implies that whilst there is a reflective awareness of the issue of caste there is a reflexive habit of reverting to the (evacuated) tradition of caste amongst people of higher caste status.

CONCLUSION

The arguments, strategies, and tactics employed in the governing of caste can be seen in terms of a privileged section of society protecting their own caste identity that brings advantages against a redefinition involving the creation of a more equal society that conflicts with their interests. In the past, the justification of caste was made valid through an appeal to tradition. In contemporary Indian society, this position is becoming less valid. A new justification has been invented appealing to the new 'tradition' of a capitalist global economic order in which the privileged continue to enjoy economic success at the expense of the poor and marginalised. The key issues remain, that the governing of caste is a vexed issue for India evidenced in contradiction between top-down policy responses and the bottom-up entrenched logic and habits of caste perpetuated by those people who belong to higher castes. As a result, inequality remains the mainstay of India's social and economic system. Equal opportunities will remain imaginary, unless India takes adequate steps towards capacity building in disadvantaged societies. Furthermore, resource distribution and the creation of an inclusive environment remains a critical challenge.

REFERENCES

Beck, U., Giddens, A., & Lash, S. (Eds.), *Reflexive Modernization: Politics, Tradition and Aesthetics in the Modern Social Order*, Cambridge, Polity Press, 1994.

—, *"The reinvention of politics: towards a theory of reflexive modernization"*, in Beck, U., Giddens, A & Lash, S. (Eds), Reflexive modernization: politics, tradition and aesthetics in the modern social order, Cambridge, Polity Press, 1994, pp. 1-55.

—, *Democracy without enemies.* Cambridge: Polity Press, 1998.

Beck, U., & Beck-Gernsheim, E., *Individualization: institutionalised individualism and its social and political consequences,* London, Sage Publication, 2002.

Burnad, F., The rights of the Dalit people: a women's perspective, *Lola Press* No. 16, 2001, p. 34.

Chandra, R., & Mittra, S., *Dalit Identity in the new millennium: Untouchability and the Law,* New Delhi, Commonwealth Publishers, 2003.

Deshpande, A., "Does caste still define disparity? A look at inequality in Kerala, India", *The American Economic Review,* Nashville, Vol. 90 No 2, 2000, pp. 322-326.

Galambos, L., "Recasting the organizational synthesis: structure and process in the Twentieth and Twenty-First Centuries", *Business History Review,* Vol. 79 No. 1, 2005, pp. 1–38.

Ghose, S., "The Dalit in India", Social Research, Vol. 70 No. 1, 2003, pp. 83–109.

Giddens, A., *"Living in a post-traditional society",* in Beck, U. Giddens, A. & Lash, S. (Eds.), Reflexive modernization: politics, tradition and aesthetics in the modern social order, Cambridge, Polity Press, 1994, pp. 56–109.

Gupta, D., "Caste and politics: identity over system", *Annual Review of Anthropology,* Vol. 34, 2005, pp. 409–427.

Held, D., & McGrew, A., *Globalization/Anti-Globalization,* Cambridge, Polity Press, 2002.

Jackson, P., " Local consumption cultures in a globalizing world", *Transactions of the Institute of British Geographers,* Vol. 29 No. 2, 2004, pp. 165–178.

Lash, S., *"Reflexivity and its doubles",* in Beck, U. Giddens, A. & Lash, S. (Eds.), Reflexive modernization: politics and tradition in the modern social order, Cambridge, Polity Press, 1994a, pp. 110-173.

—, *"Expert-systems or situated interpretation? Culture and institutions in disorganized capitalism"*, in Beck, U. Giddens, A. & Lash, S. (Eds.), Reflexive modernization: politics, tradition and aesthetics in the modern social order, Cambridge, Polity Press, 1994b, pp. 198–215.

Lukose, R., "Consuming globalization: youth and gender in Kerala, India", Journal of Social History, Vol. 38 No. 4, 2005, pp. 915–935.

McDougall, P., "Tech Powerhouse", *Information Week,* No. 1035, 2005, pp. 20-23.

Overdorf, J., "Yet another cross to bear", Far Eastern Economic Review, Vol. 167 No. 36, 2004, pp. 42–45.

Pilling, M., "Growing pains on the subcontinent", Director, Vol. 59 No. 1, 2005, pp. 41–42.

Rajadurai, S. V., Geetha, V., & Ahmad, A., "India: caste and great state nationalism an exchange", *Monthly Review,* Vol. 49, No. 2, 1997, pp. 35–38.

Rao, N. J. U., *Deprived castes in India,* Allahabad, India, Chugh Publications, 1981.

Rose, N., *Powers of freedom,* Cambridge, Cambridge University Press, 1999.

Singh, M., "The New India", *Wall Street Journal* (Eastern Edition), May 19, 2005, p. 14.

Stahl, S., "Taking a global view of innovation", *Information Week,* No. 1035, 2005, p. 8.

Thekaekara, M. M., & van der Gaag, N., "Combatting caste", *The New Internationalist,* No. 380 (July), 2002, pp. 9–12.

Webster, J. C. B., *Religion and Dalit liberation,* New Delhi, Manohar Publishers, 1999.

BIBLIOGRAPHY

Agnihotri, S., Workforce participation, kinship and sex ratio variations in India in *Gender, Technology, and Development,* Vol. 1 (1), 1997.

Ahuja, R. , *Violence Against Women,* Rawat Publication, New Delhi, 1998.

Arora, D., 'Structural adjustment programmes and gender concerns in India', *Journal of Contemporary Asia,* Vol. 29(3), 1999.

Balachander, J., 'Tamil Nadu's Successful Nutrition Effort', in Rohde, J., and Chatterjee, M. (eds), *Reaching Health for All,* Oxford University Press: New Delhi, 1993.

Bandhu, P., *Dalit Women's cry for Liberation: My Rights Are Rising like the Sun, will you deny this sunrise"?* Edited in Rao (2003). *Caste and Gender,* Kali For Women, New Delhi, 2003.

Bhalla, A., *Uneven Development in the Third World: A Study of China and India,* Basingstoke: 1995.

Bhan, G., *Questions of Agency : Nostalgia in the Indian Freedom Struggle,* Harvard University, 2000.

Bhat, E., 'Structural reform and poor women: the case of redesigning development', *Future,* Vol. 28, Autumn, 1992.

Bhoite, U. and Boite, A., "The Dalit Sahitya Movement in Maharashtra: A sociological Analysis" in *Sociological Bulletin,* 27(2), 1977, pp. 60-75.

Blauner, Robert, *Racial Oppression in America,* New York, Harper and Row, 1972, pp. 82-110.

Chakravati, V., *Reconceptualising Gender, Phule, Brahmanisam and Brahminial Patriarchy,* edited in Rao (2003) *Caste and Gender,* Kali for women, New Delhi, 2003.

Chaterjee, M., *Indian Women: Their Health and Productivity,* World Bank, Discussion Papers 109, Washington D.C., 1990.

Chitnis, V., *Human Rights of the vulnerable groups,* Futuristic Digital, Pune, 2005.

Coale, Excess Female Moratility and the Balance of the Sexes in Population: An Estimate on the number of "Missing Females, *Population and Development Review,* Vol. 17, 1991.

Das Gupta, M., 'Selective discrimination against female children in Punjab, India', *Population and Development Review,* Vol 13, 1987.

Das Gupta, M., Chen, L. and Krishnan, T. (eds), *Women's Health in India: Risk and Vulnerability,* Bombay, 1995.

Das Gupta, M., *Fertility Decline and Gender Differentials in Mortality in India,* paper presented at International Symposium on Issues Related to Sex Preference for Children in Demographics of Asia, Seoul, Korea, 1994.

Desai, S., and Alva, S., Maternal Education and Child Health, in *Demography,* Vol. 35 (1), 1998.

Desai, S., *Gender Inequalities and Demographic Behaviour, India,* New York: 1994.

Deshpande, S. and Deshpande, L., 'Gender-based discrimination in the urban labour market', in T. Papola and A. Sharma (eds), *Gender and Employment in India,* New Delhi : Vikas Publishing, 1999.

—'New economic policy and female employment', *Economic and Political Weekly,* Vol. 27(14), 1992.

Dev, S. and Ranade, A., 'Persisting poverty and social insecurity: a selective assessment', in K. Parikh (ed), *India's Development Report,* New Delhi: Oxford University Press, 2000.

Dietrich, G., *Dalit Movement and Women's Movement,* Edited in Rao (2003): *Caste and Gender,* Kali for Women, New Delhi, 2003.

Dreze, J. and Sen, A. (eds), *Employment and Unemployment in India,* Fifth Quinquennial Survey, NSS 50th Round, New Delhi (1997).

—, *Indian Development: Selected Regional Perspectives,* New Delhi : Oxford University Press, 1997.

Ghosh, J., 'Employment and labour under structural adjustment–India since 1991', *Indian Journal of Labour Economics,* Vol 38 (4), Oct.-Dec. 1995.

—, 'Gender concerns in macro-economic policy', *Economic and Political Weekly,* Vol. 29(18), April 1994.

Grecer, Colin, "Remembering Class: An Interpretation" in Colin Greer, (ed.), *The Divided Society: The Ethnic Experson in America,* New York, Basic Books, 1974. p. 35

Haddad, L., and Smith, L., *Explaining child malnutrition in developing countries,* International Food Policy Research Insititute, Washington D.C., 1997.

Heise, L. *Violence Against Women : The Hidden Health Burden,* World Bank Discussion Papers 255, Washington D.C., 1994.

Hogg, Michael A. and Dominic Abrams, *Social Identification,* Routledge, London and New York, 1998.

International Institute for Population Sciences (IIPS), *India National Health Survey 1993-94,* Bombay, 1995.

Issacs, Harold R., *India's Ex-untouchables,* John Day, New York, 1965.

Jejeebhoy, S. and Rama Rao, S., 'Unsafe motherhood: a review of reproductive health' in M. Das Gupta, L. Chen, and T. Krishnan (eds), *Women's Health in India: Risk and Vulnerability,* Bombay, 1995.

Jogdand, P., *Dalit Women, Issues and Perspectives,* Gyan Publication, New Delhi, 1995.

John, M. with Lalita, K., *Background Report on Gender Issues in India,* BRIDGE : Brighton, 1995.

Johnson, C. *et. al., Domestic Violence in India,* unpublished report to USAID/INDIA Krishnaraj, M., 'Women's perspective on public policy in India', *Gender, Technology and Development,* Vol 4(2), 2000.

Kale, R., *Kolhatyachrepor,* Granthali Publication, Mumbai, 1994.

Karolson, B.G., *Contested Belonging,* Curzon Press, Surrey, UK 2000.

Kumar, N., *Dalit Policies, Politics and Parliament,* Shipra Publication, New Delhi, 2004.

Kumar, N. and Raj, M., *Dalit Leadership in Panchayats,* Institute of Dalit Studies, Rawat Publication, New Delhi, 2006.

Kundu, A., 'Trends and pattern of female employment: a case of organized informalization' in T. Papola and A. Sharma (eds), *Gender and Employment in India,* New Delhi: Vikas Publishing, 1999.

Lipton, M. and Longhurst, R., *New Seeds and Poor People,* Baltimore: Johns Hopkins University Press, 1989.

Mahar, J. Michael, *The Untouchables in Contemporary India,* Rawat Publication, Jaipur, 1998.

Manu, *Manu Smriti: The laws of Manu with the Bhasya of Medhatithi.* Translated by Ganga Natha Jha, University of Calcutta, Calcutta, 1920.

Mayer, P., 'India's falling sex ratios', *Population and Development Review,* Vol 25(2), June 1999.

Michael, S., *Dalits in Modern India, Vision and Values,* Vistar Publication, New Delhi, 1999.

Mitra, A., *Implications of falling Sex-ratio's on India's population,* Bombay: Allied Press, 1979.

Narula. S. *Broken People: Caste Violence Against India's "Untouchables."* London: Human Rights Watch, 1999.

National Statistical Survey Organization–*Key Results on Employment and Unemployment,* Fifth Quinquennial Survey, NSS 50th Round, New Delhi, 1993-94.

Nayak, R.K. (Ed.) *The Fourth World: Appraisal and Aspirations,* Manohar, Delhi, 1997.

Omvedt, G., 'Unorganized sector and women workers', *Guru Nanak Journal of Sociology,* 1989.

Omvedt, G., *Dalit Women and Communalism,* edited in Jogdand (1995) *Dalit Women, Issues and Perspectives,* Gyan Publication, New Delhi, 1995.

Pal, R. and Bhargav, G., *Human Rights of Dalits: Societal Violation,* Gyan Publication, New Delhi, 1999.

Pandit, V., Handbook on Prevention of Atrocities (SC/ST) Vidnayak Sansod Prakashan, Ujgaon, Maharashtra, 1995.

Paswan, S. and Jaidev, : *Encyclopedia of Dalits in India* (Vol. No. 10 education), 2002.

Phalkey, J., 'Right-wing mobilization of women in India: Hindutva's willing performers', in H. Afshar and S. Barrientos, *Women, Globalization and Fragmentation in the Developing World,* New York: St. Martin's Press, 1999.

Pillai, T., *Ambedkar's Daughters: A Study of Mahar Women in Ahmednagar District of Maharashtra* edited in Michaels (1999) *Dalits in Modern India, Vision and Values,* Vistar Publication, New Delhi, 1999.

Punalekar, S., *On Dalitism and Gender,* edited in Jogadand (1995) *Dalit Women's Issues and Perspectives,* Gyan Publication, New Delhi, 1995.

Rai, S., 'Fractioned states and negotiated boundaries, gender and law in India', in H. Afshar and S. Barrientos, *Women, Globalization and Fragmentation in the Developing World,* New York: St. Martin's Press, 1999.

Rainwater, Lee, *Behind the Ghetto Walls: Black Family life in a federal slum,* Chicago Slum, Chicago, Aldine, 1970, pp. 68-69.

Ramesh, Chandra, Mitra Sangh, *Dalit Identity in the New Millennium,* Commonwealth, New Delhi, 2003.

Rao, V. and Bloch, F., *Rural Labour Enquiry, 1993-94: Report on Wages and Earnings of Rural Labour Households,* Fifth Quinquennial Survey, NSS 50th Round, Shimla, 1995.

—, *Wife-beating: Causes and Implications for Nutritional Allocation to Children,* University of Michigan, Population Studies Center, Research Report p.93-238, Ann Arbor , 1993.

Sen, G., 'Globalization, justice and equity: a gender perspective', *Development,* Vol. 40 (2), 1997.

Sharif, A., *Some Socio-Economic and Demographic Aspects of the Population according to Religion in India,* Mumbai: Center for Study of Society and Secularism, 1993.

Sharma, R.S., *Sudras in Ancient India*, Motilal Banarasidas, Varanasi, 1958.

Subbarao, K., 'Interventions to fill Nutritional Gaps at the Household level: A Review of India's Experience,' in Harris, B., and Guhan, S. (eds), *Poverty in India: Research and Policy*, Oxford University Press: Bombay, 1992.

Sunil, T., Pillai, V. and Pandey, A., 'Do incentives matter?:— evaluation of a family planning program in India', *Population Research and Policy Review*, Vol 18, 1999.

Swarup, H., and Rajput, P., *Women and Globalization: reflections, options, and strategies*, Ashok Publications: New Delhi, 1994.

Thorat, S. and Umakant, *Caste, Role and Discrimination, Discourses in International Context*, Rawat Publication, New Delhi, 2004.

Unni, J., 'Women workers in Agriculture: some recent trends in gender and employment in India', in T. Papola and A. Sharma (eds), *Gender and Employment in India*, New Delhi: Vikas Publishing, 1999.

Upadhyay, U. *India's New Economic Policy of 1991 and its Impact on Women's Poverty and AIDS* , *Feminist Economics*, Vol. 6(3), 2000.

Upadhyay, U., 'India's New Economic Policy of 1991 and its impact on women's poverty and AIDS', *Feminist Economics*, Vol 6(3), 2000.

Velkoff, V. and Adlakha, A., *Women's Health in India*, US Department of State Report, 1998.

Vlassof, C., Fertility Intents and Subsequent Behaviour: A Longitudinal Study in Rural India, in *Studies in Family Planning*, Vol. 21 (4), 1990,

Webstar, J., *Who is Dalit* edited in Michael (1999) *Dalit's in Modern India, Vision and Values*, Vistar Publication, New Delhi, 1999.

World Bank, *Improving Women's Health in India*, Washington D.C., 1996.

Zelliot, E., *Dr. Ambedkar and the Empowerment of Women*, edited in Rao (2003) *Caste and Gender*, Kali for Women, New Delhi, 2003.

Zelliot, Eleaner, *From Untouchables to Dalit*, Manohar, Bombay, 1992.

INDEX

K

L

M

N

O

P